THE WINES OF

CW01499629

THE CLASSIC WINE LIBRARY
Editorial board: Sarah Jane Evans MW,
Richard Mayson and James Tidwell MS

There is something uniquely satisfying about a good wine book, preferably read with a glass of the said wine in hand. The Classic Wine Library is a series of wine books written by authors who are both knowledgeable and passionate about their subject. Each title in The Classic Wine Library covers a wine region, country or type and together the books are designed to form a comprehensive guide to the world of wine as well as to be an enjoyable read, appealing to wine professionals, wine lovers, tourists, armchair travellers and wine trade students alike.

The series comprises more than 30 titles, including:
The wines of Australia, Mark Davidson
The wines of Brazil, Tufi Neder Meyer
The wines of California, Elaine Chukan Brown
The wines of Chablis and the Grand Auxerrois, Rosemary George MW
Côte d'Or, Raymond Blake
Fizz!, Anthony Rose
The wines of Georgia, Lisa Granik MW
The wines of Germany, Anne Krebiehl MW
The wines of Greece, Konstantinos Lazarakis MW
Wines of the Languedoc, Rosemary George MW
Wines of the Loire Valley, Beverley Blanning MW
The wines of Piemonte, David Way
Port and the Douro, Richard Mayson
Wines of the Rhône, Matt Walls
The wines of Roussillon, Rosemary George MW
The wines of central and southern Spain, Sarah Jane Evans MW

THE WINES OF
BEAUJOLAIS

NATASHA HUGHES MW

ACADEMIE DU VIN LIBRARY

Natasha Hughes MW is a London-based freelance wine writer, educator and consultant. On graduating as a Master of Wine in 2014, she won four out of the seven prizes awarded that year, including the Outstanding Achievement Award for the best overall performance in the Institute's challenging exams. Her work has been published by numerous magazines and websites, including *Decanter*, *Club Oenologique*, jancisrobinson.com and www.winescholarguild.com, among others, and she has contributed to various books, including the Académie du Vin Library's *On Burgundy*, *On California* and *On Champagne*. She first began writing about Beaujolais 20 years ago, when she became the region's section editor for Oz Clarke's annual wine guide. When not writing, Natasha leads tours to wine regions as well as hosting wine events and seminars for both consumers and members of the wine trade, and consults for restaurants, private clients, wine producers and generic bodies. She teaches both tasting and theory to Master of Wine students, and judges at wine competitions around the world, often as a panel chair. Natasha is an acknowledged expert on the on-trade and on the relationship between wine and food, and has written extensively about food and wine pairing. She was a section editor for *Square Meal*'s annual restaurant guide for many years, and worked with *Wine* magazine to develop the magazine's Sommelier Challenge.

Published in 2025 by Académie du Vin Library Ltd
academieduvinlibrary.com

Copyright © Natasha Hughes, 2025

The right of Natasha Hughes to be identified as the author of this book has been asserted in accordance with the Copyright, Designs and Patents Act 1988.

All rights reserved. No part of this publication may be reproduced, stored in a retrieval system, distributed or transmitted in any form or by any means, including photocopying, recording or other electronic or mechanical methods, and including training for generative artificial intelligence (AI), without the prior written permission of the publisher. Translation into any other language, and subsequent distribution as above, is also expressly forbidden, without prior written permission of the author and publisher.

A CIP catalogue record for this book is available from the British Library
ISBN 978–1–913141–85–1

Brand and product names are trademarks or registered trademarks of their respective owners.

Front cover: © Mick Rock/Cephas Picture Library.
Back cover © Loïc Terrier Photographe, courtesy of Domaine Lapierre

Photos: for photographic credits see the text. All uncredited photos supplied by the author.

Publisher: Hermione Ireland
Editor: Rebecca Clare
Maps: Cosmographic, recreated from originals supplied by Beaujolais Wines
Indexer: Marian Aird
Printed in Great Britain

CONTENTS

Maps

ACKNOWLEDGEMENTS

'No man is an island', wrote John Donne in 1624. What holds true for humanity also holds true for books. If, after two years of hard work, this book has finally made it on to your bookshelf, it's as a result of the support, expertise and generosity of many people.

It goes without saying – or should do – that I owe massive thanks to an entire legion of grape growers, winemakers, researchers, marketing gurus, wine importers and other experts, all of whom were incredibly generous with their time, insights and wines during the course of my research.

Much credit goes to the staff of Inter Beaujolais, both past and present, for helping me to explore their wonderful region, patiently answering my questions and putting me in touch with the people I needed to talk to when my internet searches for email addresses and phone numbers drew a blank.

There are four people in the wine community without whom I would never have been in a position to write this book in the first place. I suspect they may all be surprised to receive a name check, but gratitude doesn't come with an expiry date. Firstly, thanks to Susan Keevil, who, when editor of *Decanter*, gave me my first work on the magazine as a freelance sub-editor, and thereby became midwife to my career as a wine writer. If Adam Lechmere, who was in charge of *Decanter*'s website at the time, hadn't then given me a full-time job as his deputy and the confidence to develop my own journalistic voice, my fledgling interest in wine would have got no further than the joyful consumption of the odd bottle or two (little of it Beaujolais, I regret to say). Without the enthusiastic championing of Tim Atkin MW, then editor of wine trade magazine *Harpers*, the freelance career I embarked on when I left *Decanter* would never have got off the ground. And if Sally Easton MW hadn't insisted so forcefully and so frequently that I should sign up as a student on the Master of Wine programme, I might still be dithering about whether or not I should give it a try.

I've been lucky enough during the process of writing this book to have been able to rely on the support and encouragement of many of my fellow wine writers and MWs. To be completely honest, I've been somewhat taken aback by how positive the response has been to the news that I was working on a book on Beaujolais. If nothing else, I hope the enthusiasm my colleagues have shown for the region and its wines presages a glorious future for Beaujolais.

Particular thanks should go to all those who were generous enough not only to cheer me on, but also to cast an eye over some of the draft chapters for this book. None of the following people have read more than one chapter, but they read those chapters willingly and thoughtfully. The comments they were kind enough to send me were instrumental in refining my ideas, catching my errors and fine tuning my phrasing. This book would not be anywhere near as good as I hope it is without the feedback I received from Jo Ahearne MW, Alex Beckett, Kerrie de Boissieu, Geneviève Bonifacio, Tamlyn Currin, Alex Hunt MW, Juliette Levy, Victoria Mason MW, Michelle Paris, Siobhan Turner MW and Cathy van Zyl MW.

Books are always the product of teamwork, even if that's rarely acknowledged. I would like to take this opportunity to express my appreciation to everyone at Académie du Vin Library, from the members of the Classic Wine Library editorial board who decided to take a punt on publishing my book – Sarah Jane Evans MW, Richard Mayson and James Tidwell MS – to my publisher Hermione Ireland, and my indefatigable editor, Rebecca Clare.

Finally, I would like to dedicate *The wines of Beaujolais* to two people. My father, Frank Hughes, did not live long enough to see me achieve the success as a writer he always believed I would enjoy. He helped to kindle my life-long love for France and its food and wines, and he would have revelled in the publication of this book. I also want to pay tribute to my husband Mark Mitchell, without whose stoic and steadfast encouragement, love and friendship I would never have dared to travel so far nor reach so high.

PREFACE

For most people, Beaujolais is a region that is almost cartoonlike in its simplicity. 'Beaujolais Nouveau!' was pretty much what all my friends who don't work in the wine trade said on hearing that I was writing a book on the region. Those who've undergone formal wine education have an understanding that is a little more nuanced, but nevertheless still largely simplistic. Even some of the most educated people in the wine world believe that Beaujolais is a wine that tastes of bubblegum and candied red berries, a wine that can only last a year in bottle before it gives up the ghost of any fruit it once had. The method by which it is made is, they will tell you, carbonic maceration, and all the *cru* vineyards are planted on pink granite and all of southern Beaujolais is based on limestone soils.

When I first began visiting the region, some 20 years ago, that was pretty much what I knew – or thought I knew – about Beaujolais too. But the closer I looked, the more complex the story became. The more questions I asked of wine producers in the region, the more I got a response that ran along the lines of '… [pause]… *C'est compliqué*', it's complicated. *C'est compliqué* became the leitmotif of my research for this book, to the point at which I considered asking my editor whether she'd let me use a subtitle: The wines of Beaujolais: *c'est compliqué*. I'm joking, of course, but it's a joke that echoes a deep truth about a region that I've come to love because of – not despite – its complexity.

Beaujolais is a tiny part of the wine world in which huge variations in terroir and a multiplicity of vinification techniques (see Chapter 5) combine with one single grape variety to create a breathtaking diversity of styles. There are wines to please those who want a simple, bright-fruited quaffer that they can chill lightly and enjoy on a hot summer's afternoon, a more characterful, vibrant alternative to a sea of anodyne pale rosé. Alternatively, those looking for something more considered will also find much to enjoy in Beaujolais, from delicate wines with elegance and perfume, to fuller-bodied cuvées of great density and complexity, both styles that can reward ageing by unveiling themselves fully over time.

This heterogeneity, allied to a notion of terroir-driven differences, is not, on the whole, what most of us expect from Beaujolais. The pervasive image of a region fit only for the production of simple, unsophisticated wines dates back less than 40 years, as you'll discover in Chapter 1 on the region's history. Beaujolais's identity crisis is a relatively recent one, a melodrama in which both the people that live there and the vineyards they tend became victims of hubris and changing fashions.

By the time of my first visit to Beaujolais 20 or so years ago, the region was depressed, economically. Its wine growers were demoralized. Even I, a relative newcomer to the world of wine, could see that there was no way that the region's steep hillsides and low-trained bush vines could produce wines that were among the cheapest available on supermarket shelves, and still pay its farmers a living wage. Few of the producers I met back then had visited wine regions outside of Beaujolais, or drunk wines from elsewhere in France, never mind the rest of the world. And although there was a spirit of mutual practical aid, the exchange of ideas was rare.

It's been refreshing and rather wonderful to return to Beaujolais two decades later and, over the course of the multiple visits and many weeks of research it took to write this book, to find it transformed and yet, in its essence, fundamentally the same. The people who live and work here are, for the most part, warm and genuine. Airs and graces are in short supply, and wineries are usually happy to throw open their doors to interested visitors who want to taste their wines and learn about their terroir and their history. What has changed, though, is the attitude of the current crop of winemakers working these hills, people who are leading the charge in terms of creating a new, improved image for the region. Some of them have come to Beaujolais from elsewhere in France – or even further afield. Others are the sons and daughters (more often the former, it's true) of families who've been embedded in the landscape for generations. Many of them have studied at college with future winemakers from other French viticultural regions, establishing links that create a greater understanding of the country's diverse wine offering. And a significant number of Beaujolais's current crop of producers have worked overseas, travelling to South Africa, California, Chile, New Zealand and elsewhere before returning home with new ideas and a broader perspective. Perhaps even more importantly, they share not just viticultural tools and a helping hand in the vineyard when needed, but ideas and wines too. I quoted to many of the producers I met a dictum many wine lovers ascribe to Napa's Robert Mondavi (although it's highly likely he wasn't the first to say it) about a rising tide floating all boats. Few of them had heard of Mondavi, but all recognized the sentiment. They know that they have to work together to ensure that their region continues to thrive.

It would be naïve of me to suggest, however, that everything in the Beaujolais garden is coming up roses. The area of the region planted with vines shrinks with every passing year. In 2005, there were nearly 21,000 hectares of vineyards in Beaujolais. Ten years later the figure was closer to 16,000 hectares, and at the time of writing (in May 2025) the most recent data suggested that plantings had dropped to 13,000 hectares (although most growers believe the figure is closer to 12,000 hectares). As older vignerons retire, their vineyards are either sold on, grubbed up or abandoned. Sadly, in many cases, the vines that pass into oblivion are the twisted, gnarled veterans planted on the most vertiginous slopes. These are plants that have the potential to make world-class wines, but they are difficult and expensive to farm and give low yields, and are therefore difficult to justify in economic terms. As the table of average prices fetched by bulk wines from Beaujolais's various appellations in 2024 (see below) suggests, there is no premium paid for farming grapes in tricky, inaccessible locations. The value of the wine is, instead, dictated by consumer demand (and, to a lesser extent, the volumes produced). Although these prices are for wines sold on to négociants and cooperatives, the principle holds true for producers working with smaller volumes and bottling their own wines, even if their efforts carry a higher financial premium. This is a bitter pill to swallow for those who seek to preserve the region's viticultural heritage. It's also a poor recompense for the work undertaken by farmers in the region, whose average cost of production per hectolitre ranges from around €220 to €325. Bear in mind, too, that these costs can double or even treble if you're farming hillside vineyards by hand.

Average prices for bulk wines, as sold to négociants in Beaujolais, in 2024
(prices in euros per hectolitre)

Appellation	Price (€/hl)
Beaujolais rouge/rosé	250
Beaujolais Villages	275
Beaujolais blanc	310
Régnié	330
Chénas	340
Chiroubles	340
Brouilly	350
Côte de Brouilly	360
Fleurie	360
Juliénas	360
Morgon	380
Moulin-à-Vent	420
Saint-Amour	450

In addition, in Beaujolais – as elsewhere in France – a convoluted and inflexible bureaucracy often serves to hamper innovation instead of fulfilling its intended role of providing a framework for enhancing quality. When you factor in local politics, along with the opposing priorities of artisanal producers and large-scale enterprises, the mix can (and frequently does) become a source of frustration and simmering resentment within the region.

Furthermore, the prevailing economic and political climate around the world is causing most people to tighten their belts. Wine, now regarded by most as a luxury purchase rather than an everyday necessity, has become a casualty of current affairs. Beaujolais is far from the only region to be affected by cut-backs to household budgets, but neither has it been aided in its attempts to climb back into the wine world's spotlight by the unfavourable headwinds.

And yet, despite the challenges, there is much cause for optimism in today's Beaujolais. The first of these has been touched on above. The growers' sense of community and their recognition that they need to work together to promote their region first and themselves second is fairly unusual in France. The virtues of this approach have already proven themselves in terms of improvements in both viticulture and winemaking practices in Beaujolais. With any luck it will be extrapolated out to the creation of a collective strategy for the elevation of their region in the eyes of wine lovers around the world. In addition, the old prejudices that tarnished the region's reputation are rapidly fading in the rear-view mirror as consumers forget the taint of bland, mass-produced Nouveau (even though many of them are yet to recognize the high quality of wines now made in the region). It is a stroke of luck for the producers of Beaujolais that the seeds of a rising awareness of the quality of the wines they make coincides with the spiralling prices fetched by Burgundian cuvées. Some of the most switched-on oenophiles I know have swapped out at least some of their purchases of Pinot in favour of Beaujolais, citing their growing recognition of the amount of bang they can get for their buck by allowing their purchasing power to travel a few kilometres south. Sommeliers – often the bellwethers for trends in the wine world – have fallen in love with Beaujolais in recent years. Those working in Michelin-starred establishments cite the fact that Beaujolais – especially Cru Beaujolais – can fill a food-friendly niche on their lists at levels once occupied by *village*-level Burgundy (now priced out of contention). Wine buyers for younger, hipper eateries tune in to Beaujolais's ability to offer bottles produced in a way that aligns with their customers' interests in minimal-intervention wines and a quest for artisanal production.

My hope is that the pages of this book serve not only as a love letter to a region I have long admired and an encouragement to its producers to continue on their path towards greater recognition, but also as a guide to those seeking to explore Beaujolais's diversity and to improve their understanding of this unexpectedly complex but rather wonderful region.

A quick note on how this book is organized

The producers featured in this book have all been visited by me during the course of my research into the region, but not all the producers I met have been mentioned in the pages that follow. A small percentage of my visits turned out to be dead ends for one reason or another. Some were to producers who were on the verge of retiring, while I found that other producers made wines that simply did not live up to expectations. I felt that it was important, however, to provide readers with an overview of the heterogeneity of wine domaines in Beaujolais, and to that end, I have tried to include profiles of those working at all scales of production, from the teeny-tiny to those with worldwide distribution and a global reputation. This book includes accounts of producers making experimental cuvées and natural wines as well as those who espouse a more conventional philosophy. I wanted to make sure that the region's most established names were featured, but also took care to ensure that I gave some of Beaujolais's less recognized producers a look-in, too, as well as flagging up members of a younger generation of winemakers who I believe to be among the region's rising stars.

Sometimes it's been easy to work out in which chapter of this book a winery should be featured. When you're based in Villié-Morgon and all you make is Morgon – as is the case with so many of the producers based in the *cru* – the decision is self-evident. Other producers make things a bit more complicated by making several cuvées based on grapes grown in a number of *crus*. Here, my pragmatic approach has been to consider which *cru* a producer is most strongly linked to, or to follow the logic suggested by their largest vineyard holdings, wherever possible. Where this has not been possible, the positioning of a producer in a particular chapter has been, of necessity, a rather arbitrary decision.

Organic viticulture – whether certified or otherwise – is another recurrent theme in this book, perhaps surprisingly given that fewer than 15 per cent of producers in the region farm this way. This is not because I have actively sought out producers who work organically. However, having toured and tasted extensively across the region, what I have found is that many of the people who think deeply about how to farm in harmony with nature are also those who care enough to think deeply about how to create wines of high quality.

The most astute and observant readers will probably notice that a number of the producers featured in this book have a minimalist approach to winemaking that some might categorize as 'natural'. Many of the winemakers concerned actively and vocally reject that label, which has now become freighted with too many negative connotations, with most placing emphasis on the work they do in the vineyard in order to produce high-quality grapes rather than on addressing problems with the raw material they harvest by means of manipulation in the winery.

A further note, this time about sources

When I began researching Beaujolais in detail in the summer of 2023, I discovered that written sources were thin on the ground. In fact, no books have been written specifically about the region in English, and the most recent French publications about Beaujolais's wines date back to the 1980s (with the exception of a hagiography of the négociant Georges Duboeuf, see p. 235, published a decade or so ago). In short, there was no point in creating a bibliography of sources consulted when researching this book as published material is thin on the ground. Where I have had recourse to articles, academic or otherwise, or historical sources, these have been referenced in the text.

Nevertheless, I owe a debt of immense gratitude to Jon Bonné's magisterial work, *The New French Wine*, published in 2023 by Ten Speed Press. Bonné's love of Beaujolais and his deep-rooted knowledge of the region shines through in its pages and has provided me with both insights and inspiration, particularly in the context of the area's oenological history.

1

THE PATHS TO THE PRESENT

Like many self-respecting French wine regions, Beaujolais traces its viticultural history back to trade between what was then known as Trans-Alpine Gaul and the Roman Empire (and possibly even the Etruscans before that). The Saône River, a tributary of the Rhône, long a major trading route, was pressed into service as a highway along which wine was traded. The vineyards that came to thrive along its banks were often the fruits of the labours of retired soldiers, who were granted land in return for long military service. Local legend suggests that Florus and Brulius (or, in some accounts, Brulliacus), both former soldiers in Julius Caesar's army, are now memorialized in the name of three of Beaujolais's *crus*, Fleurie, Brouilly and the Côte de Brouilly.

As the Roman Empire segued into the Dark Ages, both monasteries and city bishops became critical not only to the maintenance of the early vineyards, but also to the development and expansion of viticultural knowledge. Monks, particularly those associated with the Benedictine order, were the first to formally identify those portions of the landscape that appeared to yield the grapes that made the best wines, thus kick-starting the search for terroir. Much of their focus in this part of the world was on the vineyards of Burgundy, helping to establish early on the prestige of the sites that would eventually become the region's *crus*. Beaujolais, too, had its monastic champions. During the tenth and eleventh centuries there were 183 priories in the region, which derived their authority from the Benedictine abbeys of Cluny and Tournus, as well as from the Bishop of Mâcon. These links certainly contributed

1

towards an understanding of the region's better sites, and a handful of the region's most historic properties are built on sites that once belonged to the Benedictine monks.

A BAD AND DISLOYAL GRAPE

By the tenth century, the region had come under the control of the lords of Beaujeu, whose fiefdom ran from the Mâconnais in the north (which at the time included four of the future *crus* of Beaujolais: Juliénas, Saint-Amour, Chénas and Moulin-à-Vent) through to the Lyonnais in the south. An echo of their *seigneurship* can be heard in the name of the region, Beaujolais. Five centuries later, however, the last duke of Beaujeu died without issue, and their lands passed into the hands of France's ruling dynasty. But geographical and viticultural proximity meant that the region was also linked closely to the Duchy of Burgundy – ties that still have some relevance today.

The most famous story told about the region's viticulture in this era suggests that the Gamay grape, which at the time was almost as widely planted in Burgundy as it was in Beaujolais, came under aristocratic scrutiny and was found wanting. Philippe le Hardi (Philip the Bold), Duke of Burgundy, passed an ordinance in 1395 in which he described Gamay as a 'very bad and disloyal' grape and decreed that the vines should be ripped out and banned from the region in perpetuity.[1] Gamay, thought the duke, not only made people ill due to the bitterness of the wine it produced, it was also responsible for ruining the good reputation of his region's wines.

There's currently a fair amount of academic debate as to why the duke had taken such a visceral dislike to the grape. Was it merely a matter of personal taste? Was it a simple recognition that Gamay vines,

---

1 The text of the edict reads '... un très-mauvaiz et très-desloyaulx plant nomméz Gaamez, duquel mauvaiz plant vient très-grant habondance de vins ... Et lequel vin de Gaamez est de tel nature qu'il est moult nuysible a creature humaine, mesment que plusiers, qui au temps passé en ont usé, en ont esté infestés de griez malaise ... car le dit vin qui est yssuz du dit plant, de sa dite nature, est plein de très-grant et horrible amertume ... Pour quoi nous ... vous mandons ... sollempnellement à touz dilz qui ont les diz plans de vigne de diz Gaamez, que yceulx coppent ou fassent copper en quelque part qu'ilz soient en nostre dit païs dedens cinq mois'. (... a very bad and very disloyal plant called Gaamez, from which come abundant quantities of wine ... And this wine of Gaamez is of such a kind that it is very harmful to human creatures, so much so that many people who had it in the past were infested by serious diseases ... as the said wine from said plant of said nature is full of significant and horrible bitterness... Therefore we solemnly command you ... all who have vines of said Gaamez to cut them down or have them cut down, wherever they may be in our country, within five months.') Translation, author's own.

when planted in Burgundy's relatively fertile soils, tend to yield copiously, thereby reducing the plant's capacity to ripen its grapes properly? Was he trying to protect the value and prestige of the wines made from grapes grown on his lands? Or was it an attempt to bolster a local wine trade that was navigating stormy commercial waters in the latter half of the fourteenth century? Historian Bart Van Loo, in *The Burgundians: A Vanished Empire*,[2] speculates that the young duke was flexing his fiscal muscles in a power showdown with the aldermen of Dijon by creating an artificial scarcity of wine.

One thing that should be borne in mind is that most vineyards at the time were planted with what would now be referred to as 'field blends', and that for centuries to come many different varieties were planted in both Burgundy and Beaujolais (as they were elsewhere in France). In his 1896 work, *Culture de la Vigne en Côte-d'Or* (The Cultivation of the Vine in the Côte d'Or),[3] Eugène Durand references no fewer than 14 varieties of Gamay, which were planted in the region in the late nineteenth century. It is, therefore, probable that the grape (or grapes) that had attracted the duke's ire is unlikely to map precisely onto what we now know as Gamay.

Regardless of the reasons behind the outburst, the duke's edict had set the tone for Gamay's reputation. For much of its recorded history, the grape would be despised by some as a 'lesser' variety, fit only for the labouring classes. Ordinances banning the grape from the Côte d'Or would be published with monotonous regularity over the centuries – testament, if nothing else, to Gamay's continuing popularity with the local peasantry. In 1855, Jules Lavalle, a medical doctor and botanist of note, published the *Histoire et Statistique de la Vigne de Grands Vins de la Côte-d'Or* (The History and Statistics of the Vineyards of the Great Wines of the Côte d'Or), in which he describes Gamay as a 'common' and 'ordinary' grape. He went on to say that the grape had 'invaded' the region, complaining petulantly, 'God knows how awfully active the vulgar plant has been in driving away the fine plant [Pinot Noir], and what progress it makes every day! Our ancestors would have been appalled!'[4]

---

2 Bart Van Loo, *The Burgundians: A Vanished Empire*, translated by Nancy Forest-Flier, Apollo, 2021.

3 Eugène Durand, *Culture de la Vigne en Côte-d'Or*, Hachette BNF, 1896.

4 Marion Fourcade, The Vile and the Noble, *Sociological Quarterly*, 2012, 53 (4), pp. 524–545.

Despite the snobbery, it wasn't until the twentieth century, and the arrival of appellation law, that Gamay loosened its grip on the wider Burgundian imagination, giving way to today's dominant varieties, Pinot Noir and Chardonnay. Nevertheless, Gamay retains a toehold in the north, where it is used to make Bourgogne Passetoutgrains (a blend of Pinot Noir and Gamay) and the wines of the recently established AOP of Côteaux Bourguignons. (It's worth noting that until relatively recently – at least until the post-phylloxera era, if not the advent of the appellation system – both Burgundy and Beaujolais enjoyed a far wider repertoire of grape varieties than is the case today.)

Beaujolais's commercial prospects were further blighted by its geographical situation. At a time when the main ways of transporting bulky goods involved either loading them onto a wagon to travel slowly over rutted roads (never good news for delicate wines) or sailing them to their destination, Beaujolais was at a disadvantage. Routes northward to Paris, with its thriving markets and its aristocratic courts, were largely blocked. From the fourteenth century onwards, until well into the sixteenth century, the duchy of Burgundy imposed a ban on non-Burgundian producers, with the exception of those from Fleurie and Romanèche-Thorins, prohibiting them from using the Saône to ship their wines.

As the Saône follows its course southwards, it feeds into the Rhône. But although in theory this allowed Beaujolais's producers access to the nearby city of Lyon, that city's vinous needs were already being met by the fruit of the vineyards situated in closer proximity to its walls. Nor was there any point in attempting to sell wines to the east or the west of Beaujolais as there were no large cities within easy travelling distance. In short, whatever the direction of travel, shipping the region's wines simply wasn't worth the time, expense and effort for Beaujolais's producers or for France's nascent merchant class.

This situation of not-so-splendid isolation meant that well into the eighteenth century Beaujolais was a relatively poor region. Furthermore, its farmers were not specialist wine growers. Instead, the local economy largely consisted of polyculture – most families lived on smallholdings where they grew some grain and beans and tended a few rows of vines and a small vegetable garden. If they were lucky, they had access to a small orchard, and maybe they even kept a few animals on their property. Most of the wine produced in the region was consumed not just locally, but by the very people who'd made it.

CHANGING FORTUNES

Change came slowly to Beaujolais. By the seventeenth century, Lyon had a thriving silk industry, and the wealth that created gave rise to a growing demand for the good things in life – and that included wine. But it wasn't until the revolt of the *Canuts*, the name given to the city's silk workers, in the 1830s that Beaujolais really got an opportunity to expand its customer base. One of the major concessions awarded to the workers was payment in wine, and the source of much of that wine was southern Beaujolais. The other factor that strengthened the ties between Lyon and the wine-growing region to its north was the rise in popularity of the city's *bouchons* in the nineteenth century. These informal restaurants, with their generous portions and cheap prices, were popular with the city's workers. The hearty meals they served needed plenty of wine to wash them down, and Beaujolais became the working man's drink of choice in many of these establishments.

This arrangement was enshrined in a trading agreement. Lyon was to receive the wines of southern Beaujolais. The region's northern vineyards, on the other hand, were traded northwards to Paris, largely by means of the network of canals that had begun to criss-cross the country in the seventeenth century.

Beaujolais now had ready markets for its wines, and production began to grow in importance in the region, with a few growers making the transition from generalist farmers to viticultural specialists. The region's ability to trade beyond its immediate boundaries picked up pace with the advent of the railways in the middle of the nineteenth century. France was relatively slow to adopt the iron horse, but by the start of the 1860s, Beaujolais's producers had access to markets in most of the country's major cities thanks to a railway line with freight stations in the town of Romanèche-Thorins and in Villefranche-sur-Saône.

Even more money flowed into the region when wealthy Lyonnais began to buy land and build houses in the region. In part these were holiday homes, but they were also agricultural investments. The largely absentee landlords needed local help to manage their estates, and the system of *métayage*, sharecropping, began to play a prominent part in the Beaujolais economy. *Métayage* had been practised in France for at least 1,000 years by this stage – possibly even longer – but it took root in Beaujolais so strongly that traces of it still survive in the region, although new *métayage* agreements were abolished by law in the 1970s.

The *métayer* typically performed all the labour in the vineyards and made the wine, in return for a half share of the production and free on-site accommodation. The landlord was responsible for all investments to the property, from the initial planting of the vineyards to upgrades to technology in the *cuvage*, as well as the maintenance of the buildings. When *métayage* worked well, it could be a win–win situation for landowner and tenant. The former could enjoy their country property in the knowledge that it was being managed to the mutual benefit of both participants. The tenant, in return, lived on the estate rent-free and derived an income from their labour. In many cases, though, *métayage* turned sour. If landlords failed to invest adequately – as so many did – the property entered into a downward spiral, with diminishing wine quality and diminishing financial returns. Some *métayers* also failed to uphold their end of the deal, performing their tasks at the level of the bare minimum required to scrape by.

CLASSIFICATION

The region was, regardless, on the rise, both economically and in terms of the reputation of the wines being made there. The first evidence for this came in 1816, when André Jullien published his *Topographie de Tous les Vignobles Connus* (an abridged version was published in English eight years later under the title *A Manual and Guide to all Importers and Purchasers in the Choice of Wines*). In it, he classified the wines of [Les] Thorins in Moulin-à-Vent and Chénas as first class (on a par with some of the most famous wines of Burgundy, including Richebourg and Clos Vougeot), while the wines of Fleurie were rated as second class (on a level with Burgundy's Vosne and Volnay).

In 1874 a Lyonnais engineer, Antoine Budker, sketched out a detailed map of the vineyards of the Côte Chalonnaise, the Mâconnais and Beaujolais in which individual *lieux-dits* were not only defined and depicted, but also ranked by quality, from fifth through to first class. Budker's classification wasn't based on local knowledge, but rather on the results of a local wine competition. Nevertheless, it was a valid – and valuable – first attempt at a systematic categorization of the quality of the region's terroirs in an approach that echoed the *cru* system of the Côte d'Or.

Budker's work became the inspiration for Victor Vermorel, an industrialist and local politician, who was president of the *Comice Agricole et Viticole du Beaujolais* (the local agricultural and wine fair) as well as the director of the *Station Viticole de Villefranche* (Villefranche's viticultural station). Vermorel, together with Réné Danguy, a professor at the viticultural college in Beaune, published *Les Vins du Beaujolais, du Mâconnais et Chalonnais* (*The Wines of Beaujolais, the Mâconnais and Chalonnais*) in 1893. This book built on the foundations established by Budker, enhanced by local understanding of the quality of the region's terroirs, to create a ranking of hundreds of Beaujolais's *lieux-dits*.

It would be tempting to dismiss the work of Jullien, Budker, Vermorel and Danguy as just another example of the Victorian era's passion for hierarchization and the creation of lists, were it not for the fact that the ranking of *lieux-dits* that emerged from the process maps closely on to contemporary understandings of the relative quality of these sites. *Lieux-dits* such as Carquelin in Moulin-à-Vent, the Haute Ronze in Régnié and Les Moriers in Fleurie were highly valued sites 150 years ago and are still prized by producers today.

In addition, documented evidence exists that the wines from some of these *lieux-dits* – or from zones that would eventually become *crus* – were just as highly prized by wine lovers as they were by the people who made the wines. A catalogue of wine prices published by the Burgundian négociant Louis Jadot in 1895 reveals that a 212-litre barrel of Moulin-à-Vent 1892 would have set you back 420 francs, while a 228-litre barrel of Volnay or Pommard 1er Cru would cost 620 francs and a similar volume of Mercurey or Givry would have fetched 360 francs. (Why the difference in the size of the barrels? Tax. The smaller barrels could be shipped, tax-free, along the Canal de Briare all the way to the Loire, and then on to Paris via the Seine.) A rough approximation suggests that the Burgundian *premier cru* carried a premium of slightly less than 30 per cent relative to the cost of the Moulin-à-Vent, while the appellations of the Côte Chalonnaise were just under 15 per cent cheaper. These days you're unlikely to find a Moulin-à-Vent at more than £35, even if it's a parcel selection from a top producer, and the reds from the Côte Chalonnaise start at around the same price. Your bottle of *premier cru* from the Côte de Beaune, on the other hand, could easily cost you over £120.

BEAUJOLAIS NOUVEAU AND ITS LEGACY

So what happened between the end of the nineteenth century and the early twenty-first century to cause the value of the wines from Beaujolais to fall so precipitously relative to those of their northern neighbour (and elsewhere)? Blame is usually laid at the door of Beaujolais Nouveau. It's true that these wines had a big part to play in the region's changing fortunes, in both a positive and a negative way. But it's facile to ascribe all the region's problems to one simple cause.

Beaujolais's race to the bottom began in the post-war period, although its roots ran deeper, back to the phylloxera crisis of the late nineteenth century. Like most wine-producing regions, Beaujolais's vineyards were devastated by the louse. Although vines were replanted on American rootstocks, production didn't really hit its stride until the period between the two world wars, at which point the Great Depression of the 1930s affected not only the volumes of wines sold but also the prices they fetched. During the Second World War, the agricultural economy of Beaujolais, which was located in Vichy France (which is to say that it was not under Nazi control), was effectively ruined. By 1945 there was, quite literally, not a single barrel of Beaujolais available for sale. From that point onwards, Beaujolais travelled pretty fast down the road towards the production of cheap table wine rather than towards the heights of more premium offerings. It was rare, at the time, for producers to bottle their own wine. Instead they preferred the quick economic hit of producing in bulk and selling their grapes (or wines) either to local cooperatives or to négociants. Quantity, not quality, became the modus operandi throughout much of Beaujolais.

Meanwhile, back in the *bouchons* of Lyon and the *zincs* of Paris, another trend was emerging. The tradition had long been to ship barrels of Beaujolais to both cities (rather than bottles), but the owners of the restaurants – and their customers – were aware that these wines were at their vibrant best shortly after harvest. By the end of each year's production cycle, the wine remaining in the barrels was beginning to look, and taste, rather jaded. Restaurateurs and *cavistes* took to putting out billboards as soon as the new wines arrived in their cellars every year. *Le Beaujolais Nouveau est arrivé* was the slogan used to advertise the fact that the latest vintage was available on tap. The race to get the Nouveau in as early as possible became so exaggerated that quality was compromised. In 1951 the INAO stepped in and legislated that the earliest that Beaujolais *primeur* could be sold was on the stroke of midnight on the third Thursday in November.

The Beaujolais-based négociant Georges Duboeuf took the idea and ran with it, big time. He started off in the 1960s by hosting parties celebrating the new vintage, first at his winery in Romanèche-Thorins, then in Paris and, eventually, around the world. He would invite famous chefs and restaurateurs, along with celebrities and politicians, causing a buzz of excitement and generating publicity both for his business and for the *primeur* wines he was selling. The world fell in love with Beaujolais and its zesty, fruity wines. (It's worth remembering that this all happened in the days before New World wines hit the markets in a big way, so easy-drinking, juicy wines were a novelty for many.) Within a decade of Duboeuf launching his new-wave Nouveaus, every négociant and cooperative in the region had jumped onto the Nouveau bandwagon alongside him.

The wacky Nouveau races

The idea of a race to be the first to celebrate the new vintage wasn't long in coming. The notion was born during a dinner enjoyed in a hotel in Romanèche-Thorins in November 1970 by Duboeuf's British wine importer Joseph Berkmann and the MP and newspaper wine columnist Clement Freud. By the end of an evening washed down with copious quantities of local wine, the two had laid a bet with each other as to who would be the first to get a case of the stuff back to London. In a way that would be considered highly illegal nowadays, both men got into their Rolls-Royces at midnight and roared north up the *autoroute* and back to London. (Berkmann won, by the way.) What began as a private bet became an established competition open to all comers. By the 1980s, fleets of trucks and planes were being drafted in to ship Beaujolais around the world so that it would be available for uncorking at midnight on the designated date. Some outlets went to drastic lengths to be the first to receive their shipments – and to bask in the glow of media attention thanks to their efforts. The most extreme example of this may well be London's Savoy Hotel, which drafted in the Red Devils to parachute their supply in one year.

The winemakers of Beaujolais revelled in their new-found riches and the fame the wines brought to their region. So important did Beaujolais Nouveau become for the region's economy that around a third of all the wines produced in Beaujolais in the 1980s and 1990s were destined for sale by the end of the very same year in which the grapes were grown. Unfortunately, the very success of Beaujolais Nouveau sowed the seeds for the region's eventual downfall. To begin with, many of the growers – particularly those based in the southern *Bas Beaujolais* zone (see p. 213) – got as hooked on the easy money to be had from growing grapes for Nouveau as teenagers do on the sugar and fat rush that comes with a fast food meal. Alongside the hit of cash came a decline in quality of the wines being made. In order to produce vast quantities of wine very quickly, shortcuts were being taken in both the vineyards and the winery.

The easiest way to produce lots of wine very cheaply is, of course, to crop at high yields. If you're going to do so, though, you're likely to need the support of pesticides, fungicides, herbicides and fertilizers. And that's exactly what happened across Beaujolais's vineyards, where the vines were routinely sprayed with all kinds of treatments throughout the growing

Les Beaujolais Nouveaux sont arrivés – an event that's still worth celebrating every November (photo courtesy of Nicolas Dormont/Beaujolais Wines)

season. The use of vast quantities of weed killers became so entrenched in the local psyche that one grower told me that when he converted his vineyards to organic viticulture in the early 2000s, allowing competing grasses to grow between and beneath his vines, his father reproached him for having 'untidy' vineyards. In the southern part of Beaujolais, in particular, the drive towards the use of chemical aids to viticulture mandated a wholesale grubbing up of old-school, densely planted bush vines in favour of trellised plantings, which were far easier to mechanize.

In the rush to vinify huge volumes of wine quickly and efficiently, the region's traditional vinification methods were eschewed in favour of technical winemaking that not only allowed for speedy processing of the raw material but also standardized flavours and aromas. Thermovinification and the use of cultured yeasts, in particular 71B, were used to create wines with deep colour, little tannin and flavours of bubblegum and candied fruits.

When the tide of fashion turned against Beaujolais Nouveau in the early 2000s, it did so with a speed and a violence that took the region by surprise. During the boom years of the 1990s you couldn't buy a vineyard in the region for love or money, but within a decade, vineyards were being left to lie fallow as it simply wasn't worth the time or the money it took to cultivate them. Worse still, there's plenty of anecdotal evidence to suggest that suicide rates among Beaujolais vignerons rose as many of them, thinking the good times would last, had stretched themselves financially well beyond their ability to repay their debts. The final – and most enduring – legacy of the Nouveau era was the tarring of all the region's wines by association. The very idea that Beaujolais could be complex, characterful and long-lived became risible.

Chauvet and the Gang of Four

In the 1970s, at the same time as Beaujolais Nouveau was rising to become the economic motor that drove the region's economy, something else was happening in Beaujolais, initially on a much smaller, quieter scale. A small, resolute group of winemakers was beginning to hold out against the almost overwhelming tide of Beaujolais Nouveau. Arguably, this group set an agenda for change that has now come to dominate the prevailing philosophy of many of the most quality-focused producers in the region.

Marcel Lapierre, Jean Foillard, Jean-Paul Thévenet and Guy Breton, all of whom were based in the *cru* of Morgon, have now been memorialized in accounts of Beaujolais's history as the 'Gang of Four'. Like all good stories, though, there's more than an element of myth making to this account of what has been widely seen as the start of Beaujolais's natural wine movement. To begin with, the term 'Gang of Four' was invented wholesale by US importer Kermit Lynch as a way of marketing the four growers he imported. Not only did the group not think of themselves in these terms, many other producers, all motivated by a similar philosophy, worked alongside them, among them key figures such as Joseph Chamonard, Yvon Métras and Georges Descombes. And in order to examine the influence of this group on the region you have to travel even further back in time to the 1950s.

Jules Chauvet was a respected négociant based in the northern fringes of Beaujolais from the 1940s onwards. He dreamed fondly of the Beaujolais he remembered from his youth – juicy, fruity wines with vibrant acidity and modest levels of alcohol. Chauvet was not just a négociant, though, he was also a respected winemaker and a chemist. He spent much time trialling approaches that would allow for the creation of the kinds of wines he was interested in, considering the simple, bubblegum-scented Beaujolais Nouveaus made in the region from the 1960s onwards, and the quasi-industrial processes that produced them, to be both an aberration and an abomination. Among other avenues of experimentation, Chauvet was interested in the possibilities of carbonic maceration, a technique Louis Pasteur had first explored in the 1870s, and which was part of the portfolio of winemaking processes used widely in the Beaujolais of Chauvet's youth. Chauvet also questioned the need to use chemicals in viticulture, investigated the microbiology of fermentation, advocated for the use indigenous yeasts, and, perhaps most famously, was a keen critic of the over-use of sulphites in winemaking.

Chauvet's contribution to the debate about the role of sulphites is widely misunderstood. Although he is widely regarded as the father (or at least the godfather) of the anti-sulphite movement, Chauvet had nothing against the use of the compound as a preservative in winemaking per se – what he railed against was its over-use, particularly when it was deployed at harvest (when it might inhibit the ability of indigenous yeasts to dominate the aerobic part of the fermentation). He was a firm believer, instead, in the use of scrupulous hygiene in the winery so as to prevent spoilage organisms from taking hold of the vinification process.

Nevertheless, it was Chauvet's scepticism about the over-use of sulphites that first drew the attention of Beaujolais's most rebellious winemakers, Marcel Lapierre and fellow travellers, to him in the late 1970s. Eventually the results of Chauvet's research into all aspects of winemaking were to become the bedrock of a new paradigm in the region, along with a growing emphasis on organic viticulture. It's easy to see, in retrospect, why the message Chauvet preached was so attractive to producers in search of an escape route from the grinding labour and poor economic returns that came from catering to the Nouveau market.

If you fast forward several decades, it's clear that Chauvet and his acolytes continue to influence the direction of viticultural travel in Beaujolais. Many of the producers you'll meet in the pages of this book either have organic certification or are in the process of conversion to organics. The winemaking practices espoused by the Gang's members – and their sympathizers – have become routine for many of the region's best producers, regardless of whether they consider themselves to be 'natural' winemakers or not. The use of sulphites is generally minimal, typically relegated to almost homeopathic doses just prior to bottling. Some estates do make a 'no-sulphur' cuvée, but this is often part of a broader range rather than being widely considered to be the gold standard.

The use of indigenous yeasts in the latter stage of fermentation, too, is now widely practised by wineries working on an artisanal scale, and even some of the larger domaines. And although some wineries produce cuvées in which the influence of new oak is marked, most Beaujolais still puts the emphasis on fruit character, with maturation taking place in stainless steel or cement tanks, older oak (often large-format barrels) or, increasingly, amphorae and concrete eggs.

The industrial, technical winemaking techniques that were such an anathema to Chauvet and his followers are still practised in Beaujolais, but in terms of driving the region's image today, the Gang – however many members you care to include – has arguably won the turf war.

FIRSTS AMONG EQUALS?

Albert Einstein once wrote that the distinction between past, present and future is only a stubbornly persistent illusion. Although this chapter is largely about Beaujolais's history, the past – as ever – has a bearing not only on what is happening in the region now, but also on its future. In 2024 the producers of Fleurie officially applied for seven of the *cru's* *lieux-dits* to be elevated to *premier cru* status. The application process requires a *dossier*, a file of evidence that details, among other things, evidence of each *lieu-dit's* history and critical recognition over time and data pointing to current market demand. The *lieu-dit*'s boundaries will be specified, along with details of its terroir and the specifics of its viticultural and vinification practices, along with all the regulations relating to its current status, from planting densities to minimum yields.

The application is unlikely to be successful immediately. The INAO, the government body with oversight of the French appellation system, tends to take its time over such decisions. Investigators are sent to regions that apply for such changes in status, and they examine each *lieu-dit* in excruciating detail, making recommendations for adaptations to the *dossier*. Blind tastings will take place to ensure that the quality of the wines made in the candidate *lieux-dits* is up to scratch. The region will have to adapt its *dossier* according to the stipulations of the INAO's experts and then, keeping its metaphorical fingers crossed, refile its application, which will again be scrutinized in detail. Further recommendations may be made, to which the *cru* will need to get a buy-in from its growers. The entire process is mind-numbingly slow, often taking ten years or more from start to finish.

Nevertheless, a number of other Beaujolais *crus* have thrown their hats – or, rather, their *dossiers* – in the ring, with Moulin-à-Vent and Brouilly filing for *premier cru* recognition for their best *lieux-dits*, and the Côte de Brouilly, Juliénas and Morgon currently contemplating following suit.

These applications have already been in the offing for a considerable period of time – since well before the start of my research for this book in 2023. My initial response to the notion of creating *premiers crus* in Beaujolais was that it was, unequivocally, a great idea, and one that could only bring benefits to the region. Now, having discussed the concept with producers around the region, I'm slightly less convinced and can see arguments both for and against the creation of Beaujolais *premiers crus*.

Reasons why having *premiers crus* in Beaujolais might be a good idea

Having *premiers crus* will serve as a reminder to wine lovers everywhere that Beaujolais has some truly world-class terroirs.

Having the words '*premier cru*' on a label may permit producers to charge more for at least some of their wines. True, this is not an unalloyed benefit for the end consumer, but Beaujolais is currently desperately under-valued relative to any other high-quality wine region in France (and the rest of the world, for that matter), and as things stand, most Beaujolais producers are struggling to make ends meet. The ability to earn an extra two or three euros per bottle for *premiers crus* might make the difference between staying afloat and succumbing to the financial tides for many producers.

Receiving a higher financial reward for their best wines could potentially allow for greater investment in the region's vineyards and *cuvages*. This, in turn, might result in the production of even better wines.

If a *cru* does not apply for *premier cru* status for some of its *lieux-dits*, the *cru* as a whole may lose out, both commercially and in terms of status, relative to those appellations that do have *premiers crus*. Imagine a scenario where, in 10 years' time, you're handed a restaurant wine list, and you're given the choice of, say, a Fleurie *premier cru* Grille-Midi or a Chénas Aux Blémonts. All other things being equal, which are you going to assume is the better wine?

Reasons why having *premiers crus* in Beaujolais might not be a good idea

A number of producers have mentioned their belief that *premiers crus* belong to Burgundy and have nothing to do with Beaujolais's culture or traditions.

In a region that has had to learn the hard way that everyone needs to pull together to promote the region as a group, the creation of a notional quality barrier that raises one neighbour over another is, perhaps, invidious.

The creation of *premiers crus* does not automatically earn those who farm these vineyards the right to raise their prices. Some regions have found, to the contrary, that the net effect of introducing a new, superior quality level is to depress the prices of wines from the same region that do not have *premier cru* on their labels.

The creation of *premiers crus* does not necessarily mean that a wine produced as a *premier cru* will be a qualitative improvement on a wine without that designation. Most wine lovers are familiar with the notion that there are producers in nearby Burgundy whose *village*-level wines are far superior in quality to *premiers crus* from lesser producers. This, then, begs the question of the real value of any such classification system.

Unless the notion of *premier cru* is linked to real criteria associated with the production of high-quality wines, the classification itself will be meaningless, and may even undermine the image of Beaujolais overall. When speaking to me many producers have placed particular emphasis on the need for any *premier cru* status to be associated with organic farming and due consideration being given to appropriate levels of yield.

The insistence on a glorious record of market demand and critical praise for a *lieu-dit* in the *dossier* places undue emphasis on those vineyards that have successfully ripened fruit in an era when most wines from Beaujolais were routinely chaptalized. These are typically the sunniest, best-exposed sites, and therefore may not be the best vineyards in any given *cru* in an era of climate change.

My belief is that some of these arguments, both for and against the introduction of *premiers crus* to Beaujolais, can be taken with a heavy pinch of salt – or that work-around solutions can be found to the problems that arise. Either way, *premiers crus* are almost certainly coming to Beaujolais, whether, on balance, we come down in favour of them or not. The true challenge will be in ensuring that the criteria on which they are selected, the constraints that are imposed on them and the way producers use their *premier cru* status are truly relevant to enhancing the image of Beaujolais and its *crus*.

2

THE SONGS OF THE EARTH: BEAUJOLAIS'S TERROIR

As you drive south through the Mâconnais, Burgundy blends seamlessly into Beaujolais. For most of the year, until *veraison*, when the dark colour of the Gamay berries takes over from the green hue of the Chardonnay, the only clue that you've crossed the border between the two regions is the transition between trellised vineyards and a landscape dominated by bush vines.

THE LIE OF THE LAND

From the northernmost *cru* of Saint-Amour to the furthest flung villages of the *pierres dorées* in the south, Beaujolais is just over 70 kilometres in length, and measures around 20 kilometres across at the widest point of its east–west axis. As wine regions go, therefore, it is pretty bijou.

Beaujolais is split roughly in half between the zone in the north containing the *crus*, and the southern zone, which is dominated by the area that produces AOP Beaujolais. There are 10 *crus* – specific, delimited production zones, each with their own distinctive terroir and history. The *crus* produce wines that are widely considered to represent a significant jump in quality above that of basic AOP Beaujolais in terms of both concentration and complexity. Running from north to south (approximately, as they don't lie in a conveniently straight line) the *crus* are Saint-Amour, Juliénas, Chénas, Moulin-à-Vent, Fleurie, Chiroubles, Morgon, Régnié, Côte de Brouilly and Brouilly.

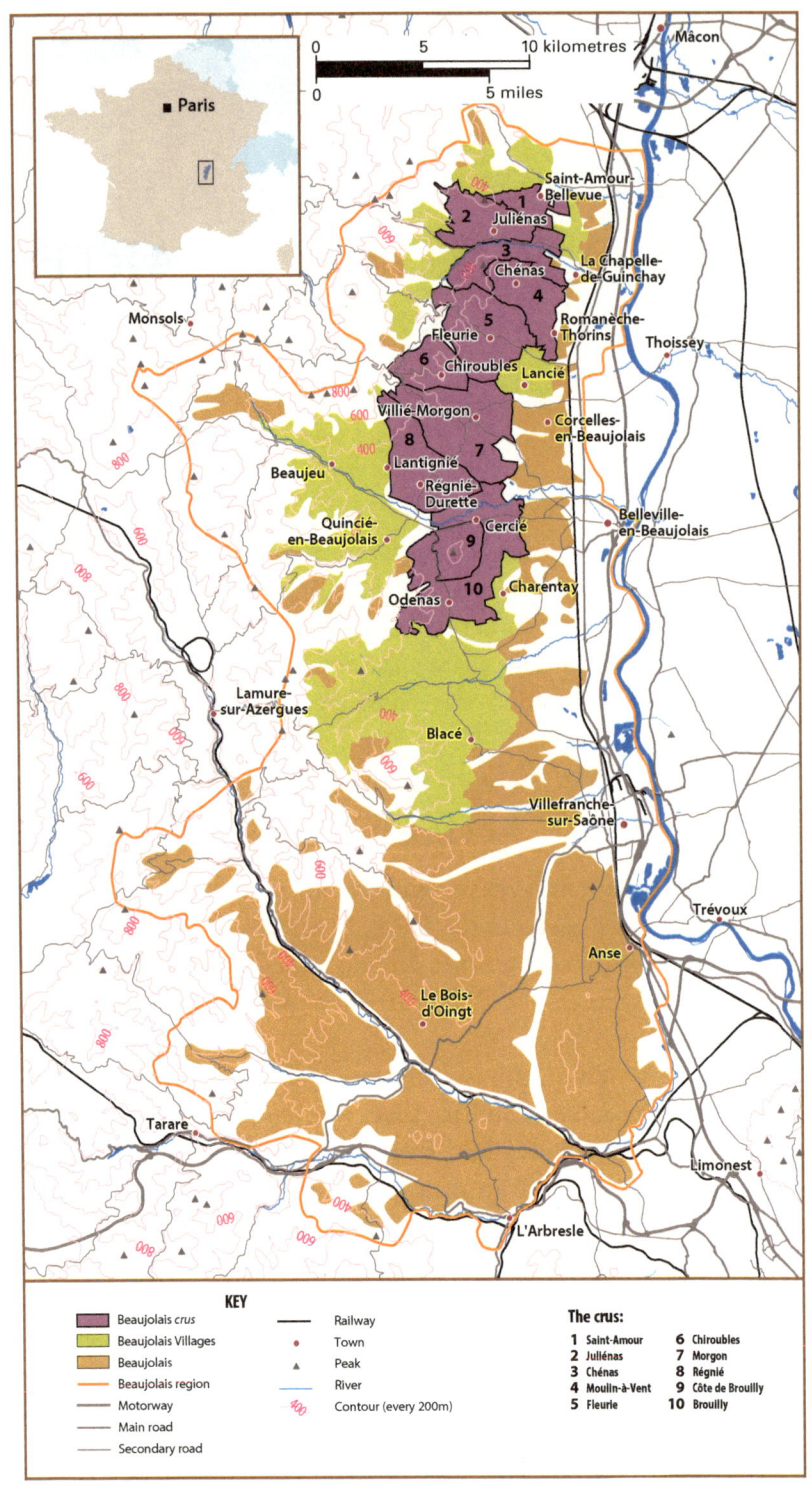

Map 1: The Beaujolais wine region

Contrary to popular belief, Beaujolais Villages isn't some kind of souped-up appellation awarded to better-than-average basic Beaujolais. It is actually a discrete – if scattered – production zone spread out across 38 often hilly communes. Most of the villages curl protectively around the western flank of the *crus* or act as a girdle that separates the *crus* from the *Bas Beaujolais* to the south.

Within this framework lies another layer of cartographic complexity. The *crus* in particular, but the rest of the region to a lesser extent as well, are further subdivided into a series of named parcels known as either *lieux-dits* or *climats*.

The term *lieu-dit* (the nearest translation is 'named place') or *climat* refers to the designation given to a specific parcel of land within a larger zone such as a vineyard or appellation. There's a good, practical reason for the existence of *lieux-dits* and *climats*. It is far more convenient to be able to tell your family that you'll be spending the day pruning vines in Douby, for instance, rather than to specify that you might be found in the far south-eastern corner of Chiroubles, just below the little stream that runs down into the Morgon vineyards. It is also helpful to be able to single out the characteristics of any given plot of land when planning your viticultural management strategy – knowing that Grille-Midi is warmer and sunnier than Les Labourons, for example, may well help to determine the way you manage the canopy of the vines in these plots.

This practice of naming specific parcels occurs throughout the wider Burgundian region. In Burgundy itself, the term *lieu-dit* is typically used to refer to sites situated in *village*-level vineyards, while a *climat* often refers to larger parcels (sometimes whole vineyards) of all quality levels. To confuse matters further, there may be a number of *lieux-dits* within a *climat*, the latter typically being larger than the former. Broadly speaking Beaujolais has adopted this naming practice, with particular emphasis on *lieux-dits* rather than *climats*, and there are more than 500 *lieux-dits* spread out across the *crus*, *villages* and Beaujolais zones. Of course, given that this is Beaujolais (remember, *c'est compliqué*), one *cru* – Morgon – has, in the past, eschewed the use of *lieux-dits*, opting instead to subdivide itself into larger *climats*, although each of these can be further subdivided into *lieux-dits*. This distinction would be of purely academic interest under most circumstances, but it has a direct – and unexpected – consequence for the debate over the issue of whether or not to apply for *premier cru* status for certain parcels (see p. 14), as well as a recent controversy to affect the growers of Morgon (see p. 145).

THE STORY OF THE SOILS

One of the key differences between the terroir of the *crus* and that of the Beaujolais AOP production area lies in the typicity of their soils. Anyone who's ever undertaken any formal wine education will have been told that the northern half of the region has granitic soils, while the south is dominated by limestone-rich clays. But while this is broadly true, the reality is far more complex. In 2009, a team of workers led by the geologists of Sigales, a soil-mapping agency, began to take soil samples and dig pits at regular intervals across the entire region. Over the course of nine years, some 1,000 trenches were dug – that's one for every 20 hectares of land – and micro-trenches were assayed every 1.5 hectares.

Growers were invited to participate in weekly sessions in which they were encouraged to peer into the pits and join discussions led by the surveyors in order to gain a greater understanding of the underlying geology of their vineyards. Nevertheless, when the final results of the study were published, they astounded everyone. More than 300 different soil types had been identified in the region. To simplify matters these were grouped into 25 broad categories according to the dominant type of rock, the depth of the topsoil, the degree of decomposition and other criteria. The information gathered has not only helped to educate growers, it has also been used to create a series of incredibly detailed geological maps of the region.[5]

These maps show that the pink granite so closely associated with the *crus* is widely found across the north of Beaujolais – it accounts for around 38 per cent of all planted areas – but its distribution is far from even. A solid seam of granite runs down the western side of the *cru* zone and on into the hills of the Beaujolais Villages. Granite dominates Fleurie and Chiroubles – but these are the only two *crus* where granite is the main soil type. Elsewhere in the *crus* you'll find rich deposits of diorite, a bluish-tinged hard volcanic rock, known locally as *pierre bleue*, with concentrated outcrops situated in Juliénas as well as on Mont Brouilly and Morgon's Côte du Py, in addition to scatterings along the western slopes of the *villages* vineyards. The eastern flanks of the *crus* are rich in alluvial and colluvial deposits. And while some of the *cru* zones are fairly homogeneous in terms of their geology, others – most notably Saint-Amour and Brouilly – appear to be a palimpsest of geological complexity. The

---

5 To explore all of Beaujolais's gelological maps in detail, visit the homepage for the appellations: www.beaujolais.com/decouvrir/nos-12-appellations/

southern part of the region, although dominated by richer limestone-inflected soils, also has its fair share of diorite, granite, marl and clay. No wonder UNESCO awarded Beaujolais status as one of its Geoparks in recognition of the geological diversity uncovered by the researchers.

It is possible to make a rough generalization about the typical expression of these soils when it comes to the wines they produce. Although both the granite and the diorite are poor in organic material, the blue stone typically holds a bit more water than the free-draining pink granite. Both impose curbs on Gamay's natural vigour, and are therefore – in theory at least – terrific soils for anyone looking to make high-quality wines. Having said that, both types of soil are associated with specific challenges, particularly in hot vintages, when the limited water-holding capacity of the pink granite (particularly the decomposed sands derived from the stone) can render the vines vulnerable to stress. In the same vintages, conditions in the vineyards planted on blue stones can become

Granite bedrock rising to the surface in the vineyards of Fleurie

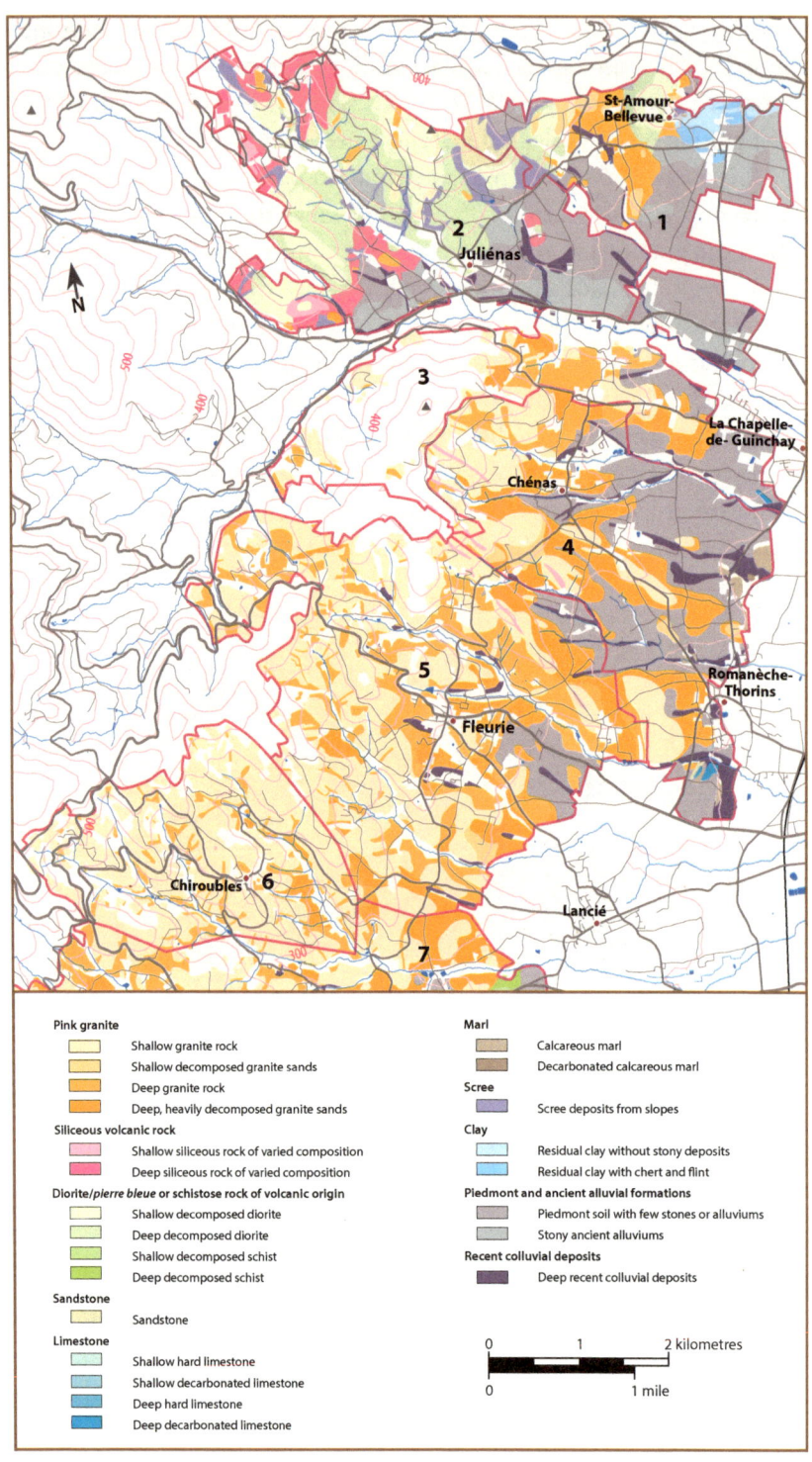

Map 2: The geology of the northern crus

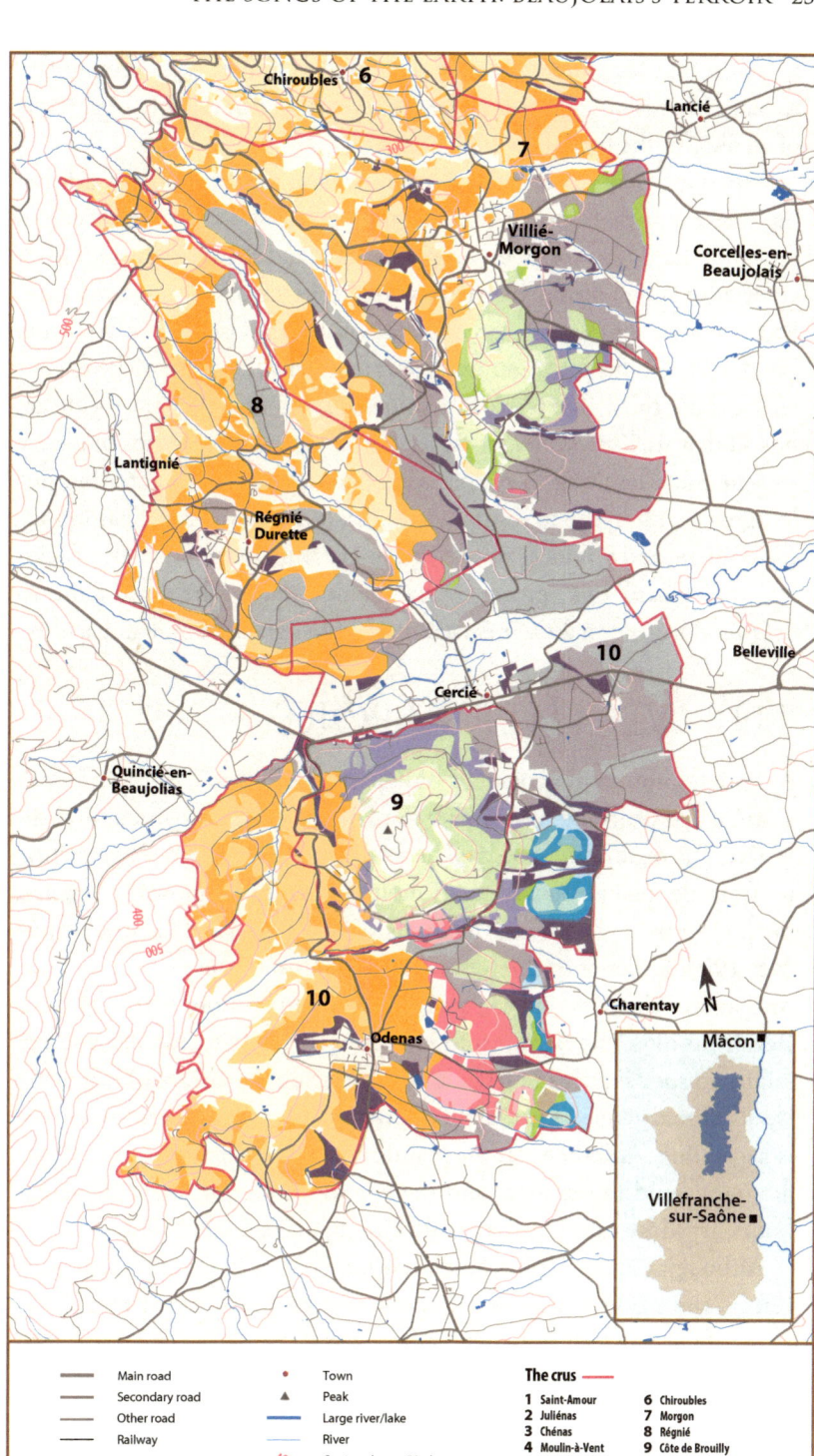

Map 3: The geology of the southern crus

so warm that the grapes ripened there have a tendency to accumulate sugars extremely fast, which in turn can result in undesirably high levels of alcohol in the finished wines.

Typically, wines made from grapes grown on granite tend towards being linear and perfumed in character, while those derived from grapes grown on hard blue rocks are more muscular and dense. The wines from vineyards planted on alluvial and colluvial soils are often quite broad and fleshy in style, but as their precise geological composition is often quite variable, with different amounts of clays and sands, it can be tricky to generalize about them. The fertile limestone soils to the south of the region are not all that well suited to Gamay as they encourage the grape's tendency to generosity, resulting in simple wines and a lack of concentration unless growers intervene to restrict yields. On the other hand, Chardonnay thrives here, and produces wines with bright fruit and good levels of acidity, while Chardonnay grown on the granitic soils of the north tends to over-produce and make wines lacking in both concentration and acidity.

THE WEATHER REPORT

Although important, geology is only part of the terroir story, and both altitude and exposure have a part to play in Beaujolais's viticultural diversity. The region's vineyards all lie to the west of the Saône River, rising up from the plain into a series of mounded hills that grow ever steeper the further west you travel. The mountains of the Massif Central lie just over 100 kilometres to the west, while the Alps, to the east, are so close by that on a clear day you can see the snowy cap of Mont Blanc from the Beaujolais hills. (Vignerons told me about this view repeatedly, and my failure to spot France's tallest mountain during the course of my many weeks of research led me to believe that my informants were, somehow, exaggerating. And then, on the penultimate day of my research, I drove around a bend in the road, and there it was, towering above its neighbours, its white cap tinged a gentle pink by the sunset.)

Although the north of Beaujolais is hillier than the south, the French refer to the region as *la petite Toscane*, little Tuscany, because the combination of the gently undulating landscape and the warm honey-coloured stone that dominates the local architecture, particularly in the south, is reminiscent of central Italy. But beautiful as these hills might be, they have a deeper significance in viticultural terms; growers can play not only with altitude but also with aspect to achieve varying degrees of

The hills of Beaujolais extend out towards the Massif Central,
gaining in altitude as you travel west

ripeness in their grapes. Altitude and exposure therefore have a key part
to play in creating complexity in the region's wines, but also in dealing
with climate change – of which more later.

First, though, it's important to consider the region's climate in more
general terms. Beaujolais lies at one of France's great crossroads. The
city of Lyon – widely seen as the point where northern France tips over
towards the warmth of the Mediterranean – lies about a half hour's drive
south from Villefranche-sur-Saône, the biggest town in the Beaujolais
area. As a result of its location Beaujolais enjoys a semi-continental
weather pattern of cold, often rainy winters – there might even be the
occasional dusting of snow – and summers that tend to be slightly hot-
ter and drier than those in Burgundy's Côte d'Or.

The climate in Beaujolais was once considered to be marginal in
terms of its ability to bring Gamay to the peak of ripeness. Producers often found that they had to chaptalize (add sugar to) their musts in order
to bring the finished wines up to an acceptable alcohol level of 12% abv
or more. Some of the struggle to get grapes up to the required levels of
maturity may well have been due to the growers' competing desire to
pick generous volumes each year, especially during an era when quantity
was considered to be at least as important as quality. High yields may
have been good for the bank balance, but it also meant that the vines

struggled to accumulate sugars in each individual berry. Nevertheless, it is clear that in Beaujolais – as elsewhere – summer temperatures are climbing, and this affects levels of ripeness. (For more on the changing climate's effects on Beaujolais's grapes see p. 36.)

These pages are not the appropriate arena for rehearsing detailed arguments about climate change and its effects on viticulture worldwide – or even specifically in Beaujolais – but it is important to note that growers in the region appear to be facing some very specific challenges. Violent hailstorms are now a regular feature of the growing season, typically occurring in summer, sometimes several times a year. Beaujolais is no stranger to hail – although the frequency of these storms has increased in recent years – but what has changed is their route. Where once the ice-bearing clouds bypassed most of the vineyards, the destruction of a coppice of trees on the top of a hill a few years ago seems to have altered their path, and there is now a hail-prone belt that runs right through Régnié, on into the heart of Fleurie and up onto the hillsides of Chiroubles. Other parts of the *crus* can also be affected by hail, although not with the frequency and the viciousness of the storms that sweep

Storm clouds gather over the vineyards (photo courtesy of David Large)

through the belt, the worst of which are described by growers as torna-does of hail. There can be few things as heartbreaking for a grower than to nurture their vineyards through most of a growing season, only to see bunches and leaves alike torn to shreds in the space of a few devastating minutes, often just weeks away from harvest. In some years growers may lose 50 per cent or more of their grapes. In addition, levels of rainfall are at a historical low, and the water table is not always replenished over winter – although this was not the case in either 2021 or 2024, when epic levels of rain throughout the growing season brought both fungal disease and reduced yields. When summer brings high temperatures and drought – as it so often seems to do these days – vines planted on free-draining granite sands, in particular, are susceptible to water stress. This is particularly true for younger vines or those with the shallow root systems associated with the use of fertilizers and herbicides.

One interesting impact of the changing climatic conditions in the region has been a re-evaluation of some aspects of the Beaujolais terroir. Many growers are beginning to see value in terroirs that were once dis-missed as being incapable of fully ripening their bunches, among them vineyards planted at higher elevations or those whose slopes face away from the sometimes blistering heat of the afternoon sun. In particular, this has benefited producers of Beaujolais Villages, whose vineyards are often situated at fairly high altitude. On the other hand, given the his-torical weight that has been afforded to sunnier sites that could bring grapes to full maturity in the most marginal of vintages, vineyard own-ers are understandably reluctant to reappraise the value of these sites in a changing climate.

The graphs overleaf chart the dates of key events in the annual growth cycle in Beaujolais over the course of nearly 55 years. Some broad pat-terns can easily be observed here, foremost among them the way that, from the 1990s onwards, bud break, flowering, veraison and harvest typically take place far earlier than was the case in the 1970s and 1980s. Don't be fooled by the citation of 'average' dates here – with very few exceptions, from the 1990s onwards, key events in the cycle typically happen *before* the average date. Another point to note is the compres-sion of the growth cycle. If you take a typical year in the 1970s or 1980s, bud break took place at some point during April, while harvest typically started in the third week of September, creating a gap of 22–24 weeks to allow for flowering, the development of the bunches and eventual ripening. By the 2010s, bud break usually occurred around 31 March,

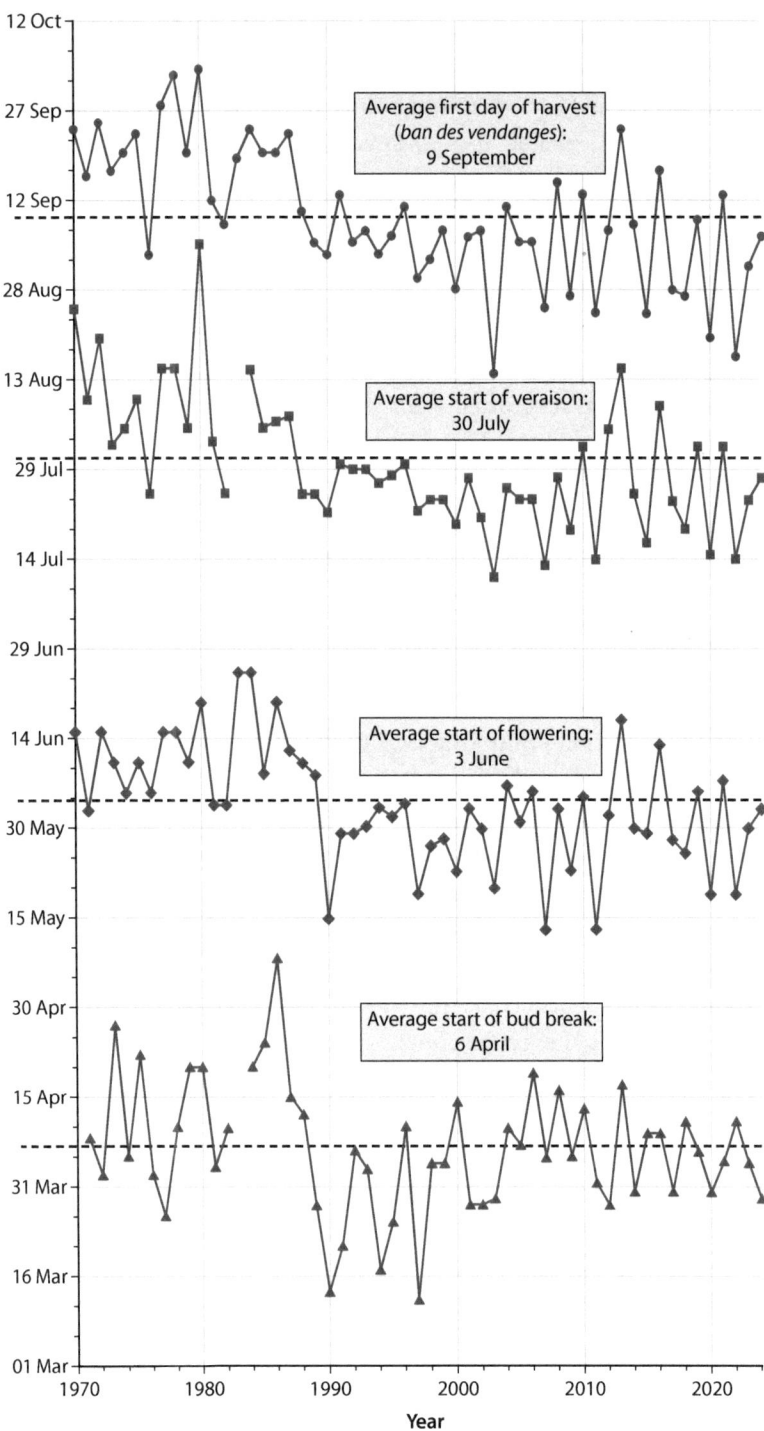

Dates of key events in the annual growth cycle in Beaujolais (1970–2024),
courtesy of IFV-SICAREX Beaujolais

with harvest taking place in the last two weeks of August, compressing the growing season by a week or two. The final point to note is that with key events in the cycle happening earlier in the year, the vine is exposed to different climatic conditions at critical phases. Bud break and flowering take place at a time when late frosts pose a greater risk to the developing structures, while harvest happens during periods where intense heatwaves are still likely. These changes are due, of course, to climate change, with further, more dramatic, shifts to growing patterns possible in years to come.

Is Beaujolais part of Burgundy?

On the face of it, the answer to this question seems obvious. The only problem is that for those on one side of the debate, it is crystal clear that Beaujolais is part of greater Burgundy, while to others it is equally evident that it is not.

The clues available to resolve the issue are equivocal. It has been noted earlier that the vineyards of the Mâconnais flow into those of Beaujolais with no natural boundary to separate the two. However, in administrative terms, the northern tip of Beaujolais's *crus* – Saint-Amour, and part of Juliénas, Moulin-à-Vent and Chénas – mostly lie within the Saône-et-Loire department of the Bourgogne-Franche-Comté region. Once you're south of this border, though, you're in the Rhône department and the Auvergne-Rhône-Alpes region. So, technically speaking, most of Beaujolais does not actually lie within Burgundy's boundaries.

Geologically, too, there are massive differences between the largely volcanic or igneous soils of the *crus* and the limestone-rich vineyards of Burgundy – although the southern part of Beaujolais has a lot of limestone too. The climate is broadly similar in Beaujolais and Burgundy, although summers are often slightly warmer in Beaujolais than they are in the heart of the Côte d'Or. The landscape of Beaujolais is very different to that of the Côte d'Or: the largely south-east-facing scarp of the latter is replaced in the south by a series of rolling hills – but the Mâconnais countryside is just as undulating and wiggly as that of Beaujolais.

The evidence of the grape varieties grown in Burgundy and Beaujolais is also ambiguous. There's little Pinot Noir grown in Beaujolais – apart from in a few, largely experimental vineyards. The ever-adaptable Chardonnay, though, is almost as much at home in Beaujolais as it is elsewhere within the wider Burgundian region. And for many years, the Chardonnay of Beaujolais could be sold as Bourgogne Blanc (see p. 34), although now wines made from recent plantations (those dating from 2016 or later) must be labelled Beaujolais Blanc. Indeed, much of the Chardonnay grown in the southern part of Beaujolais is used to make Crémant de Bourgogne, the region's take on traditional method fizz. It might be easy to point to Gamay's ubiquity in Beaujolais and cite that as a point of difference. However, despite Philip the Bold's centuries-old edict (see p. 2), and subsequent attempts to legislate Gamay out of the Burgundian vineyards, the grape is still grown in the region. In contrast to Beaujolais, however, you can't make mono-varietal wine from Gamay in Burgundy (at least not if you're working outside of the Côteaux Bourguignons, and even then 100 per cent Gamay is rare). Instead, the grape must be blended with Pinot Noir (which must account for at least 30 per cent of the blend, while Gamay, the junior partner here, needs to account for no more than 15 per cent) to make a wine known as Bourgogne Passetoutgrains.

Beaujolais was once linked to the Duchy of Burgundy in a complex web of feudal, agricultural and trading relationships during the Middle Ages. But although farming and trade continued to tie the two regions together, the Duchy itself ceased to exist in the sixteenth century. As a result, you might well think that any formal ties between the two regions are, well, history. There's far more evidence, instead, to tie most of Beaujolais tightly to the culture and economy of the Rhône.

And when you ask producers about whether or not they consider Beaujolais to be part of Burgundy you should bear in mind that their opinions might well be inflected by commercial considerations. Generally speaking, large négociants seem to be keen to bind Beaujolais tightly to Burgundy. Many of them have vineyards in the Mâconnais and the Côte Chalonnaise – and even further north – and emphasize the commercial advantages of hitching Beaujolais's star to that of its more expensive northern neighbour. Smaller growers, on the other hand, tend to place their emphasis on affirming Beaujolais's identity as a unique, discrete region apart.

3

GAMAY AND OTHER GRAPES

GAMAY

Gamay – or, to be more precise, Gamay Noir à Jus Blanc (Black Gamay with White Juice) – is Beaujolais's main grape, accounting for around 95 per cent of all wines produced in the region. So why bother specifying the black skin and white (actually clear) juice? It turns out that Gamay has a *teinturier* relative, the Gamay Teinturier de Bouze, whose pulp is more deeply coloured than that of 'regular' Gamay (although not as deeply coloured as that of most *teinturier* varieties). To all intents and purposes, though, it is safe to assume that when people talk about Gamay, they're referring to Gamay Noir à Jus Blanc and not the very rare red-fleshed variety.

Gamay is an incredibly ancient variety, which means that there is an immense amount of clonal variation in vineyards planted with the grape. DNA analysis has revealed it to be closely related to the wider family of Burgundian grapes, including all the Pinots, Chardonnay, Aligoté, and Melon (once more widely known as Melon de Bourgogne, a variety which, despite the name, is now most closely associated with the Atlantic delta of the Loire). It is likely that Gamay's parents were Pinot Noir and Gouais Blanc, an obscure white grape variety whose neutral character has largely seen it relegated to the footnotes of history and a handful of vineyards in Switzerland and Slovenia.

A generous variety that buds and ripens early, Gamay needs to have its natural fecundity limited in order to give of its best, which is why it turns in its best performance when grown on the poor soils of Beaujolais's *crus*. Too much organic matter in the soil – or soils that allow Gamay to grow profusely – means that the vines run riot, producing copious numbers of heavy bunches that yield dilute, unripe flavours, high levels of acidity and low levels of alcohol. That tendency towards early ripening also means that the grape works better in cool or moderate climates – too much warmth can tip it towards rapid sugar accumulation and jammy flavours. This has proven to be a challenge in recent years as producers have found that the grape can tip from under-ripe to over-ripe in a matter of two or three days, especially in conditions of extreme heat.

The grape fares well beyond the borders of Beaujolais, most notably in the volcanic soils of the Auvergne and in Touraine in the Loire. But a recent growth of interest in the grape – and its relatively light-bodied, refreshing wines – has seen plantings expand to the New World, with particular interest being shown by producers in Oregon, Canada, South Africa and Australia.

Gamay bunches are typically medium in size, with tightly clustered berries
(photo © Château du Moulin-à-Vent)

Gamay is typically described as being red-fruited in nature, but the reality is that its flavours and aromas vary widely, largely depending on levels of ripeness and terroir. Regardless of aromatic character, there is always something sappy and refreshing about good Gamay, and levels of acidity are often high. Beaujolais that's made for youthful consumption tends to have pretty low levels of tannin, but wines from the *villages* or the *crus* can be surprisingly firm and structured. Typically, though, Gamay's tannins have a subtly raspy edge to them – less fine and silky than those of Pinot Noir but nowhere near as grippy as those associated with Cabernet Sauvignon. Depending on how the wines are made, Gamay can often show a hint of smoky reduction when recently uncorked, but rarely tips over into the excessive boiled cabbage character some other grapes are prone to.

In an era of growing disenchantment with big, boozy, over-oaked reds, it may well be that Gamay is a grape whose time has come. Sommeliers in upmarket restaurants have led the charge (as they often do), driving demand for lighter, fresher, food-friendly reds. Pinot Noir may well have been the torch bearer for the trend, but as Pinot prices rise, there's been a growing realization that anything Pinot can do (in food matching terms), Gamay can do just as well.

Lighter, fruitier styles of Gamay can be lightly chilled in summer or served at room temperature in colder months. Either way, the freshness of these wines allows them to pair well with charcuterie and salads as well as richer fish (think tuna or swordfish). Bolder Gamays with more structure and more depth of flavour can take on heartier foods, and are good with roast chicken or duck, game and even beef. A glass or two of Beaujolais always goes down well with the smoky flavours of a barbecue, and you can even open a bottle with mildly spiced dishes (think curries and tagines) as the supple tannins and lack of overt oak mean that the wine won't fight with any heat from chillies or other spices. In short, Gamay is a really versatile grape to bring to the table.

And forget any preconceived notions that the wines need to be drunk young. It is true that Beaujolais Nouveau and most basic AOP Beaujolais are at their best in the relatively short term, but many of the better wines can be enjoyed either in their first flush of primary-fruited youth or cellared for an astonishing amount of time, which allows them to acquire the complexity that comes with age. The most structured Beaujolais – particularly those from the *crus* of Juliénas, Fleurie, Moulin-à-Vent, Morgon and the Côte de Brouilly – can improve over the course of many decades – and even lighter *crus* can benefit from a decade or more of maturation. During the course of my research for this book, I've been astounded by the number of producers who've told me of tastings of Cru Beaujolais dating back 50 years or more, with the wines showing well despite their venerable age.

CHARDONNAY

Chardonnay barely needs any introduction to this book's readers. It is the world's most ubiquitous white grape, planted in pretty much every wine-producing country in the world. Chardonnay is the only white variety officially permitted in Beaujolais, but it frequently comes disguised. Wines produced from grapes planted before 2016 can be sold as Bourgogne Blanc, while later plantings have to make their origins clear by bearing the Beaujolais Blanc label. It is worth bearing in mind, though, that not all wines sold as Beaujolais Blanc come from younger vines – for many growers, acknowledging the true source of their grapes is a matter of pride.

Regardless of the nomenclature, Chardonnay grown in Beaujolais tends to be riper in fruit character than might be typical in Burgundy, but the fact that it is typically planted at altitude or on limestone soils can help it to retain some acidity and also curbs alcohol levels. Having said that, the best examples are rarely those from granitic soils, which seems to deplete acidity in these wines. While Beaujolais Blanc tends to have relatively modest levels of acidity, freshness is rarely a problem as good levels of minerality and, quite often, a hint of pithy bitterness on the finish helps to create an overall sensation of balance in the wines.

When it comes to winemaking, Chardonnay in Beaujolais is a shapeshifter, as it is elsewhere. Expressions range from simple, fruity wines fermented in neutral tanks (usually made of stainless steel) to weightier, more textural examples that have been fermented and aged in wooden barrels (although large amounts of new oak are rarely used). You might even find the occasional orange wine being made from Chardonnay, although typically this will be classified as a Vin de France rather than Beaujolais AOP.

Most of the Chardonnay grown in Beaujolais, though, is not identifiable as such. This is because much of it goes into Crémant de Bourgogne, a traditional method sparkling wine. It is estimated that somewhere in the region of 60 per cent of the fizz bottled as Burgundian is sourced from growers in Beaujolais.

OTHER VARIETIES

In terms of appellation law in Beaujolais, all grapes other than Gamay and Chardonnay are off limits – for the moment, at least. Nevertheless, many growers have started planting small experimental vineyards where, for the sake of variety or with one eye on climate change, they are trialling a range of new varieties. Any wines made from these grapes have to be labelled as Vin de France, so their origin will be clouded.

Syrah is probably the most widely planted of all these new varieties. The proximity of the vineyards of the Northern Rhône to Beaujolais and the analogies between the granite soils in both regions are too compelling for some inquisitive growers not to feel like they should take a punt on the grape. These wines are a work in progress, and at the moment there is no clear identifiable style that can be linked to Syrah grown in Beaujolais – instead you'll find all sorts, from sinewy, peppery, cool-climate styles to wines made from grapes that have been allowed to hang on the vine for far longer, resulting in bigger, bolder, riper wines. Oak use, as ever in Beaujolais, tends towards restraint. There's also a little bit of Pinot Noir grown in Beaujolais, although I have encountered very few bottlings that make my heart beat that little bit faster.

Other grapes of growing interest (if you'll pardon the pun) are white grapes from the Rhône – both Roussanne and Marsanne seem to be attracting attention, while Viognier is already a firm alternative favourite – and aromatic varieties from Alsace, including Muscat. Aligoté, a close cousin of Gamay being also the result of a crossing between Pinot Noir and Gouais Blanc, is currently flavour of the month in Burgundy, with growers belonging to the group of Les Aligoteurs doing a great job of publicizing the virtues of this once-despised grape. Some producers in Beaujolais, inspired by their example, have begun planting the grape in their own vineyards, hoping that its kinship with Gamay and its characteristically high levels of acidity will work in their favour as the climate warms. Another high-acid variety that's turning heads down south is Chenin Blanc, although plantings are, once again, in the early stages and it's too soon to tell whether the grapes will take to granite soils in the way that growers hope.

When it comes to reds, crosses and hybrids like rot-resistant Gamaret and Chambourcin, as well as late-ripening Marselan are also finding favour with producers keen to mitigate the worst excesses of climate change. Typically, though, these grapes are more bit-part players in blends rather than the stars of the show, and their take up has been relatively slow.

Rosé

Around one per cent of all the wines made in Beaujolais are pink, so why haven't I written any of these wines up in my producer profiles? There are a few reasons behind the lack of rosé representation in these pages. The first is pragmatic. Not only is there very little pink wine made in the region, very little of what does get made is sold beyond Beaujolais's borders. There's little point in recommending wines that readers stand little chance of enjoying for themselves.

Another challenge to finding noteworthy rosé in Beaujolais is that very little of what I tasted was distinctive in character. (By which I mean distinctive in a good way – I certainly tasted a few Beaujolais rosés that, while striking, were not recommendable.) Even when the rosés I tasted were drinkable, many were dull. In a number of cases, producers seem to be seeking to make rosés that are similar in colour to the pastel-hued Provence pinks. The trouble is that, in order to achieve such fashionable pallor, you need to strip a lot of Gamay's personality away (not a good thing, I concluded).

Until such time as Beaujolais's producers decide that their pinks should pack a punch – and step up the volumes they produce – the wines will, I suspect, remain of limited interest to most of us.

4

VITICULTURE: THE CRAFT AND SCIENCE OF GROWING GRAPES IN BEAUJOLAIS

As I write this chapter, the French doors of my rented gite are flung wide open and I have a view out over the mounded hills that roll away towards the Chapel of the Madonna, which overlooks the vineyards of Fleurie. It's spring, and the first tender leaves have unfurled on the vines, creating a pointillist haze of green that covers the nearest slopes. If you zoom out to the hills in the middle distance, though, what stands out is a patchwork effect that transposes vivid green blocks with strips of earthy brown, an impression that is even more stark in the dead of winter, when no leaves are present on the vines to blur the boundaries. It's not obvious to the casual observer, but the difference in colour marks one of the most fundamental frontiers in Beaujolais, the demarcation between different viticultural ideologies.

The bare brown soils are evidence of the use of herbicides, products used to nuke any plants that might grow between and under the rows of vines and compete with the latter for the resources buried underground, whether they be water, minerals or other nutrients. In many cases, the use of herbicides often stands proxy for the use of other chemical treatments – fungicides, insecticides and fertilizers, in particular. When I first came to Beaujolais over 20 years ago, almost all the region's vineyards were farmed like this, a method often referred to as 'conventional agriculture'. Now, though, more and more of the vineyards have a soft carpet of green, evidence not only of a growing understanding of the

In springtime it's easy to see which vineyards are being sprayed with herbicides and which growers favour the use of cover crops

importance of inter-row vegetation, but also of growers farming their land in a way that is environmentally sustainable (at the very least), and quite possibly organic, biodynamic, regenerative or a combination of elements derived from all these practices.

You may be wondering why inter-row vegetation is now regarded by many as an adjunct to healthy grape-growing rather than the enemy. There's a growing understanding among many vignerons that the plants that grow alongside their vines – whether grasses, flowers, legumes or a whole botanical compendium of species – can make a positive contribution to the health of their crop. One way in which they do this is that when these plants die back (or, more frequently, are cut down) they release organic matter back into the soil. This in turn furnishes the growing vines with the nutrients they need to grow healthy grapes and allows underground fauna to thrive, including earthworms, whose activity improves soil health.

True, these plants can compete with the vines for water, an issue of particular importance in the free-draining granitic sands that dominate much of the area in the *crus*, but if they are cut back before the height of the summer and allowed to rot down gently where they fall, they can actually help to preserve moisture in the soil by preventing evaporation. This layer of dead grasses can even help lower the soil temperature

Many growers are increasingly interested in promoting biodiversity in their vineyards (photo courtesy of Fabrice Ferrer/Beaujolais Wines)

around the trunks of the vines, reducing rates of transpiration. These last factors have come to be of increasing importance in the hot, dry summer conditions now prevalent in Beaujolais.

Increased organic content in the soil also helps to sustain the microbiome that many now believe to be vital not only to vine health but also to fostering a healthy population of yeasts on the skins of the grapes. This, in turn, helps to ensure a good chance of a strong alcoholic fermentation, reducing the risk of unwanted microbial life taking over the process and generating unwanted aromatic characters in the wine. One last advantage is also worth mentioning: given that Beaujolais's best terroirs are characteristically both poor in organic content and steeply sloping, improving soil quality can help to prevent erosion. Regular ploughing was once seen as the main way of achieving this, but many growers are now looking to alternative ways of improving soil, such as mowing, the rolling of cover crops or permaculture.

The improvement in soil life is one of the key goals for all producers farming organically or biodynamically. Unfortunately, systematic improvements to soils are often at odds with another of Beaujolais's key viticultural characteristics. Along with Languedoc-Roussillon, in the south of the country, Beaujolais is one of the two French viticultural areas with the greatest wealth of old vines. This is particularly true in the *crus*, where it is far from unusual for vineyards to clock in at around 50 years old. Many vineyards are even older. I've heard vignerons referring to their 30-year-old vines – an age which would qualify them for labelling as 'vieilles vignes' (old vines) in other regions – as '*les plantiers*', the recent plantings.

Farming old vines is a two-edged sword. On the one hand old vines tend to cope better with hydric stress brought on by drought, maintaining their equilibrium in part thanks to the ability of their root systems to seek out underground reserves of water. The grapes they produce often offer not only greater concentration of flavours than grapes from younger vines, but also better balance of structural components such as acidity and sugars. That concentration in flavour, however, tends to come at the expense of yields. Also, like octogenarian humans, octogenarian vines are fragile creatures. They may be more vulnerable to some diseases (although they may be more resistant to others), and they can be badly damaged by a glancing blow.

This last has proven to be a particular challenge for those farming some of the older vineyards. Back when the old vines were planted, the local tradition was – and still is in many *cru* vineyards – to train them as bush vines, with the trunks kept low to the ground. In some of these old vineyards, the bunches of grapes are often carried a few centimetres off the ground. In addition, the arms or branches of these vines were not

Bush vines in early spring

Horse-drawn ploughing is increasingly in vogue in Beaujolais
(photo courtesy of Fabrice Ferrer/Beaujolais Wines)

trained (or trellised) to run in neat lines, as they often are these days. Nor were vines planted in tidy rows, as is now the custom. When you add in the high densities of plantation typical back then – around 10,000 vines per hectare – what you often end up with is a higgledy-piggledy vineyard with vines dotting the landscape in a random pattern, and with the bunch-bearing arms pointing every which way. This makes these vineyards impossible to manage with machines, or even with the horse-drawn ploughs that many organic producers have now adopted. Working the vineyards by hand and on foot still carries a risk that one misstep or wrong turn will result in a fragile vine losing one or more of its arms.

All work in these old vineyards, whether pruning, ploughing or harvesting, is therefore a labour-intensive process. For those with vines planted on the vertiginous inclines that dominate some of the *crus*, the work is back-breakingly hard. I've heard producers talking about members of the older generation, physically wrecked by the age of 60 from the sheer effort of maintaining their vineyards. Unfortunately, exhaustive – and exhausting – soil work is a prerequisite for organic or biodynamic certification. I've lost track of the number of growers who've told me that they're 'more or less' organic, with the exception of an old-vine parcel planted on steep slopes. They'll say, with a regretful shrug, that it's impossible to farm these vineyards organically.

Bush vines en eventail, *with the fruiting zone raised off the ground and canopy trained on wires (photo courtesy of Domaine les Garçons)*

The truth is that organic farming of even the oldest parcel of vines planted on the steepest slopes is not impossible. It's merely incredibly hard and time consuming. Farming old vines on slopes takes about two or three times the work hours that it would take to tend younger vines in flatter vineyards – and is therefore difficult to justify on a purely financial basis. It is possible to restructure these old vineyards, and that is just what some producers have done – but that, too, is a laborious, expensive project.

Nevertheless many growers are keen to maintain the traditional shape of their bush vines, explaining that the flow of sap it encourages helps to keep the vines healthy for far longer than would be possible with trellised vines. There are solutions, though, for those looking for alternatives. Those back-breakingly low bush vines can be trained a little higher, and their arms can be persuaded to lie along a wire in a horizontal plane, a system known as *goblet en eventail*, a fan-shaped goblet. This helps to protect the plant from trunk diseases, while allowing for greater ease of passage between the rows of vines. Other growers are looking south to the escarpments of the northern Rhône for inspiration, and have adopted the *échalas* training system, in which a stake driven into the soil next to the vine's roots provides a structure that allows for the canopy to be raised above the fruiting zone. Another strategy is the introduction of the wire-based training systems more commonly found outside Beaujolais, such as cane pruning or double cordon royat. This is the easiest option for those replanting their vineyards, not least because it allows for a greater degree of mechanization in the vineyards. It doesn't hurt, either, that grants are available from the EU to allow farmers to change the structure of their vineyards in this way. Alternatively, some *vignerons* have chosen to retain their old bush vines but to remove some of them so

Many of Beaujolais's vineyards are vertiginously steep
(photo courtesy of David Large)

as to align the remaining plants in a more practical grid. Some growers have pushed this even further, aiming to reduce the density of planta-tion to a more manageable 6,500 plants per hectare (the legal minimum in the *crus*, while in AOP Beaujolais this can be reduced even further to 5,000 plants per hectare) by creating a grid with two-metre gaps be-tween rows, and 80-centimetre gaps between plants within each row.

In the *Bas Beaujolais* in the south, the pressure to mechanize means that few old vineyards remain, and Gamay there is typically tamed, pruned (both Guyot and Cordon systems are used) and trellised in wide-ly spaced rows. And while hand picking is still the norm in the north, most southern Gamay is harvested by machine. This, in turn, means that semi-carbonic maceration cannot be used to vinify these grapes.

VITICULTURAL CHALLENGES

The viticultural challenges facing Beaujolais are manifold – as they are in wine regions elsewhere. Climate change has brought in its wake one year after another of unusual weather patterns. Mild winters challenge the dormancy of the vine and even milder springs see bud break and flowering happen earlier than was once the norm. When this is followed either by long periods of extreme heat and drought – as seen in 2020, 2022 and 2023 – or heavy, prolonged bouts of summer rainfall – in 2021 and 2024 – growing conditions become challenging. (This is just a citation of the most recent vintages in the region, but swings between drought years and years of downpours have been the new norm in the region for a while.)

In the hot, dry years, the vines grown on granitic soils face exagger-ated levels of water stress as the free-draining sands wick moisture away from the plants' roots. Depending on the timing and severity of the drought, this can have a negative impact on both yield and wine quality, particularly with reference to phenolic ripening and the accumulation of sugars in the berries, and may even result in reduced yields in future vintages (by affecting the development of future buds). Vines grow-ing on diorite are slightly less affected by water stress due to the better water-carrying capacity of these soils, but the hard blue stones accumu-late heat during the day, reflecting it back onto the bunches, which can send sugar levels spiralling out of control. It's not unusual, these days, to see wines made from grapes grown in these terroirs topping out at 15.5% abv. (Remember that the days when growers struggled to get

Old bush vines just before harvest

their grapes to 12.5% abv are well within living memory.) And, regardless of the soils on which the grapes are grown, poor canopy management in such solar years can result in the berries becoming sunburned or shrivelled.

In the rainy years, fungal diseases run rampant through the vineyards. For growers still using chemical fungicides this is, potentially, less of a problem than for those with organic certification. These *vignerons* only have recourse to sulphur and copper sprays in order to protect their crops. Leaving aside issues about the potential toxicity of over-use of copper, the use of these chemicals in very rainy years carries an inherent risk, which is that they wash off fairly easily. If a grower sprays their vineyards and it rains the next day, they will have to spray again. Some growers treated their vines on more than 20 occasions during the disastrously rainy summer of 2024, and many of these still lost a substantial proportion of their potential harvest to mildew and rot. Although the data has yet to be published, anecdotal evidence suggests that 2024 may have delivered the *coup de grace* to many growers' ambitions to farm organically. Given that prior to 2024, only around 15 per cent of all producers in Beaujolais were certified organic – a fairly low percentage compared to many other viticultural areas in France – this represents a significant setback to the region's environmental credentials.

The risk of late frosts in Beaujolais is not unusually high – although when these occur they can have a significant adverse effect on that year's yields – but what is striking is the high risk of devastating hailstorms, particularly in the *couloir de grêle* (the hail corridor) that sweeps northward through Régnié and Fleurie up towards Chiroubles (although other parts of Beaujolais often suffer from hailstrike too). Romain Zordan (see p. 113), who makes wine in Fleurie, says that he's lost varying proportions of his crop to hailstorms in eleven out of the past twelve vintages. Pauline Passot of Chiroubles' Domaine de la Grosse Pierre (see p. 136) says that in 2023 a hailstorm swept through the vineyards closest to her winery, wiping out 70 per cent of that year's crop. It's little wonder that some producers are now experimenting with hail netting, which is incredibly expensive (costing somewhere in the region of €15,000 per hectare to install), but may well pay for itself over time. (It's worth noting that netting can only be installed in trellised vineyards, which imposes a practical limit on its use in many of the oldest and most fragile vineyards in the *crus*.)

There is one further scourge that afflicts the vineyards of Beaujolais, and that is the growing incidence of flavescence dorée, a phytoplasma disease whose initial symptoms are delayed bud break and shoot growth. The leaves of an infected vine turn red or golden yellow (as a result, flavescence is one of a group of diseases collectively referred to as 'grapevine yellows') and curl downwards. The grape bunches either fail to set or, if the plant is infected later in the cycle, drop from the vine, and any surviving berries shrivel and develop a bitter taste. Once a plant is infected, it will almost certainly die off. There is no cure for flavescence once it has developed in a plant, and the only option available to a grower who has detected its presence is to uproot the vine lest the disease spread to nearby plants. In theory the spread of the disease can be controlled by focusing on eliminating its vectors – the main culprit is an insect known as a leafhopper, a Californian species that has migrated to France, broadcasting flavescence widely in its wake. Once again, however, organic producers are left with some difficult decisions to make when addressing the risks of flavescence, as certification makes it impossible for them to use the necessary insecticides. In such instances, an ounce of prevention is worth a pound of cure, and many producers now organize regular group searches in order to create a firebreak between infected plants and their own vineyards.

5

WINEMAKING IN BEAUJOLAIS ... AND ITS UNEXPECTED COMPLEXITIES

MAKING WINE IN BEAUJOLAIS – BROAD BRUSHSTROKES

The one thing that most people know (or think they know) about Beaujolais is its wines are made using a technique called carbonic maceration. At best this is a half truth. In reality, there are a number of vinification methods used in the region, each of which has a big impact on the style and structure of the wines it produces. When considered together, the incredible variety of winemaking techniques employed in Beaujolais makes the region one of huge oenological complexity.

While most alcoholic fermentations depend on yeasts to metabolize the sugars present in ripe grapes to produce alcohol and carbon dioxide, in Beaujolais a different kind of fermentation is more typically practised. Both carbonic maceration and semi-carbonic maceration are based on intracellular fermentation (albeit to differing degrees, see below). Intracellular fermentation occurs when enzymes within uncrushed grape berries transform the sugars present into alcohol without the need for yeasts or for oxygen (intracellular fermentation is an anaerobic process). In tandem with the conversion of sugar to ethanol within individual grapes, the enzymes that steer the process also produce a range of aromatic compounds as metabolic byproducts. These, in turn, contribute to the fruit-forward profile of wines made in this way. Mathieu Lapierre of Domaine Lapierre in Villié-Morgon describes these reactions as being similar to the enzymatic processes at work when meat is hung by a butcher in order to develop a broader and deeper array of flavours than might be found in recently butchered cuts. In addition, intracellular fermentation is a less efficient way to convert sugar to alcohol, and this typically results in more modest levels of alcohol in the finished wines, although the difference between a wine made this way and one that undergoes a more conventional alcoholic fermentation is typically less than 1% abv.

Pure carbonic maceration (often referred to in Beaujolais as 'dry' maceration) is rare. When large volumes of grape bunches, still attached to their stems, are tipped into a fermentation tank, the bunches at the bottom tend to get squashed, and will therefore expel juice. In order for the fermentation process to be entirely intracellular, therefore, winemakers wanting a dry maceration need to withdraw any juices pooling at the bottom of the tank on a regular basis (these juices are typically fermented separately and may be back blended into the finished wine). Winemakers will also need to pipe carbon dioxide into the top of the tank, where it sinks down into the tank, forming an inert blanket of gas that protects the whole bunches from the formation of mould or attack from bacteria and other unicellular undesirables. While the latter step is easy to implement, the rigorous withdrawal of juices from the bottom of the tank means that true carbonic maceration is a technique that can only be employed by artisanal producers making small volumes of wine each year.

Producers who've decided to work with semi-carbonic fermentation (the majority of winemakers in Beaujolais) have an altogether easier life. Not only do they not have to worry about drawing off the must from the bottom of their tanks, they typically don't need to pump much, if any, carbon dioxide into their tanks (apart from in the first day or two of the fermentation process). Once the juices at the bottom of the tank start to ferment, winemakers can rely on the action of the yeasts in the fermenting must to release carbon dioxide into the tank, thereby protecting the liquid from any risk of oxidation. Typically, in a tank where semi-carbonic maceration is taking place, there are three types of fermentation going on at the same time. At the bottom of the tank, 'normal' (alcoholic) fermentation takes place, with yeasts metabolizing the sugar in the must to produce alcohol. At the top of the tank, whole

Hand sorting bunches before they go into tanks is vital to ensure that only the healthiest berries are used (photo courtesy of Arnaud Bertrand/Beaujolais Wines)

bunches remain intact, and therefore all fermentation in this part of the tank is 'true' carbonic maceration. What takes place in the middle of each tank, though, is often a bit of a mix, with whole bunches undergoing intracellular fermentation, albeit at a slower rate than at the top of the tank, while floating in a soup of fermenting must. It should be noted that while this account provides an overview of the essential processes at work in a semi-carbonic maceration, there are as many variations on the theme as there are winemakers, and some of the key inflection points will be discussed below.

It's worth noting that the boundary between 'true' carbonic maceration and semi-carbonic maceration is a blurry one, particularly in warm vintages where the berries' thick skins means that they don't squash all that easily and so maintain their structural integrity even at the bottom of the tank. The upshot in these instances is that what was originally intended as a semi-carbonic maceration becomes, de facto, a more or less dry, full carbonic maceration – at least during the earliest parts of the process. (In such cases, if semi-carbonic maceration is what's required, the producer may press some of the bunches to ensure that juice is released.) Furthermore, many producers in Beaujolais have different definitions of where the boundary between carbonic and semi-carbonic macerations lies. For some producers, the winemaking technique can

The impact of intracellular fermentation on bunches and within individual berries over time (photo courtesy of Domaine Lapierre)

only truly be called carbonic if the juices at the bottom of the tank are regularly drawn off to create a dry maceration, while for others it's a carbonic maceration if the tank is blanketed in carbon dioxide and sealed at the start of the fermentation process and no *remontages* are used, even if there is juice being fermented by yeasts at the bottom of the tank.

Either way, in the case of both carbonic and semi-carbonic maceration, the enzymatic fermentation in the whole berries doesn't typically run to completion but grinds to a halt leaving some unfermented sugars present in the grapes. The *jus de tire*, the liquid portion, is drawn off from the bottom of the tank and stored separately, while bunches are pressed to create the *jus de presse*. This pressing process releases sugar-rich juices that are free to complete their alcoholic fermentation in the presence of both yeasts and, initially at least, oxygen, which gives the unspent yeasts an energy boost. The *jus de tire* and the *jus de presse* are typically blended together to finish the ferment.

It is worth knowing that the kind of fermentation employed in most wine regions around the world is also practised in Beaujolais, particularly – but not exclusively – in the *crus*. In this technique, often referred to in Beaujolais as 'Burgundian' winemaking, the bunches of grapes are de-stemmed on arrival at the winery and lightly crushed before being tipped or pumped into the fermentation vessel. Yeast – either cultured or 'indigenous' (that's to say the yeasts carried in from the vineyards on the skins of the grapes and those already present in the winery) – metabolize the sugars present in the must to produce alcohol and carbon dioxide, a process typically referred to as alcoholic fermentation. This practice typically allows for more vigorous extraction of tannins and colour than would be the case with any other winemaking method used in Beaujolais, and also creates a different suite of aromatic characters as there is no intracellular fermentation.

A extra layer of nuance is created by the use of an additional technique that further blurs the boundaries between Burgundy and Beaujolais. Since I started my research for this book, I'd found myself wondering about the difference between the use of whole bunches for carbonic and semi-carbonic maceration (techniques associated with Beaujolais) and the use of whole bunches in fermentations for Pinot Noir and Syrah, as practised in Burgundy and the northern Rhône, as well as in other regions where these grapes are grown. (Whole-bunch fermentation is also practised with other grapes, although less frequently than with Pinot and Syrah.) It's not uncommon, particularly in ripe vintages, where the stems that hold the bunches together are well lignified (ripened to a point where they have lost all or much of their 'green' character) for growers to include a varying proportion of whole bunches in their ferments to lend freshness and focus to their wines. Given that producers can cite up to 100 per cent whole-bunch use, how, I wondered, did this technique differ from those practised in Beaujolais? The answer is *foulage*. The difference between the use of whole bunches associated with carbonic or semi-carbonic macerations and fermentations described as whole bunch (but not carbonic or semi-carbonic) is that in the latter case the whole bunches are gently pressed in tank to allow juice to be released, a technique known as *foulage*. This, of course, creates an immediate difference as there is no enzymatic fermentation here, but there is a lot of contact between the fermenting must and the stems. You may be wondering by now why I've meandered into a digression about winemaking as practised on other grapes in other regions. The reason is that it turns out that a number of producers in Beaujolais practise *foulage* themselves to varying degrees.

There's a further vinification technique used in Beaujolais, although typically winemakers don't tend to talk about it much because of its strong association with wines of modest quality. In thermovinification, the juices from the crushed grapes at the bottom of the tank are drawn off into a heat exchanger, where they are warmed to temperatures of around 60°C and then gently sprayed over the bunches remaining in the tank, *remontage*-style. Alternatively, the must from de-stemmed grapes may be passed through the heat exchanger and then piped into a tank. Either way, the heating process usually lasts for a few hours before the tank is chilled down and fermentation – whether alcoholic or semi-carbonic – can then proceed. The application of heat at this initial stage of the winemaking process helps to release a number of compounds, ranging from anthocyanins that lend a more intense colour to the wine to low levels of supple rounded tannins. Thermovinification also, typically, helps to suppress unripe, green flavours in order to achieve a homogeneous, if somewhat bland, fruity profile in the finished wines.

This suppression of undesirable aromatic characters may help to explain why thermovinification was adopted with enthusiasm in the past. The pressure on négociants to make vast lakes of Beaujolais Nouveau at the peak of global demand for these wines meant that they, in turn, pushed growers to supply massive quantities of grapes at low prices. As a result, the grapes that were being used to produce these entry-level wines typically came from high-yielding vineyards where vines struggled to fully ripen their bunches. In addition, thermovinification is a useful tool for eliminating any trace of off-flavours derived from rot in the bunches. This was an absolute blessing in rainy vintages, where growers would otherwise have to get rid of a sometimes significant proportion of their production. In both instances, thermovinification is a key weapon that winemakers would have at their disposal to allow them to use fruit that would otherwise be deemed unfit for purpose.

Thermovinification has one further advantage. The technique helps speed up the winemaking process, and speed has always been of the essence to producers aiming to go from picking grapes through to bottled wines in the short window of time before the Beaujolais Nouveau deadline of the third Thursday in November. This technique is still widely used for the production of many Nouveau styles, although the *primeur* wines made by more artisanal domaines are made using brief semi-carbonic macerations rather than thermovinification.

The above account of the four main winemaking processes used in Beaujolais appears to suggest that each technique exists in its own separate silo. This is not necessarily the case. Some producers make cuvées that blend elements of various winemaking techniques – it's not uncommon, for instance, for a winemaker to routinely use both whole bunches and de-stemmed grapes in varying proportions in their ferments. Others might blend a little thermovinified juice in with wines made from semi-carbonic fermentation after fermentation is finished, or mix the issue of de-stemmed and semi-carbonic fermentations together. Yet others adapt the winemaking techniques they use according to what they perceive to be the requirements of each individual vintage.

THE INFLUENCE OF WINEMAKING ON STYLE AND STRUCTURE

While the link between winemaking technique and end result is obvious in thermovinification, producers using any of the three alternative methods to ferment their fruit can inflect them to influence both the style and the structure of their wines.

Fermentation temperatures can have a surprisingly profound influence on a wine's personality. Many of the more 'natural' producers in Beaujolais like to chill their grapes overnight prior to starting a slow, low-temperature fermentation, sometimes peaking at temperatures as low as 17–18°C. (These temperatures are more typically associated with white wine fermentations, while red wines are usually fermented at higher temperatures.) The aim is twofold. Firstly, by fermenting at such cool temperatures, winemakers are looking to produce wines with a very bright, fruit-driven palate and less tannin and alcohol than might otherwise be the case. The other factor that they're hoping to exploit is that the lower temperatures result in slower fermentations (chemical processes – even ones associated with yeast metabolism – tend to slow down when cool or speed up with the application of heat). The idea is that the slower fermentation will allow for the development of more varied aromatic characters, creating greater complexity in the wines.

On the other hand, starting a fermentation at warmer temperatures (within limits) helps to get the fermentations bubbling along vigorously right from the start, helping to eliminate the risk of noxious yeasts gaining an upper hand in the fermentation tank, thus lowering the risk of the wine developing unwanted aromatic characters. Higher temperatures may also be helpful in terms of extracting colour from the grape skins. The downside of the use of higher temperatures is that they may promote rather cooked fruit characters and exacerbate high levels of alcohol if the fermentation takes place in a closed tank. Furthermore, a really fast fermentation may result in a fairly simple wine as the yeasts may not have the time to metabolize a range of aromatic precursors in the grapes. Definitions of high or low fermentation temperatures are, of course, in the eye of the beholder – and where fermentation temperature is particularly relevant to the style of the wine being created, it is mentioned in the texts on individual producers.

While all intracellular fermentation is an enzymatic process that occurs within whole berries, any alcoholic fermentation in Beaujolais (as it is elsewhere) is derived from the action of yeasts. Winemakers have the choice of adding cultured yeasts to the tank for this phase of the process or of letting indigenous yeasts carry out the fermentation. The advantage of using cultured yeasts is that the fermentation is likely to proceed smoothly and that a winemaker knows pretty much what the end result will be as yeasts can be purchased 'off the peg' to achieve specific aromas and textures – or even to be as neutral as possible, to allow the grapes to express their own inherent aromatic characters.

Winemakers who favour a more hands-off approach in the *cuvage* tend to favour letting the indigenous yeasts (also known as 'wild' yeasts) do their thing. In this instance the idea is that fermentation will be achieved not by a single species but by a whole suite of yeasts, each of which thrives at different phases of the fermentation. As each yeast contributes different metabolic products to the finished wine, the aim of the exercise is greater complexity. But the use of wild yeasts carries its own risks, not least of which is that unwanted yeasts may take over a fermentation, contributing undesirable flavours to the wine. The best known of these species is *Brettanomyces bruxellensis*, aka 'Brett', which can introduce characters into a wine that range from compounds reminiscent of cloves to those that smell of the altogether more undesirable mouse droppings. In the worst cases, Brett can strip a wine of its fruit almost entirely, leaving an unpleasant drying sensation on the palate. The other risk associated with the use of indigenous yeasts is that of 'stuck' fermentations, when – as the name suggests – the fermentation process grinds to a halt. The risk, once again, is that unwanted bugs develop in the tank. In this instance the main risks are *Acetobacter*, a genus of bacteria which prompt the development of acetic acid (volatile acidity) in the wine, turning it into vinegar, or the creation of acetone, a chemical which can make a wine smell like nail polish remover.

An intermediary solution, and one used fairly frequently in Beaujolais, is the creation of a *pied de cuve*. A small amount of grapes are harvested around a week before the scheduled start of the main pick and are encouraged to ferment using the ambient yeasts on their skins and in the winery. This ferment is monitored to ensure its microbiological health, and is then used as a 'starter culture' to get fermentations off to a healthy start. The idea behind the use of a *pied de cuve* is that it creates the complexity of a wild ferment while ensuring that the population of yeasts is healthy enough to get the fermentation underway smoothly and efficiently.

The other factor that should be borne in mind when considering the actions winemakers may choose to take during the course of fermentation is that of tannin extraction. Generally speaking, the aim of producers working with carbonic or semi-carbonic maceration is to extract very little tannin from their grapes, and most use a technique called *remontage*, usually translated as pump-over. Juices are drawn off from the bottom of the tank and pumped (or in some cases hand sprayed, watering can-style) over the cap, the floating mass of whole bunches that rises to the top of

Remontage *(pump-over) helps to ensure the cap is kept wet*
(photo © Château du Moulin-à-Vent)

each tank. The aim is twofold – in the first instance, the liquid being sprayed over the cap helps to keep it moist, and the importance of this will be explored below. The second reason producers do this is that the fermenting juices help to extract tannins from the stems that hold the bunches together. The vigour with which the *remontage* is performed – and its frequency – help to determine the level of extraction.

While *remontage* can also be used as an extractive technique when fermenting de-stemmed grapes, producers often incorporate *pigeage*, the rather violent-sounding punch-down, in which the cap is forced (gently or otherwise) under the surface of the liquid. The aim here, once again, is to extract tannins – although in a totally de-stemmed fermentation these come from the skins of the grapes rather than the stems holding the bunches together. *Pigeage* is not typically used in carbonic or semi-carbonic macerations because the plunging of the cap can hasten the end of the enzymatic fermentation phase by crushing the grapes and releasing the juice.

A further method of extraction rarely seen outside Beaujolais is the traditional *grillage*, in which a grille, often but not always made of metal, is inserted at the top of the tank and used to submerge the cap. Those employing it say the technique allows for a gentle tannin infusion into the fermenting liquid, likening it to steeping a tea bag in hot water, while others critique it for its potential to extract harsh tannins from the stems.

A final point to be made about extraction in Beaujolais is that the cap – the solid mass of whole bunches – must be pressed off at the end of the intracellular phase of the fermentation. The firmness with which this is done influences the amount of tannin that is extracted, as well as its quality – too firm an extraction and the winemaker will create an unpleasant bitterness in the wine, too gentle an extraction and the wine may end up lacking focus or the ability to age. This latter point is not necessarily a disadvantage in a simple Beaujolais, made for youthful consumption, but is undesirable in a more 'serious' wine that is destined for ageing.

THE REWARDS AND RISKS OF CARBONIC AND SEMI-CARBONIC MACERATION

It used to be thought – and taught – that semi-carbonic maceration was what gave Beaujolais its typical aromatic character, described by

English wine tasters as 'bubblegum' and by French wine tasters as 'banana'. The truth is that this distinctive note was far more likely to have been derived from a particular strain of yeast widely employed in the region in the past (less so these days), although some winemakers believe this character is strongly associated with particular terroirs. (I've yet to see any evidence of the latter, but I'm prepared to believe that specific *lieux-dits* I've yet to encounter may produce these estery aromas.)

For most contemporary winemakers in Beaujolais, though, the use of carbonic and semi-carbonic maceration is what gives their wines a distinctive, bright-fruited character while also creating supple tannins. In addition, the inclusion of stems in the ferment adds aromatic complexity to the wines that would not exist if they were not present.

The techniques are not without their drawbacks, though. To begin with, the stems themselves, while capable of creating their own suite of aromatic characters, can add an undesirable, under-ripe 'green' note to the wines if they are insufficiently ripe at the time of harvest. Unripe stems can also contribute to an astringent bitterness in the wine. For this reason, many winemakers de-stem more in cooler, wetter vintages.

The presence of stems also influences the level of acidity in the wine. The high levels of potassium they contain can result in tartaric acid precipitating out of solution, thereby reducing the overall amount of acid in the wine and raising the level of pH. Gamay is a variety with good levels of acidity, and in a high-acid vintage this reduction in overall levels can help to create better balance in the wines. In warm, ripe vintages, though, the depletion of acidity can not only harm balance but also make the wine more vulnerable to the development of a range of microbial nasties, which thrive in high pH conditions. Stems can also contribute to an overall impression of balance and zestiness in a wine by adding aromatic notes that most palates 'read' in a similar way to the freshness that comes from acidity.

The risk of *Acetobacter* developing in a carbonic or semi-carbonic fermentation is also raised due to the fact that the matrix of stems and berries in the cap helps to create small pockets of air in which microbial life can flourish. This is one of the key reasons that the blanket of inert carbon dioxide is such a vital adjunct to this style of fermentation as it helps to prevent the *Acetobacter* from accessing the oxygen-rich environment they need to thrive. These bacteria – and other forms of microbial life – also tend to multiply if the cap dries out, which is one reason why producers who conduct semi-carbonic macerations tend to employ gentle *remontages*, which help keep the cap moist.

In many regions the way winemakers might address these microbial challenges is via the use of judicious doses of sulphites, but many producers in Beaujolais – particularly those working in a more 'natural' style – avoid using sulphites during the fermentation process. Some add a little to the wine after malolactic conversion or just prior to bottling to ensure stability, while others use no sulphites at all. Instead, the standard measures taken in Beaujolais involve a combination of scrupulous hygiene (the cleaner the winery, the less risk you run of populating it with an undesirable microfauna) and the use of carbon dioxide (which prevents any microbes present from gaining access to oxygen). More importantly, perhaps, is a painstaking surveillance of each tank. Many of the best winemakers monitor their vats with the kind of attention more typically administered to patients in an intensive care unit, refusing to leave their winery during the most critical phases of fermentation. Their observations involve the senses of smell and taste, but also sight and even sound (a healthy fermentation apparently has a different sound to one that has been taken over by microbes). If a winemaker is in any doubt, they will conduct inspections by means of microscopy and chemical analyses. If a problem is detected, remedies can be employed, although the appropriate one will depend on the nature of the problem and its extent. The aim, however, is to nip any problem in the bud before it becomes a deeply entrenched issue.

Producers working with carbonic and semi-carbonic macerations face one further problem not typically encountered in standard alcoholic fermentations, which is that malolactic conversion (the process in which sharp malic acid is converted to softer lactic acid by the action of lactic acid bacteria) can often kick off before the enzymatic fermentation has come to completion. This typically happens towards the end of fermentation, as the yeasts begin to tire. The risk is that instead of metabolizing the acid in the ferment, the bacteria will instead gain the upper hand over the flagging yeasts and begin to consume the sugar, producing that familiar and undesirable byproduct, acetic acid. Caught early enough, the solution is to gently press any whole bunches in the tank as the juice they express contains enough sugar to spur the yeasts into renewed action, or to dose the sluggish tank with some liquid from a more active ferment, in which case the resulting vigour of the fermentation prevents the lactic acid bacteria from producing further volatility.

Whose tradition is it anyway?

One thing that I've learned to be wary of during my visits to Beaujolais is any reference to 'traditional vinification'. Traditional is in the eye of the behold-er, and is used, variously, to refer to fully carbonic, semi-carbonic and de-stemmed 'Burgundian' styles of winemaking.

Both semi-carbonic maceration and 'Burgundian' fermentations have a claim to be regarded as Beaujolais's traditional way of making wine. Fully car-bonic macerations – especially those inflected by the use of very cool temper-atures – have less of a right to be regarded as the ur-style of winemaking in the region for the very simple reason that the ability to pipe carbon dioxide into a tank and chill it right down has come with relatively recent advances in technol-ogy. True, the warm temperatures that prevail around harvest-time in Beaujolais are a relatively recent phenomenon, so fermentations may once have started at cooler temperatures, but refrigerating grapes down to 10°C or so prior to the start of fermentation or ensuring that active fermentations are chilled down to below 20°C takes access to electricity and sophisticated cooling mechanisms.

There's definitely a case to be made for the antiquity of the 'stack-it-in-a-tank-and-let-it-ferment' approach to vinification that finds echoes in semi-carbonic fermentation (albeit with contemporary inflections in most cases these days). Nevertheless, there are also valid arguments to be made that alcoholic fermen-tation and firm(ish) extraction also has a rich tradition in the region, and it is likely that this was the dominant way in which wine was made in Beaujolais during the nineteenth century, and probably well into the twentieth century. Some producers in Beaujolais have never made wine any other way.

It's perhaps worth noting that many practitioners of the latter style of winemaking argue – some with more vehemence than others – that by de-stemming their grapes and allowing for a full alcoholic fermentation, they are permitting their wines a wider range of aromatic expression. In doing so, they believe, they are making wines that are more capable of interpreting the ter-roir than wines that undergo an enzymatic fermentation, which tends to pro-duce a more limited range of characters.

In any case, there is no real benefit to be had in being didactic about which of the two fermentation practices has the better claim to be Beaujolais's 'trad-itional' method of winemaking. Nor, for that matter, is it appropriate to take a position about which is 'better'. Wine lovers should, instead, rejoice in the huge variety of approaches to vinification seen in Beaujolais, which only serves to increase the extraordinary diversity of wines made there.

MATURING THE WINES

Although a few producers mature their Beaujolais in new oak barrels – or at least a proportion thereof – this is not the norm in the region. Most winemakers believe that Gamay is at its best when its fruit shines through unmasked. Wines destined for youthful consumption are typically aged in inert vessels – stainless steel or cement tanks for the most part – prior to bottling. In the case of Beaujolais Nouveau, this maturation period is, of necessity, brief, but in most cases maturation lasts a few months at most.

Wines with more structure and more complexity are matured for longer in a range of containers, with individual winemakers having their own preferences. Stainless steel tanks are rarely used as vessels for longer-term maturation, with many winemakers preferring cement or oak. Cement tanks are the traditional option for fermentation and, in many cases, the ensuing maturation of the wines. Most of the older *cuvages* – and many more recent ones – have an array of these. These can either be lined with an impermeable coating, which protects the wine from oxygen as it ages, or unlined. Many winemakers prefer the latter as the pores in the cement allow for a little gentle airflow, which helps to tame Gamay's reductive tendencies and integrate the tannins into the body of the wine. Oak barrels of various sizes, mostly sourced second-hand from producers in Burgundy or elsewhere in France, are also traditional maturation vessels in Beaujolais. Once again, the porosity of the wood helps soften tannins and round out the wines as they age. More than a few producers are also turning to large amphorae, often made from sandstone, concrete or terracotta, each with varying permeability levels. Finally, egg-shaped vessels made from concrete or fibreglass can be used with the aim of helping the fine lees circulate through the liquid as the wine ages, fleshing out the mid-palate.

Ageing in Beaujolais typically lasts a few months, although some producers will mature wines for more than a year prior to bottling, especially when it comes to more structured wines from specific sites within the *crus*.

6

SAINT-AMOUR

Year in which *cru* status was awarded: 1946
Total vineyard area: 310 hectares
Altitude: 240–340 metres
Average altitude: 335 metres
Notable *lieux-dits*: En Paradis, A la Folie, Côte de Besset, Les Ravinets, Hameau des Billards, Vers l'Eglise, Aux Terres de Guinchay, Clos du Chapitre, La Pirolette, Au Breuil.

The most northerly of the Beaujolais *crus*, Saint-Amour lies hard up against the southern frontier of the Mâconnais. Its shallow slopes offer greater geological diversity than any other *cru*, with the exception of Brouilly (albeit packed into a much smaller area). Yes, you'll find a band of Beaujolais's iconic pink granite sands here, as well as outcrops of blue diorite, but there's also sandstone, clay, strands of alluvial deposits and even a tiny patch of limestone. As a result, it's incredibly hard to generalize about the characteristic identity of the wines made in the *cru*.

The *cru* takes its name from that of a Roman soldier, a convert to Christianity, who fled to Gaul in the third century, where he founded a monastery on a rocky outcrop overlooking the Saône River. These days Saint-Amour's romantic associations create an irresistible attraction for tourists from all around the world. In summer it's not unusual to stumble across couples queuing up in order to take selfies in front of the name panel at the entrance to the village of Saint-Amour Bellevue.

That romantic aura permeates the commercial realities in the *cru*, too. In France, in particular, wines from Saint-Amour are frequently

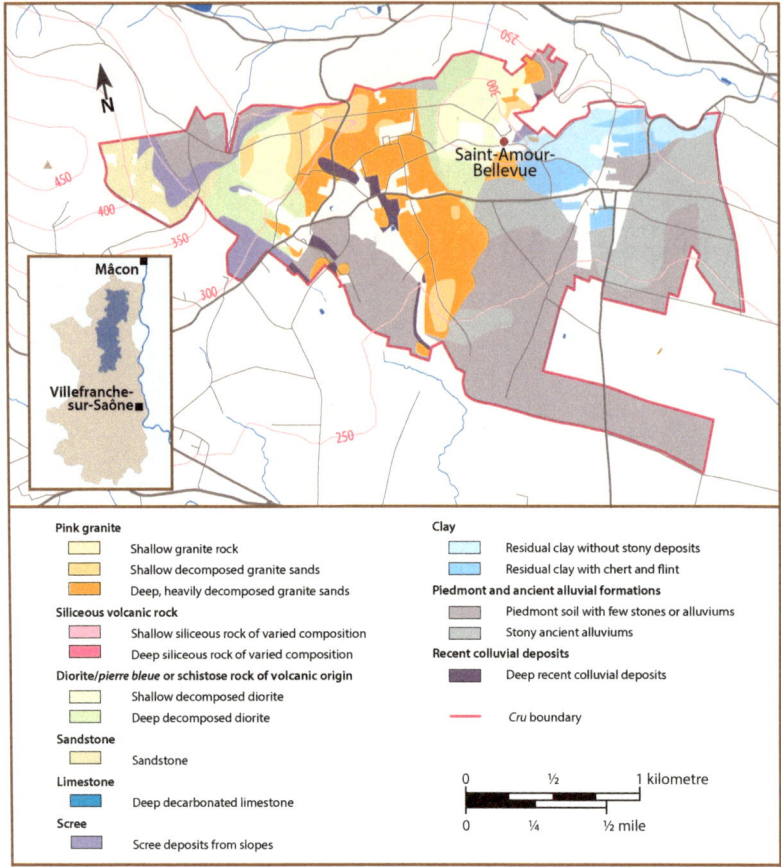

Map 4: The geology of Saint-Amour

purchased for weddings and anniversaries. And négociants have not been slow to cotton on to the opportunities afforded by the name, placing huge emphasis on the marketing of these wines in the run-up to Valentine's Day. There are also strong links between the *cru* and producers in the Mâconnais, and many of the vineyards are owned by producers whose ties to Burgundy are closer than their links to Beaujolais. So strong is demand – and so easy is it to sell Saint-Amour – that négociants pay a higher price, on average, for its wines than for those of any other *cru*. Nevertheless, Saint-Amour doesn't have much in the way of prestige domaines, producers whose names add a premium to the purchase price of a bottle, so although it's rare to find cheap Saint-Amour, it's equally rare for the *cru* to feature prominently in collectors' cellars.

The vineyards of Saint-Amour are among the flattest of all Beaujolais's crus, while those of nearby Juliénas are among the hilliest (photo courtesy of Fabrice Ferrer/Beaujolais Wines)

Producers

Domaine Chardigny

www.domaine-chardigny.com

The Chardigny vineyards, which straddle the border between Beaujolais and the Mâconnais, have been in the family since the eighteenth century, but it was only in 1995 that Catherine and Jean-Michel Chardigny decided to build their own winery and bottle their production. Up until that time, like many local growers, they'd sent their grapes to be vinified at the local cooperative.

However, Domaine Chardigny, as it's currently constituted, didn't take shape until 2015, when Catherine and Jean-Michel's three sons, Victor, Pierre-Maxime and Jean-Baptiste, bottled their first wine. Jean-Baptiste used to work for Burgundy's Domaine Leflaive, and he now farms the 20 hectares of vineyards organically, with a view to seeking biodynamic certification in the near future. Victor trained as a wine-maker, while Pierre-Maxime earned his commercial chops while working for a property in Bordeaux.

The domaine's vineyard holdings are divided fairly equally between the Mâconnais and Beaujolais, with 6 hectares of Saint-Amour and another 3.5 hectares of Beaujolais Villages vineyards in Leynes. Although the latter is vinified using a semi-carbonic maceration, Leynes' burly, dark-fruited, broad-shouldered character shines through. There are two Saint-Amour cuvées. The Clos du Chapitre comes from a parcel perched on a promontory and whose soil is characterized by an abundance of stony alluvial deposits. The grapes for this wine are partially de-stemmed (around 50 per cent, depending on the vintage) and then chilled down for a cold pre-fermentation maceration, which gives the wine aromatic richness – there are notes of blueberries and blood plums on the palate – and depth of colour. Finally, the finished wine is aged in *demi-muids* to soften and integrate the rather firm, dusty tannins. The A la Folie comes from a nearby parcel with similar soils to the Clos, but the vines are planted on a gentle slope. In terms of winemaking, there's a touch more active extraction practised here, and the wine is matured in a mix of large and small old oak barrels, as well as stainless steel tanks. It's a wine with a plush, plump, spicy mid-palate and noticeable tannic grip, although there's a welcome burst of bright acidity on the finish to liven things up. Both Saint-Amours deserve a bit of time in bottle to open up and show at their best.

Domaine de Fa

Instagram @antoinegraillot

While most of the investment in Beaujolais from outside the region trickles south from Burgundy, the Domaine de Fa bucks the trend. It's an outpost of the Graillot family's viticultural empire, a name familiar to anyone with an interest in the wines of the northern Rhône. In truth, the Graillots have had links with Beaujolais for many years. Alain Graillot's mother grew up near Tournus, and her family home became the Graillot's holiday house. Initially Graillot wanted to replant vines in the area, but the INAO turned down his application to do so, so the family began looking further afield.

In 2013, Graillot's sons, Antoine and Maxime, found 5 hectares of vines in and around Saint-Amour, buying another parcel of vines in Fleurie the next year. Five years later, they decided to expand the range with a white wine, and found a couple of small parcels of Chardonnay to add to their portfolio. These vineyards are now all managed organically – as are the Graillot holdings in the Rhône – but in actual fact their practices are now biodynamic, just without the official seal of certification.

It may come as a surprise to learn that the Graillots practise more semi-carbonic fermentation in Crozes-Hermitage than they do in Beaujolais.

Instead they crush the berries but retain the bunches, effectively making their fermentations whole-bunch, allowing juice to be expressed freely. This also allows for gentle extraction of the tannins via occasional *remontages*. This technique was a response to a challenging first round of winemaking in 2014 when, says Antoine Graillot, they didn't really understand Gamay and thought the variety was far more fragile than it actually is. As a result, they stacked whole bunches into the tanks and expected that those at the bottom of the tank would be crushed by the weight. Instead the berries stayed intact, the fermentations didn't start, and *Acetobacteria* activity ensured that levels of volatility went through the roof. Nowadays, in addition to lightly crushing the bunches, they ensure fermentation gets off to a good start by gently heating the tanks. Given that the Graillots are often among the last to pick, towards the end of the season, this helps to counteract the typically cool ambient temperatures in the cellar. After the fermentation comes to an end, the wines are aged for around a year in a mix of old oak barrels.

The two whites are fermented and aged in old oak barrels, and the Beaujolais Blanc Les Magnons, which comes from young vines planted on granite soils, is rounded and rich, with peachy fruit but the relatively modest acidity typical of Chardonnay grown on granite. The Saint-Véran Les Crais is more focused and fresh thanks to its limestone soil, and shows a little more minerality and elegance. The Beaujolais En Besset is a far better wine than its simple appellation designation suggests. It's very fine boned and perfumed, with heady notes of cherries and violets, as well as some stony minerality. It's not concentrated or very long, but it's an absolutely joyous wine. The Saint-Amour Côte de Besset is made of sterner stuff. Broader and fuller on the mid-palate, its tannins show more chewiness, and in its youth there's a hint of smoky reduction, although the palate opens up on aeration to show tangy plums and summer flowers. Defying all expectations about the delicacy of Fleurie, the Roche Guillon is the most structured of the three reds, with focused, gravelly tannins and abundant red fruits with a twist of orange zest.

The wines are a delight in their youth, but one can't help but feel a thrill of excitement on discovering that the Graillots have taken the decision to retain 10 per cent of their Fleurie production in order to age it for a decade. This late release, of which the first will be the 2015 vintage in 2025, is a resounding vote of confidence in Gamay's longevity.

Château de Lavernette

www.lavernette.com

The Château de Lavernette lies, quite literally, on the borderline between Beaujolais and the Mâconnais, with vineyards from both regions facing each other from across a narrow track. The property originally belonged to the monks of Tournus, but at the end of the sixteenth century passed into the hands of the lords of Lavernette, and now the twelfth and thirteenth generations of the same family live on the estate and manage its lands. In a meet-cute worthy of a Hollywood movie, Xavier de Boissieu met his wife, Kerrie, an American, while on his way round the world, studying and doing *stages* in the Rhône, New Zealand and California. Kerrie, who was working at Saintsbury in Carneros, was charged with taking the young French winemaker under her wing and showing him a thing or two about the American way of growing grapes and making wine. Xavier is happy to admit that even now, some 20 years later, he's still learning from Kerrie.

It wasn't all that long before Kerrie moved to rural France, where she and Xavier set about quietly revolutionizing the Château's approach to both viticulture and winemaking. Xavier admits that although he'd always wanted to farm organically, he was rather prejudiced against bio-dynamics, thinking that it was founded on airy-fairy notions rather than being grounded in science. Kerrie, an ardent advocate of the ap-proach, helped to change his perspective on the topic, and by 2008 the entire 13.5-hectare estate was being farmed biodynamically. Realizing that there was no point in growing beautiful biodynamic grapes and then using oenological additives, the couple also altered the family's winemaking practices. Xavier says that his father was initially wary of the change in approach, but has become increasingly positive thanks to the changes in quality he's seen in the wines produced at the Château.

Most of the wines made at Lavernette are built for the long haul, and a tasting of the Beaujolais Blanc going back as far as 1996 proves the cuvée has a remarkable ageing capacity, particularly in cooler vintages, where acidity is retained. The wine is now aged in tank for two years prior to bottling, which means that the wine has time to reach its poten-tial before it hits the market. Even in warmer years it has good levels of freshness as well as a stony mineral quality, enlivened by notes of white blossom and juicy pears.

Of the two Beaujolais Leynes wines (both are Beaujolais Villages, but the de Boissieus, like many producers in Leynes, choose to specify the name of the village, see p. 195), my preference is for the more lightly oaked Le Clos. It's vinified by means of layering whole bunches and de-stemmed grapes, topped off with more whole bunches, then aged for a few months in barrel, of which around 5–10 per cent is new oak. The palate is plush and generous, with lashings of dark berry and plum fruit, spice and a little hint of salty liquorice on the finish. There's a bit of grip here, but not too much. The Jadis, from the same vineyard planted on diorite, but made from a parcel of old vines, enjoys a longer maceration period, more extraction and up to 30 months of ageing in oak, of which up to 30 per cent is new. It's a bold, concentrated wine that will take time to settle into its maturity.

There are two Saint-Amours as well. En Chatenay is a de-stemmed cuvée made from grapes grown on granitic sands and a bit of sandstone. In its youth, the tannins are quite chewy, but there's plenty of bright acidity for balance, and a suggestion of mintiness on the finish helps reinforce an overall impression of freshness. Le Chatelet, on the other hand, undergoes a semi-carbonic fermentation and tannins are gently infused, then the wine is aged in a mix of sandstone amphorae and old oak barrels. The result is a wine that shows an elegant silkiness of tannin, and a long, juicy, dark-fruited finish that benefits from a twang of Campari-like bitterness.

Domaine Pierre Van Oost

Instagram @domainevanoost

Pierre Van Oost is a newcomer to winemaking in Beaujolais in many respects. Growing up in the Vosges mountains, his only contact with the region and its vines came in the holidays, when he came to visit his grandparents, who lived in Saint-Amour. Van Oost had always wanted to work in agriculture, but had no inclination to farm cattle or grow wheat, so he followed his heart south to work in the vineyards.

In between official training courses, he worked part-time at the Château de Lavernette (see p. 66) and by 2021 felt ready to take the plunge with his own venture. He was lucky enough to find vineyards located right by his grandparents' house, where he'd built himself a rudimentary winery (he's about to move into a bigger space in Leynes). He has 6 hectares of vineyard on long-term leases in and around Saint-Amour, and recently bought his first parcel of vines, a small plot of Chardonnay in Leynes.

Van Oost is still trying to find his signature winemaking style, and is experimenting with techniques ranging from dry carbonic maceration through to semi-carbonic macerations with a bit of *foulage*. In terms of ageing the wines, his whites see a little old oak, while the Saint-Amour, Le Clos de la Brosse, even has a small amount of new oak (no more than 20 per cent). This cuvée comes from a parcel grown on hard diorite rocks, which lends a characteristic richness to the fruit, and this in turn helps absorb the oak influence, which is noticeable only in a suggestion of vanilla on the finish. Given that the 2022 I tasted was only Van Oost's second vintage, its poise and precision is remarkable. The texture is silky and the tannins, though present, are well integrated into the wine. He makes two whites, both Beaujolais Blancs, both based on vines planted in 2016 and both fermented then matured for six months in old oak barrels. The Aux Arserons comes from clay-rich loams and is more mineral and intense than the brighter, more fruity La Côte 114, which is derived from soils with more limestone content.

Taken all together, these wines presage serious intention on Van Oost's behalf, and may well signal the rising of a new star in Beaujolais's winemaking firmament.

Clos Sauvage

clossauvage.com

Sophie and David Devynck, as the surname might suggest, are not native to the Beaujolais region. They travelled southwards from northern France, having worked for a number of producers along the way, mostly in the south-west of the country. They were looking for a region where they could afford to buy their own vineyard – not just any vineyard, but one with good terroir, where they could work organically and make wines with freshness and tension. After a year of searching in Beaujolais, they stumbled across a place hidden away in the forest of Leynes. Perched on a hill at 450 metres above sea level, the house and its vineyards had run wild, abandoned by its former tenants, who'd managed it on behalf of a large négociant. Inspired by its untamed abandon, they named it the Clos Sauvage.

The property came with 7 hectares of vineyards, but most of them were in such a bad state that the Devyncks grubbed them up, leaving them with 2 hectares of Beaujolais Villages in Leynes. This has now been supplemented with a further 6 hectares of vineyards, spread across sites in Saint-Amour and Juliénas, as well as Leynes. These are all, as per the Devyncks' original intentions, farmed organically, with biodynamic trials being conducted. 'But,' says David, 'the decision about whether or not to pursue this has to be a scientific one, based on rigorous observations.'

Having learned how to make wine in the south-west, the Devyncks inflect their fermentation practices with those learned outside of Beaujolais, including the use of a significant proportion of de-stemmed fruit. In cold vintages they may use as little as 30 per cent whole bunches in order not to extract green characters from the stems, while in warm vintages the proportions of de-stemmed fruit to whole bunches might well be reversed. They want to ensure that the fermentations last long enough to extract properly, so they're conducted at a fairly modest temperature, starting at 14°C and climbing up to about 24–25°C towards the end. *Pied de cuve* yeasts are used to ensure the fermentations get off to a good start.

The entry-level wine is 9 Mois Après, a Beaujolais Leynes, which is made with semi-carbonic fermentation and a single *pigeage* at the end. It's a juicy wine with dark berry fruit, notes of smoky tobacco leaves and very supple, restrained tannins. The Saint-Amour La Cocagne comes from a north-facing parcel planted on blue stones on the heights of the *cru*. The initial impact is all about perfume and bright, layered fruit, but this cloaks some serious, grippy tannins. Precise and well-defined, it's utterly delicious.

There are two further wines from Beaujolais Leynes. The Fauve is made from 60-year-old vines grown on a plot where the clays of Mâcon meet the granitic sands of Beaujolais. It's smoky, spicy and tightly wound in its youth, but the vivid red fruit and floral notes on the long finish promise well for its future. A small parcel of this wine is aged for 22 months, of which a year is spent in *demi-muids* and the rest in stainless steel, to create the Fauve Longue Elevage. Aromatically, it's quite similar to the straight Fauve, but better integration of the tannins creates a wine with greater elegance.

7

JULIÉNAS

Year in which *cru* status was awarded: 1938
Total vineyard area: 540 hectares
Altitude: 200–450 metres
Average altitude: 330 metres
Notable *lieux-dits*: Les Capitans, Les Mouilles, La Bottière, Vayollette, Bessay, En Rizière, Beauvernay, Bois de la Salle, Cotoyon

Juliénas is one of the least well known of Beaujolais's *crus*, at least outside France, where it has a small but devoted following. This lack of renown is due to a number of factors, none of them related to the quality of the wines that can be made in this relatively remote northern *cru*, but it probably doesn't help that around 80 per cent of the *cru*'s production is sold at knock-down prices in supermarkets.

Situated on the north-west fringes of the Beaujolais zone, much of Juliénas – whose name ultimately derives from Julius Caesar – is isolated and rural (a strange concept given that the *cru* lies around 15 kilometres south-west of the bustling city of Mâcon). The feeling of isolation is enhanced by the fact that the approach to the pretty village of Juliénas, from whichever direction you happen to be travelling, lies along narrow roads that switchback over a series of hills and valleys.

With around 540 hectares of vineyards, Juliénas comes pretty close to the mean size of the 10 *crus* overall. (If you want to be truly picky, the mean is actually 568 hectares, but what's 28 hectares between friends?) It's one of the hilliest, affording growers a variety of expositions, of which the most prized are generally those that face south and south-east. Altitude has a part to play in the character of the wines, too, as vineyards run from around 200 metres above sea level to as much as 450 metres, and slopes are often steep. This topography can make it tricky to farm, and it's unsurprising (although rather sad) to see that herbicides are more widely used in these hillside vineyards than they are in many places elsewhere in the *cru* zone. It's perhaps understandable, though, given that Juliénas's lack of prestige (or, more importantly, the relatively high prices that come with critical kudos and consumer demand) means that growers can ill afford to lavish the time-consuming attention required to farm their fragile elderly bush vines organically.

Of all the *crus* in Beaujolais, Juliénas has the lowest amount of the pink granite soils so typical of the region. Instead, a significant portion of the area under vine is planted on diorite-rich soils, which lend the wines a certain breadth on the palate and firmness of tannin. On the southern and eastern fringes of the *cru*, alluvial soils mark out the course of an ancient river bed, and there are also isolated outcrops of pink granite and flints dotted around.

Producers

Domaine de Boischampt
www.domainedeboischampt.fr

The Domaine de Boischampt has a venerable heritage, with buildings dating back to the seventeenth century, but by the time Antoine and Thibaud Baudin moved in to manage the property on behalf of its new owners in 2018, it's fair to say that the property was not in the best of states. It had been owned by a négociant, but the estate's poor profits had meant that its vineyards and buildings were badly in need of restructuring.

The Baudins have been given a free hand by the new owners to revive the Domaine's fortunes in whatever way they see fit. Since their arrival, 12 hectares of vineyards, out of a total of 18.5, have been replanted. These vineyards, of which 6 hectares are in Juliénas, with the remainder scattered across Morgon, Fleurie, Moulin-à-Vent, Chénas and Beaujolais Villages, are now organically certified. The renovated *cuvage* has been outfitted with smartly liveried cement tanks and gentle pneumatic presses, while a vaulted cellar is dedicated to ageing some of the wines in large old oak barrels.

Thibaud Baudin has already earned his chops at the head of Chablis's Domaine d'Henri, so is no stranger to high-quality winemaking. There's

The village of Juliénas gives the surrounding appellation its name (photo courtesy of Fabrice Ferrer/Beaujolais Wines)

plenty of proof of his ability to work with Chardonnay, as evidenced by the Beaujolais Villages Blanc, which shows not only ripe citrus and orchard fruit on the palate, but also some stony minerality and balancing bright acidity. Oak has been used, but its influence is restrained and subtle. The reds are vinified using semi-carbonic macerations, which are kept at around a cool 20°C to preserve fruit and ensure a long fermentation. There's a Beaujolais Villages Rouge, which shows good acidity, soft tannins and a pleasing twist of pithy bitterness on the finish. The Juliénas blended bottling is a step up in concentration and quality, with stony tannins gripping a generous, red-fruited palate enlivened with notes of wild herbs and Campari bitters. Les 4 Cerisiers is another Juliénas, from a parcel grown on a steep, windy, east-facing slope. It's heady and wild in the way that only Juliénas can be, with chunky, dusty tannins that exert some grip on the finish. The Juliénas Vayolette comes from grapes grown on a north-facing parcel, which gives it a much tighter, austere personality, and generous but very fine tannins and bright acidity. This is a wine that's going to take time to unpack and reveal its layered palate in full. The Saint-Amour cuvée, Tête de Bonnet, is juicy and attractive, but lacks the focus for the long haul, while the Moulin-à-Vent Au Michelons shows the *cru's* typical elegance and focus, along with stony minerality and peppery spice.

Domaine du Clos du Fief

closdufief.com

The Domaine du Clos du Fief, like many of the older winemaking properties in Beaujolais, was once owned by wealthy silk merchants from Lyon. Francis Tête, the great-grandfather of Sylvain, who currently helms the property, was the on-site manager of the domaine for the hands-off proprietors.

When the silk industry began to founder in the inter-war period, Francis bought the property, along with 6 hectares of vineyards in Juliénas, and passed it on to his descendants. Things have changed since the time of great-grandfather Tête. The vineyard holdings have expanded to 17 hectares, of which Juliénas still forms the heartland, with the remaining hectares spread out across the *crus* of Saint-Amour, Moulin-à-Vent and Chénas, as well as substantial holdings in the *villages* zone and even as far north as St Veran in Burgundy (a kind of reverse takeover in terms of the usual pattern of vineyard ownership in the region).

Sylvain Tête's time spent working overseas, mainly in Australia and New Zealand, would probably have been considered a bit unusual by his progenitor, but Tête feels that he benefited from his time abroad, returning with a new perspective on the best way to make and market his wines.

Flexibility is the order of the day at the Clos du Fief, both in the vineyard and in the winery. Semi-carbonic maceration is typical of the house style, but in some years Tête deems that a certain amount of de-stemming is necessary, particularly in those vintages where sugar levels in the grapes are rising rapidly but the stems are still green. Most fermentations and maturations take place in cement tanks, which allow for some gentle oxygen ingress to counterbalance Gamay's tendency towards reduction, but the top two cuvées are aged at least partly in older oak barrels (Tête is not a fan of oaky flavours in Gamay).

Of these two top bottlings, only the Tête de Cuvée is vinified in the Burgundian style, with full de-stemming and vigorous extraction of the tannins. This cuvée is only made in years in which Tête thinks the quality of the juice he extracts from a plot of very old vines grown on the slopes of Juliénas warrants it. It's a dense, deep black hole of a wine, with firm, chalky tannins that benefit from being allowed a few years to unwind in the bottle. Les Berthets, another Juliénas, is made from vines planted somewhere around 1910–15, and which are reaching the end of their lives, but Tête is loath to grub them up while they produce wines with this level of concentration and poise.

The other wines also share the same hallmark of poise, despite the richness afforded by recent vintages. There's a fine, nervy Chénas Gandelins made from vines grown on pink granite soils, while the Moulin-à-Vent Les Deschanes is tight and austere in its youth, but blossoms into elegance and perfume over the long-term. The St Amour Les Capitans appears ripe and generous on first impression, but all that generosity of fruit cloaks fine, grippy tannins. Tête's Beaujolais Villages, both white and red, show good structure and some complexity, punching well above the weight you might expect from the appellation.

Domaine le Cotoyon

Geoffray Benat is a member of the eighth generation to make wines in Beaujolais (at least if you follow the line of matrilineal descent – his father came from the Charolais region, better known for its cattle farming). Don't make the mistake of assuming he's a country bumpkin, though – he only returned to the home farm in 2019, after having spent several years living and working in London. (He's still involved in the ownership of a wine bar in London's Notting Hill Gate.)

Benat worked alongside his father for a few vintages before taking the reins solo in 2022. He's planning on making changes to the way the vineyards are managed and the wines made but, he says, he's taking it one step at a time.

One change he's already begun to implement is the replanting of the 17 hectares he farms bit by bit (half a hectare per year is all he can manage). Benat is looking to shift away from Beaujolais's traditional high-density planting to a lower density of 6,000 vines per hectare, planted on a 0.8 x 2 metre grid (two metres between rows and 80 centimetres between vines within each row). This will allow him to open up the canopy of each vine, reducing the risk of fungal diseases. The ultimate aim is to move towards a winery in which the farming is organic and the carbon footprint is as close to zero as possible.

The domaine is situated above the village of Pruzilly, which itself is the highest village in Juliénas, and one of the property's main vineyards lies nearby. A good two-thirds of Le Cotoyon's vineyards lie in Juliénas, although Benat has other vineyards in Saint-Amour. In total, he manages more than 30 parcels of vines spread out across the northern part of the *cru* zone, and currently makes half a dozen wines. The aim, eventually, is to move from bottlings based on blends of grapes from different vineyards to a greater number of site-specific cuvées, a process that has already started with Le Cotoyon and Les Mouilles.

In terms of winemaking, Benat's approach is straightforward. Semi-carbonic maceration takes place in concrete tanks, with gentle tannic extraction – the wines of Juliénas are structured enough to bypass any need to enhance the tannins, Benat believes. The top cuvées spend a bit of time in oak, mostly older barrels, with the aim of taming those tannins with some gentle micro-oxygenation.

Overall, the style of the wines is dense, deep-fruited and ripe – Benat is not afraid of alcohol, if that's what the site and the vintage combine to give him – but there's always a welcome freshness and a sense of balance. The Beaujolais Villages Pruzilly is plush and approachable, with generous layers of dark fruit and enough supple, fuzzy tannin to allow the wines to age for a few years. The Juliénas Vieilles Vignes, made from a parcel of vines aged 60 years and more grown on alluvial soils, is dark and brooding, verging on raisined in warmer years, but there's no lack of bright fruit on the finish. Of the two parcel selections, Les Mouilles is the richest, with alcohol levels that sometimes top out at around 15 per cent in hot vintages, but the balance is precise, and the deep, spicy fruit profile and sinewy tannins are reminiscent of the wines of the northern Rhône. My own favourite is Le Cotoyon, made from grapes grown at altitudes of around 400 metres, which lends the blueberry-scented wines a zesty character. There's also a sophisticated Chardonnay that eschews the simple peardrop flavours of many of the region's whites in favour of a more complex, savoury palate tinged with almonds and dried herbs.

Domaine David-Beaupère

domainedavidbeaupere.fr

Jean-Louis David took over the running of Domaine David-Beaupère in 2007, bringing the winery back under familial control after a long period of it being leased as a *métayage*. At the time, the property owned 4 hectares of vineyards, which were farmed conventionally, but by 2009 David was working organically. Hard manual labour was the order of the day – or, to be more precise, the order of a few years – as a lot of work was needed to put the vineyards in good order.

The worst plots were grubbed up and replanted as the root system of these old vines was shallow and fragile, thanks to a long-term regime of herbicides and fertilization. The aim with the new plantings was to encourage the vines' roots to dig deeper into the stony soils of Juliénas.

David says that he would have found it difficult to manage the process without the support and encouragement of some of the region's other producers, most notably Paul-Henri Thillardon.

Domaine David-Beaupère is still organically certified, despite David's occasional frustrations with the system. 'It was really important that someone should be a standard bearer for organic practices in the region,' he says. And although he's not seeking further certification as a biodynamic producer, many of his practices tend in that direction, including the spraying of herbal teas in the vineyards, the burying of cow horns full of manure and a desire to work in harmony with the lunar calendar.

Hand in hand with this respect for the environment goes a minimalist approach in the winery. No adjustments are made to the must, natural yeasts are encouraged to do their thing and the use of sulphur dioxide is kept to a minimum. Grapes are chilled on reception, right down to 5°C, in order to ensure a long, slow start to a semi-carbonic fermentation that is encouraged not to rise above about 21°C in order to ensure purity of fruit in the finished wines.

The secret to a clean fermentation, says David, is rigorous triage in the vineyard. 'The question I ask myself is whether or not I would want to eat the berries,' he explains. Any berries that are healthy but rejected as being unworthy of the still wines are used to make a sparkling pét nat.

Of the 11.5 hectares of vineyards David now manages, 7 are in Juliénas, with the remainder in Moulin-à-Vent and Beaujolais. Currently they're only planted to Gamay, but David is seriously considering adding a white to his portfolio, although, he says with a mischievous twinkle in his eye, he's not planning on planting Chardonnay. Juliénas, he says, is a great place to make white wines, and the best grape to help it reach its potential in that respect is Aligoté, which David believes to be a 'terroir sponge'.

The wines David makes all have a lightness of touch, and alcohol levels are generally restrained, without any ensuing loss of ripeness of fruit. The Trois Verres cuvée, made from younger vines grown on the loamy, stony soils of La Bottière, is packed full of pretty red fruits, tinged with summer flowers. Its older brother, La Bottière, is initially somewhat reductive on the nose, but shows a similarly floral flavour profile once it opens up. This is a wine that needs some time in bottle to fully reveal its generous, rounded palate, framed by slightly chunky tannins. The Vayolette bottling comes from a vineyard planted on dense, dark diorite, which gives the wine a kind of density, a dark richness. The palate is plush and velvety, with a darker fruit character than the Bottière, enlivened with a refreshing twist of Campari bitters on the finish.

Domaine Louis Paul Pernot

Instagram @domainelouispaulpernot

An army of Burgundians has travelled south to take on vineyards in Beaujolais in recent years, and Louis Paul Pernot is one of its foot soldiers. Unlike many from his cohort, though, this native of Pouilly-Fuissé was not born with a pair of silver secateurs in his hand. Instead his background is in the building trade, although he learned his vineyard skills from his father, who worked in the vineyards of the Mâconnais. However, attracted by the idea of working outdoors and making wines, Pernot settled in Juliénas (there was no way a novice like him could afford vineyards further north, he points out) in 2018.

His initial purchase of a 1-hectare vineyard has been extended to a total of 8.5 hectares, some of which he owns and some of which are managed on long-term leases, of which 80 per cent are in Juliénas.

Pernot's Burgundian background shows in his approach to winemaking. He starts by de-stemming and crushing the grapes on arrival at the winery, and then uses pump-overs and plunges to extract tannins from the must. The wines are then matured in barrels, and although few of these are new, many of the wines are quite marked by oak.

The one exception to the rule is Les Vayolettes, which despite being aged in oak like the other cuvées, is based on semi-carbonic maceration which is inflected by gentle Burgundian-style tannin extractions when Pernot deems these are necessary. The finished wine is noticeably more perfumed and vibrant than the other cuvées, with a promising concentration and depth that should allow the wine to age well.

One gets the impression that Pernot's winemaking is a work in progress and that he is feeling his way towards a better understanding of the new horizons he's currently exploring. To my mind, Les Vayolettes points the way in the right direction.

8

CHÉNAS

Year in which *cru* status was awarded: 1936
Total vineyard area: 220 hectares
Altitude: 200–500 metres
Average altitude: 260 metres
Notable *lieux-dits*: Les Brureaux, En Champagne, Les Journets, Les Grands Gandelins, En Papolet, Les Daroux, Aux Verchères, En Nervat, Aux Blémonts

The smallest of all the *crus* at 220 hectares, Chénas is also one of the least well-known, despite the fact that it was the source of King Louis XIII's favourite wines in the seventeenth century (allegedly he refused to have anything else in his cellar). The quality of Chénas's wines was also recognized by all the nineteenth-century cartographers of Beaujolais's *lieux-dits* (see p. 19), with an astounding six classed as first growths (only one fewer than the much larger commune of Villié-Morgon) by Vermorel, Budker or both. Part of the problem stems from the fact that the Chénas appellation does not map precisely on to the commune of Chénas, which lies partly within the *cru* of Moulin-à-Vent. Strange as it may seem, even the village of Chénas does not lie within the boundaries of the *cru* that takes its name. (Once again, *c'est compliqué* in Beaujolais.)

The topography of the *cru* is incredibly diverse, and the average altitude of 260 metres fails to capture the fact that although its eastern hills are relatively gentle, as you travel westwards, the uplands can rise to fairly dizzying heights. Soils vary, too, with the eastern vineyards planted on stony alluvial deposits, while shallow pink granites dominate in the west. As it does in nearby Moulin-à-Vent, a seam of manganese runs

Chénas's vineyards often seem remote, despite their proximity to a number of villages (photo courtesy of Fabrice Ferrer/Beaujolais Wines)

through Chénas's terroir, influencing the character of the wines made there (see p. 90). The woodlands that are believed by many to have given the *cru* its name (*chêne* is French for 'oak') have largely been cut down to make way for vineyards, although the crests of the hills and the north-facing slopes that look out towards the *Beaujolais Vert* are still green with trees. (Another possibility is that Chénas takes its name from yet another Roman, a nobleman named Canus.)

As with that other small *cru*, Chiroubles, the wines made in Chénas do not receive either the critical or commercial success they merit, and as a result its vineyard area is decreasing (down by about 15 per cent in the last two years). This may be because the amount of wine produced here is not high enough to make the *cru* very interesting to volume-driven négociants. This, in turn, means that it is rare to find Chénas in supermarkets even in France, let alone in export markets. It's a vicious circle; lack of availability leads to lack of awareness, and the resulting low demands lead to a greater reluctance on the part of retailers to stock the wines. Another reason for Chénas's woes may be that it has few big-name domaines to draw attention to its virtues. But its virtues are there, ready to be discovered. The *cru* is capable of producing wines that have depth, richness and structure, with a fruit profile that is often a little darker than is typical in many other *crus*, sometimes tinged with notes of peonies, irises and peppery spice, and tannins that can be rather firm and austere in youth.

Producers

Pascal Aufranc

www.pascal-aufranc.com

Thanks to the *cru's* switchback hills and hairpin bends, and the shaded woodlands that hug the road tightly, many of Chénas's domaines feel rather remote, a world apart even though they lie only a few brief kilometres, as the crow flies, from the small village of Chénas. That impression of living at one remove from the crowded, complex modern world is part of the attraction of the area for Pascal Aufranc, who launched his eponymous domaine in 1992 after studying in Beaune and then working in Oregon. He started out with 6.5 hectares, mostly in Chénas, and now owns 10 hectares, with land in Juliénas as well, which is where the winery is situated.

Aufranc is certified HVE (*Haute Valeur Environnemental*), saying that the risk of erosion on the steep granite soils of some of his vineyards makes it difficult to manage the soil in a way that allows for organic certification, although he tries to use as little product as possible. When it comes to winemaking, he aims for gentle infusions rather than vigorous extraction, which he achieves by using a grille to submerge the cap. His semi-carbonic macerations last between seven and 12 days, starting off at around 22°C and rising up to around 30°C towards the end to extract colour, although Aufranc explains that he monitors extraction carefully as there's a risk towards the end of fermentation of deriving bitter flavours from the stems. The wines are then matured in either cement tanks or resin eggs that help integrate the tannins into the body of the wine without affecting their flavour. He also uses micro-oxygenation to open up the wines and avoid any trace of reduction.

He makes a sulphite-free Chénas, the 'Naturellement', a wine that brings to mind a liquid Black Forest Gateau, all dark cherries and chocolate, albeit with a cooling minty element. The En Rémont, also from Chénas, is a complex wine that shows density and weight, without a trace of clumsiness. He also makes two wines in Juliénas. Les Crots comes from a parcel planted on alluvial clay soils, and it's an approachable, gluggable wine with fleshy, supple tannins. Les Chers, which comes from vines planted on diorite, is an altogether different beast. It's a layered wine with taut, focused tannins and great freshness that would repay a bit of time in bottle before being drunk.

Domaine Hadrien Houbert

Instagram @domaine_hadrienhoubert

When I met Hadrien Houbert for the first time, he was manoeuvring a large palomino horse and the plough it was pulling down a narrow strip of soil that lay between two rows of low-slung bush vines. In what may well be the most meta statement I've seen during my time in Beaujolais, Houbert was wearing a T-shirt that featured the silhouette of a horse drawing a plough, guided by a man. Beneath the image, the slogan read 'Rage against the machine'. It was clear, even before Houbert greeted me, that I was about to have an encounter with an ecowarrior.

Houbert is a relative newcomer to life as a grape grower, having already enjoyed a successful career as a maker of deluxe cabinetry in Paris. But, he says, he grew fed up of working in a luxury industry where everything he did was 'on a whim and under the cosh'. He was earning good money, but he was also stressed out. He decided to jack it all in so that he could work in an arena in which the pace was dictated by nature rather than the demands of his clients.

Having spent a fair bit of time working in the vineyards belonging to his in-laws in Champagne, he decided that viticulture was his true calling. He settled in Beaujolais (far more affordable than Champagne) and set himself up with 3.4 hectares of vineyards on a long-term lease, a scale that allows him to achieve an intense, detailed style of biodynamic farming. Houbert talks with passion about the experiments he's been conducting, trials with straw mulches to reduce the soil temperatures in his vineyards during the height of summer, and of the virtues of agroforestry. He says that he sells 90 per cent of the wines he makes in France as trying to sell his wines overseas would make a mockery of his aim of reducing his overall carbon footprint. And he's proud of the way he's managed to reduce his use of treatments – with the exception of biodynamic tisanes and silica sprays (which he references in detail on his back labels) – in the vineyard.

When it comes to winemaking – which he says is of far less interest to him than the growing of the grapes themselves – Houbert says he learned on the job in a constant process of self-questioning. He chills his grapes right down to around 12°C as soon as they arrive at the winery in order to allow him to return to the vineyard and continue to work with his pickers. Overall, he's aiming for light, fresh styles of wines made by means of classic semi-carbonic maceration, with as little intervention and extraction as possible.

He makes a light, crunchy Beaujolais Villages, which he bottles as a Beaujolais Villages Nouveau if he feels it's ready in time, otherwise it gets bottled in spring the next year at the latest. There are two Chénas wines in the line-up. The Chénas En Champagne comes from a windy, south-facing plot that is, says Houbert, difficult to manage in a hot year and which he now harvests based on acidity levels rather than phenolic ripeness. It's a wine with ripe, fleshy dark cherry fruit and a lovely bright finish. The picking date for the north-facing Chénas Les Brurreaux is less vital as the grapes hang on to their freshness for longer. This cuvée typically shows luminous levels of acidity, and focused, sinewy tannins framing a palate redolent of orange zest and slightly dried summer flowers. The weightiest of Houbert's wines is En Roche Pilée, a Morgon whose grapes come from shallow, stony soils at the lower end of Corcelette. It's a brooding, dense, Heathcliff of a wine, rich with blueberries, spice and liquorice.

Domaine Obora

Instagram @obora__

The first beneficiaries of Thibault Liger-Belair's Domaine des Jeunes Pousses (see p. 206) project were Hugo Foizel and Angela Quiblier. At the time they took up Liger-Belair's invitation to make wines in Chénas, the couple had recently graduated as oenologists from the University of Dijon, and Quiblier, who comes from the Jura, met Liger-Belair while working at the Hospices de Beaune. Impressed by the young woman, Liger-Belair offered her the opportunity to take on the Chénas vineyards. She was somewhat daunted by the idea of taking on 5 hectares of vineyards by herself, and asked whether Foizel, her partner (a native of Champagne's Aube) could join her in the project. The young couple's first vintage in Beaujolais was in 2020, and by 2021 not only had they settled into the region, they had also taken on Domaine Obora as a *métayage*. They ran the two projects – the Jeunes Pousses and Domaine Obora – side by side for a vintage, but realized that something had to give. Although grateful for the opportunity that the Jeunes Pousses scheme had given them to get to know a region and to understand how to make wines there, Foizel and Quiblier decided to focus on Obora.

They now farm 7 hectares of vineyards organically, from which they make four cuvées in a style which owes more to the mentorship of Paul-Henri Thillardon than it does to Liger-Belair, although the relationship with their erstwhile patron remains strong. On arrival at the winery, the bunches are chilled overnight then fed into concrete tanks at temperatures of about 8–9°C. The grapes are blanketed in carbon dioxode and then left to allow the initial enzymatic fermentation to begin slowly and gently. The cooler the temperature, the slower the pace of the fermentation, which carries both risks and rewards. The longer the enzymatic fermentation, the more vivid and fruity the final aromas of the finished wine are likely to be, with more layers of complexity. But the same slow pace runs a higher risk of the development of off-aromas in the wines, which means that Foizel and Quiblier need to monitor the tanks diligently, taking whatever measures necessary to ensure that the finished wines remain pure and clean.

Judging by the success of their 2023s, they manage the job well. The entry-level cuvée is Bob, a crunchy, vibrant Vin de France made mostly (around 95 per cent) from declassified Chénas grapes. They make two more wines in Chénas, both parcel selections. The En Perelles comes from a vineyard planted on alluvial soils and is a pretty, floral wine with good levels of acidity and a distinct note of wild strawberries, all supported by rounded, supple tannins. En Papolet is a well-balanced, focused wine with fine, grippy tannins and bright flavours of blood orange, plum and raspberry. Both wines show a distinctive thick texture, plush and velvety. The final wine comes from a vineyard in Juliénas that they own outright. It has a dense, rich palate with a ferrous twang of minerality on the long finish, but has plenty of ripe red fruit that helps make it both accessible and enjoyable.

Domaine Benjamin Passot

domainebenjaminpas.wixsite.com

From the heights of the village of Vauxrenard, Benjamin Passot enjoys a wonderful view out towards the vineyards of Fleurie and Chénas. On a clear day you can even see the hazy snow-topped heights of Mont Blanc in the far distance.

Most of the time, though, Passot is too busy to stop and admire the view. He's fully occupied making the most of his small domaine, which he established back in 2017. Of the 3.5 hectares he farms, some are owned outright by him, and some he leases from his family on a long-term basis, until he's paid off enough of their purchase price to own them outright. Although Passot's family hails from the Côte de Nuits in Burgundy, he wasn't born to the life of a winegrower, but fairly young, he got bitten by the viticultural bug. Realizing that he'd never be able to afford a vineyard on his home turf, Passot struck out for parts south, but not before he'd learned his craft from some of his home region's best winemakers.

His first purchase in the region was a chance buy – he'd idly typed in 'vineyards for sale' on a website, and ended up with a small plot of vines in Juliénas. For the first few vintages, he continued to work in Burgundy, trading his labour for the opportunity to make his Beaujolais in the cellars of his employers, who offered him tank space and the use of equipment and barrel. As Passot puts it, 'You really have to love what you do in order to create a winery if you don't inherit one.'

What Passot lacks in terms of silver spoons, he makes up for with an enquiring mind and sheer ingenuity. His winery features a collection of Heath Robinson contraptions based on second-hand purchases of ancient winery equipment that he's rigged up himself in order to allow him to de-stem his grapes, chill his musts, bottle his finished wines and perform a whole host of other tasks vital to the smooth running of a winery. In one corner stands a plastic container full of wines left over from tastings. He's hoping that the selenium contained in the tannins of these left-over wines will allow him to protect his crops from fungal diseases once the liquid has been diluted and turned into a spray.

By 2020, Passot had expanded his production to take in five of the ten *crus* (Chénas, Chiroubles, Morgon, Moulin-à-Vent and the original parcel in Juliénas). He also has plans to plant some Chardonnay vines on the diorite soils of Juliénas, as he believes the terroir will give him wines of great freshness and poise.

He vinifies his grapes in the traditional Burgundian manner, de-stemming them wholly or partially, depending on both vintage and terroir. He allows indigenous yeasts to ferment the grapes, and matures the wines in a mixture of old and new barrels. He manages to do this in an adroit, judicious manner, as none of the wines seem marked by obvious oak character. His wines all show fine, elegant tannins. The Chénas Au Bois Retour comes from grapes planted on the *cru*'s granitic heights, and it's a fine-boned, delicate wine with a marked floral character. The Chiroubles Cercillons is structured and closed in its youth, but blossoms into a palate notable for the purity of its raspberry fruit and its silky tannins. The Moulin-à-Vent presents a very focused, narrow palate with a long, persistent finish and a touch of peppery spice.

Domaine Thillardon

When I talked to winemakers – particularly the younger generation of winemakers – about how they learned to make wine, one name came up time and again. Paul-Henri Thillardon is a source of both inspiration and information for many, but when he arrived in the *crus* in his early twenties, he says that he, too, felt a bit lost.

Thillardon, and his siblings Charles, Jean-Baptiste and Aude, who now work alongside him at the domaine, grew up in a family of grape growers in the southern part of Beaujolais. Thillardon had moved out in order to work with winemakers in Beaujolais and the Rhône, but Chénas – where he'd found some organic vineyards to rent on a long-term lease – was a bit of a mystery. 'I could tell these were great terroirs, with granites like the ones you find in Fleurie and Moulin-à-Vent,' he says, 'but I had no template to work to as the *cru* had no image. It felt like no one know about it.' He felt comfortable with the viticultural aspect of his work, having been born to it, but, says Thillardon, vinification is different – it requires both creative instinct and the application of science.

His approach to winemaking has evolved over the years. Initially he stuck to what he saw as 'the rules', using cultured yeasts and filtering his wines, which he says you need to do in order to learn how to leave the recipe behind and make natural wines. Thillardon learned how to use a microscope (a vital tool for a natural winemaker, he says), and how to ask the right kinds of questions. 'It's fine to be romantic about winemaking, but you need to be analytical, too,' he says, 'it's about tasting and analysing and understanding. There's a knowledge base that only comes with experience – you never stop being an apprentice, but after about 10 years you begin to get the hang of it.'

Thillardon says that he seals himself off hermetically from the outside world between the harvesting of his grapes and the stage at which the whole bunches are pressed to allow for the final alcoholic phase of fermentation. He says he needs to be able to concentrate intensely as otherwise he might miss something. Every year, says Thillardon, he faces new problems, and each one of them requires a creative solution.

Thillardon has now become the reference point for anyone seeking to understand Chénas that he was looking for on his arrival in the region back in 2008. He makes a couple of fairly unusual Vin de France whites. Cuvée Georges is a blend of Chardonnay, Aligoté and the rare pink-skinned Chardonnay Rose aged for 20 months in large-format old barrels. It's a slightly hazy, deeply coloured wine with incredible acidity, stony minerality and a layered palate with notes of lemon zest, green herbs and great length. It's an astonishing wine, outclassed only by Albert, a blend of 70 per cent Chardonnay and 30 per cent Aligoté with the truly effortless complexity and precision that's only ever shown by world-class wines. When it comes to reds, Les Vibrations, a blend of different Chénas parcels, provides an introduction to Thillardon's vibrant house style. Les Blémonts comes from a parcel grown on manganese-rich clays. It's rounded and generous, with supple tannins, raspberry dark cherry fruit and a whisper of smoky reduction. Soils based on alluvial stones and flints give rise to grapes vinified as Les Carrières. Thanks to the trees and hedges that surround the parcel, it's one of Thillardon's coolest, and the wine is incredibly polished and elegant, with fine, powdery tannins and flavours of Seville oranges and strawberries. Chassignol is now a Thillardon *monopole*, and its quartz-strewn granites and centenarian vines combine to create a complex, rich wine of great depth, grace and length.

9

MOULIN-À-VENT

Year in which *cru* status was awarded: 1936
Total vineyard area: 620 hectares
Altitude: 220–275 metres
Average altitude: 255 metres
Notable *lieux-dits*: Aux Caves, Les Vérillats, Champ de Cour, La Rochelle, La Roche, Carquelin, La Tour du Bief, Le Moulin-à-Vent, Les Thorins

There's a story told about the celebrated Burgundian négociant Henri Mommessin that reveals a good deal about the changing fortunes of the *crus* of Beaujolais, and in particular those of Moulin-à-Vent. Apparently, so the tale goes, some time in the early 1930s Mommessin was asked by a friend why he looked so glum. Mommessin recounted that he'd just returned from an auction, where he'd planned on buying a vineyard in Moulin-à-Vent but had been outbid by a competitor. Reluctant to leave the sale empty handed, Mommessin settled on his second-choice vineyard, the Clos de Tart in Burgundy's Morey-Saint-Denis. In 2017, the best part of a century later, the 7.57 hectare Clos was sold to François Pinault of the Artemis Group (owners of a range of luxury lifestyle brands, including some of the world's most iconic wineries) for a figure reputed to be close to €250 million. That same year a hectare of Moulin-à-Vent would have set you back somewhere in the region of €100,000.

But if Moulin-à-Vent's star waned during the twentieth century, it's waxing once again. Demand is growing for vineyard land in the *cru*. It has attracted great interest from outside investors over the course of the

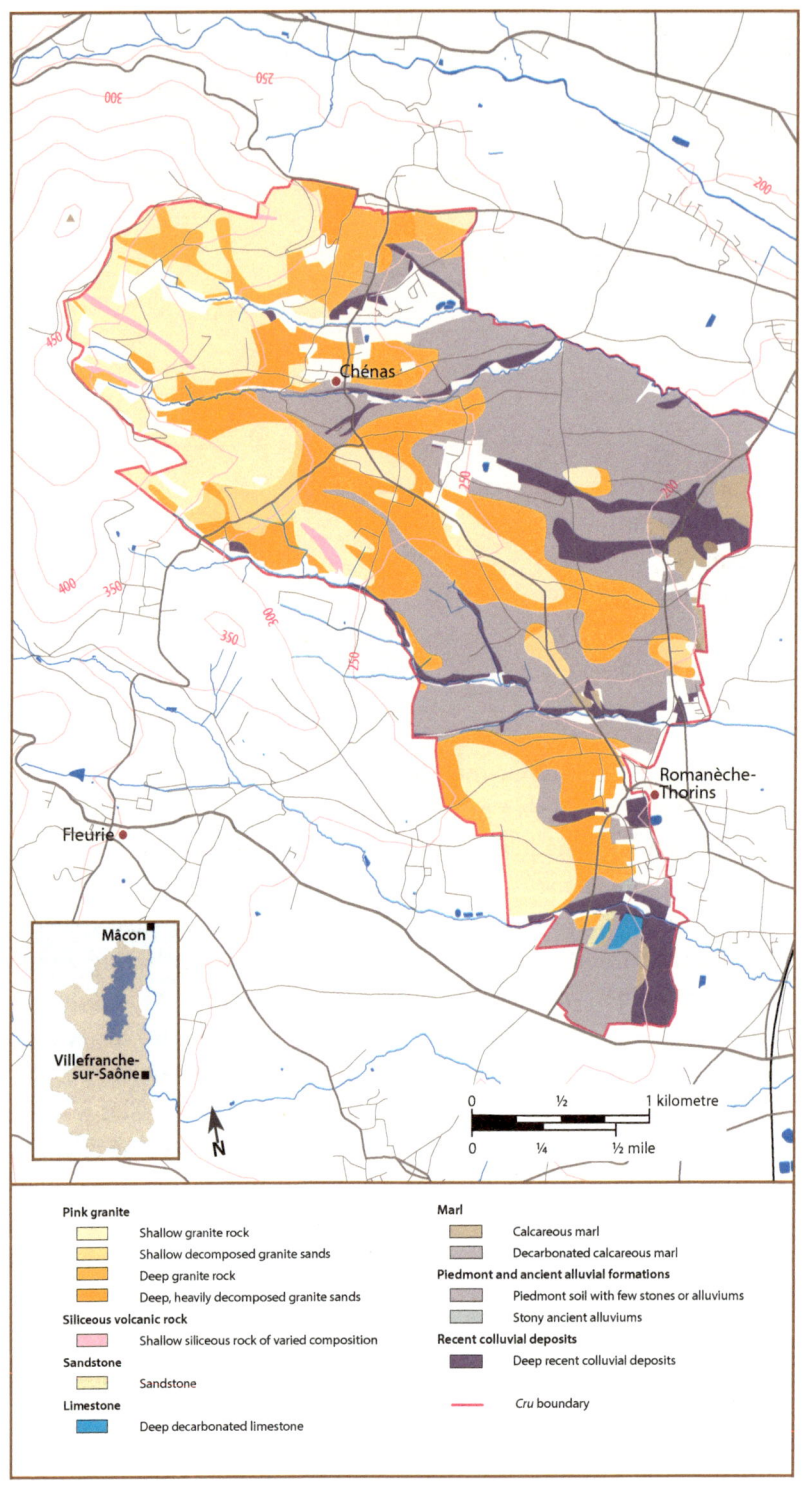

Map 5: The geology of Moulin-à-Vent

past decade or so – to the point where around 25 per cent of its vineyards are now in the hands of relative newcomers to the region, many of them from Burgundy. They're drawn by Moulin-à-Vent's reputation as a source of some of the region's most elegant and long-lived wines, and it's certainly true that many cuvées show plenty of fine but grippy tannins. The wines often show hints of peppery aromatics and, quite often, some perfumed floral notes, too. There's plenty of variation in winemaking to add to the complex patchwork of Moulin's typicity, too. The full diversity of winemaking styles can be found here, with producers using techniques ranging from the more 'natural' cool semi-carbonic fermentations to full-on Burgundian de-stemming and maturation in oak, some of which may even be new (albeit relatively rarely).

One of Moulin-à-Vent's key characteristics is that it lies at the lowest average altitude of all the *crus*, at 255 metres above sea level, and its inclines are gentler than most. Most of its slopes face south or south-east, which means that the vineyards are bathed in sunlight for much of the day, and ripening tends to be pretty homogeneous as a result. The key climatic influence here is probably the winds that blow across the slopes – it's no coincidence that the fifteenth-century windmill that gave the *cru* its name was built on a site that overlooks the vineyards. This windiness helps to mitigate the risk of fungal diseases, which in turn helps those producers who are working organically – of which there are many in Moulin-à-Vent – to reduce their reliance on repeated sprayings of copper and sulphur.

If you look at a map of the *cru*, it's tempting to see an echo of South America in Moulin-à-Vent's outline – there's the bulge of Brazil to the east, and a long southerly tail reminiscent of the way Chile and Argentina plunge southwards towards the Antarctic Ocean. Rather confusingly for anyone familiar with the names of the *crus*, the village of Chénas is actually situated in the northern part of the Moulin-à-Vent *cru* (the actual *cru* of Chénas lies to the north of Moulin-à-Vent). This is a lingering legacy of Moulin-à-Vent's historical prestige – landholders of *lieux-dits* such as Au Michelon and Chassignol, which might more logically have been labelled as Chénas, wanted to retain their rights to label their wines with the three magic words.

So prestigious was the terroir of Moulin-à-Vent in the late nineteenth and early part of the twentieth century that owners of vineyards abutting the zone were frequently tempted to sell their wines by implying that they came from these sought-after vineyards. At the turn of the twentieth century, a producer who owned a vineyard just beyond the notional borders chanced his arm once too often and was taken to court in 1924 by some of the winemakers from Moulin-à-Vent. The judge handed down a ruling that recommended that the boundaries of the hallowed zone be officially delineated. Shortly after, France launched its official appellation system, and the newly defined Moulin-à-Vent was one of the first to be officially recognized, in 1936.

The geological map shows that the Moulin-à-Vent *cru* has its fair share of pink granite, but these deposits are largely located in the northwestern sector of the *cru*. There's a tongue of pink rock that licks into the centre and south of the *cru* too. Most of the rest of Moulin-à-Vent is situated on very ancient alluvial and colluvial deposits, while a very few vineyards in the extreme east and south of the zone have younger colluvial soils or even some limestone and sandstone deposits. In addition, there's a seam of manganese that runs through the *cru* (so pronounced is it that the mineral was once mined here). Most producers believe that the presence of this mineral is what gives the wines of Moulin-à-Vent

Early springtime beneath the iconic windmill

their typicity, but few agree on how it does so. Some claim that it serves to curb yields, thus increasing concentration in the wines; others (rather vaguely) ascribe Moulin-à-Vent's 'nobility' to the mineral-rich soils; while a few suggest that the tendency of these wines to *pinote* – to become more Pinot-like – as they age is due to the manganese in the soils. The wine world is full of Just So Stories like these, and without further research it is impossible to confirm the actual impact of the mineral on the grapes grown in its presence. It is highly likely that there is some interaction between rock and root microbiome that helps to create some of Moulin-à-Vent's unique identity.

There are 69 *lieux-dits* (although two of them are split between the regions of Bourgogne-Franche Comté and that of Auvergne-Rhône-Alpes, so are sometimes counted twice, giving a total of 71). There's a broad consensus that most of the best wines come from those founded on granite soils, but even so there are exceptions to this rule – the Champ de Cour and Le Bief, for instance, are notable for the weight and density of the wines grown on their colluvial soils. As a result, a small number of these colluvial terroirs are listed among the *lieux-dits* being put forward for *premier cru* status (the initial dossier was deposited with the INAO in 2024) alongside a majority of granite-based sites (see p. 14).

As ever, there is considerable debate among the producers of Moulin-à-Vent as to what the next steps of the application should be. Should they place greater emphasis, for instance, on requirements to eschew the use of pesticides and herbicides in the future *premiers crus*, or should the focus be, instead, on the reduction of yields or the redrawing of boundaries? At the time of writing there is little producers can do, other than await the initial response of the INAO to their application. If I was a betting person, though, I'd be willing to lay good money on an eventual outcome that sees at least some of Moulin-à-Vent's greatest terroirs take their place among the pantheon of France's *premier cru* vineyards, vindicating Monsieur Mommessin's historic belief in the quality of this *cru*.

Producers

Domaine Louis Boillot

Clément Boillot is pretty much Burgundy royalty, the son of Louis Boillot and Ghislaine Barthod, both big names in the Côte d'Or. You might, then, wonder what draws him to Beaujolais, and the *cru* of Moulin-à-Vent. Originally, the family's investment in these vineyards was a sentimental one. Louis was born in Beaujolais, and even though

he's best known as a producer of fine Burgundies, Clément says his father always wanted to return to his southern roots. In particular, he says,
he was keen to buy land in Moulin-à-Vent as he was impressed by the
elegance and ageability of the wines, and the way they often come to
resemble fine Burgundies as they age.

The Boillot family began looking for vineyards in Beaujolais in 2010,
and by 2014 were making three cuvées in the region, a number that has
since expanded to nine, of which eight are in Moulin-à-Vent and one in
Fleurie. Clément began working on the wines with his father in 2015,
and in 2019 took over sole responsibility for making the Domaine's
wines (in Burgundy as well as in Beaujolais).

Winemaking here – unsurprisingly – takes its inspiration from
Burgundy. Grapes are 100 per cent de-stemmed on arrival at the winery.
Tannin management is key to the approach – fermentation is allowed
to reach temperatures of around 30°C to favour structure rather than
fruit, and tannins are extracted gently with a mixture of pump-overs
and plunging throughout the 20-day fermentation cycle. The finished
wines are then aged in 500-litre barrels for anywhere up to 18 months.

The wines are quietly impressive, with a real density to them. The
Champ de Cour, a cuvée based on grapes grown on granitic soils just
beneath the windmill, is linear and focused, with fine tannins. Aux
Caves is made from 85-year-old vines that have a tendency towards
poor fruit set, resulting in massive concentration of fruit and tannins.
The grapes for Les Rouchaux are planted on a dome of granite that rises
close to the surface, and the resulting wine is complex, fresh and long.

Famille Guerin

domaine-famille-guerin.fr

When is a natural winemaker not a natural winemaker? This is no riddle
of the sphinx, but a real dilemma for producers like Elisa Guerin, whose
minimalist approach to winemaking often sees her referred to as a member of the cohort of natural winemakers. Guerin is passionate about making wines that reflect her terroirs with as much transparency as possible.
And yet, if you talk to her about 'natural wines', she throws up her hands
in horror. Guerin is keen to distance herself from those who jump on the
minimal sulphur bandwagon out of a desire to be perceived as fashionable. And she's in absolutely no doubt about the sheer number of hours
of toil in the vineyards and the hard work in the winery that it takes to
make wines of purity and focus with as little manipulation as possible.

Guerin's path towards becoming one of the most sought-after young winemakers in Beaujolais began in the family vineyards, and yet her destination was not inevitable. Her interest in environmental studies led to time spent researching the impact of global warming on grapegrowing at the UK's prestigious Plumpton College. She then worked for an upmarket food supplier, but in the end, all roads led to the vineyards. Her eventual return to Beaujolais in 2018 saw her take over the family property, where she immediately put in place an organic management system for her vineyards.

Her approach to her work in the cellar is as hands-off as her labour in the vineyard is intensive. Freshly harvested bunches are piled into concrete tanks and blanketed in carbon dioxide. This semi-carbonic maceration, which she monitors carefully to ensure that no bacterial spoilage mars the wine's pristine flavours, eventually results in the release of juices from the softened skin. The juice is gently pumped over the cap to leach tannins and spicy flavours from the lignified stems, then the press and free run juices are blended and matured in inert vessels and some older barrels.

At the moment she makes four cuvées, a zippy, bright-fruited Beaujolais Villages and a delicate, pretty, floral Chiroubles, bursting with crunchy, herb-tinged redcurrants, its zestiness a testament to the altitude at which the vines are grown. Les Thorins is a cuvée made from grapes grown on granitic sands situated mid-slope beneath the windmill, a terroir that lends Guerin's wine a plushness of fruit that cloaks the fine, grippy tannins. La Vigne de mon Père is, arguably, the most long-lived of her bottlings, a wine that combines dark fruit with liquorice and spice. Despite its density and concentration, La Vigne de mon Père does not lack finesse, and its tightly wound tannic structure promises a long future for the wine, even in the warmest vintages.

Château des Jacques

www.chateau-des-jacques.fr

Maison Louis Jadot is another Burgundian négociant to have invested in Beaujolais in a big way. The Château des Jacques, a seventeenth-century property, was not a noted wine-producing property for much of its history, but in the 1920s its owner, Amédée Rousseau, began buying up parcels of land around the site of Moulin-à-Vent's iconic windmill. By the time Maison Louis Jadot bought the property in 1996, the Château was a significant landholder in the *cru*. Investments didn't stop then, and the Château now farms 67 hectares of Beaujolais in total, of which 34 hectares are in Moulin-à-Vent, with a further 20 hectares of Morgon, 3 in Fleurie, a 9-hectare walled clos planted with Chardonnay and a small, experimental 1-hectare parcel of Syrah in Moulin-à-Vent (vinified as a Vin de France). The winery was totally renovated in 2017, and is now one of the biggest and best equipped in the region, with rows of gleaming stainless steel tanks and pyramidal concrete *cuves*, as well as a smart barrel cellar.

The vineyards are largely farmed organically, with biodynamic inflections in the form of tisanes, with the exception of some of the more fragile old vines planted on precipitous inclines, whose soils can't be ploughed. Winemaking tends towards the Burgundian, with almost all the Gamay bunches being de-stemmed on arrival at the winery (with the exception of a Morgon cuvée that sees a little whole-bunch action). Generally fermentation temperatures are fairly modest, at around 23–25°C, although this is allowed to climb a degree or two towards the end of fermentation to enhance colour. Extractive techniques include both *remontage* and *pigeage*, although the amount of each is determined by both the vineyard and the vintage character. Many of the wines undergo around ten months of barrel ageing, often with some new oak influence.

Overall, the style of many of the Château des Jacques cuvées is denser and more structured than many wines produced within the *cru*, although there's elegance and freshness too. Of the single-vineyard parcels made in Moulin-à-Vent, the Clos du Grand Carquelin typically shows good concentration on the mid-palate and deep-pile, velvety tannins. The Clos des Thorins, planted on slightly richer soils, is ripe-fruited, with fine tannins and a generous finish. The Clos de Rochegrès is the most pure-fruited and elegant of the trio, with fine-boned, linear tannins. The Morgon Côte du Py is as chewy and broad as one might expect from vines grown on this hot, exposed terroir.

Domaine Paul Janin et Fils

www.domaine-paul-janin.fr

Despite the name – Paul Janin and Son – this domaine, based in Moulin-à-Vent, proudly bucks the local trend for properties to be passed down from one generation of men to another. Eric Janin (Paul's son, and a member of the fourth generation of Janins to farm the family plots) has recently been joined at the helm of the property by his daughter, Perrine. The pride Janin takes in his daughter's abilities is made clear on the domaine's website, which recapitulates the family's history. The most recent entries on a roll of honour that notes the purchase of particularly prestigious parcels of vines, and the years in which each family member took over management of the company, cite Perrine's work overseas in California's Sonoma County and Australia's Beechworth Valley.

Anointing a daughter as your successor at the family winery is still considered to be fairly unconventional in conservative Beaujolais, but in many other respects Domaine Paul Janin et Fils (will the name change to 'et Filles', I wonder) hugs closely to Moulin-à-Vent's traditions. Although the Janin vineyards were certified organic in 2024, the certification merely set the seal on the way the family had always worked. Nevertheless, the approach was fine tuned in the 1990s by Eric Janin, who began to take an interest in research that focused on the health of the soil and also on biodynamics, and certain key practices have been incorporated into the viticultural routine.

Winemaking *chez* Janin sees a mix of whole-bunch and de-stemmed grapes added to tanks, roughly in a proportion of 60:40, although this varies from one vintage to the next, with less whole bunch used in years when the stems fail to ripen properly. Cultured yeasts are added to the tanks – although the Janins are constrained by their organic certification in terms of which ones they can employ. Temperatures in each tank are allowed to climb, although they rarely reach more than about 28°C, preserving the fruit character. Tannin extraction is achieved by means of one *remontage* per day. Rather unusually, however, ageing is done in stainless steel tanks rather than in the old barrels or cement tanks more typical of quality producers in the region, in an effort to maintain fruit purity. Although the family vinifies and ages each plot of land separately, the wines are finally blended to create a range of cuvées with a consistent 'house style', rather than the parcel selections that are typical of many Moulin-à-Vent producers.

The Beaujolais Villages Blanc – the only wine to be aged in barrels (albeit old ones) – is labelled Argiles, a reference to the type of soil on which the grapes are grown. It's a limpid, fresh wine with some stony minerality and subtle but ripe fruit. The red Villages, the Piemont, is a subtle, slightly smoky wine with fine tannins and a little stemmy character that serves to lift the red fruit. The remainder of the family's wines are all Moulin-à-Vents. The Empreinte is made from younger vines and is designed for early drinking. The Vignes du Tremblay – a nod to the property's old name, the Domaine de Tremblay – is more complex and tightly wound, with some of Moulin-à-Vent's typical peppery spice on the palate. Héritage is a blend of grapes from two parcels, one plant-ed in 1910, the other in 1914. Dense and focused, this is a wine that needs time to open up in bottle. The final wine, Les Greneriers, comes from another parcel of 110-year-old vines, albeit planted in a different *lieu-dit* with a bit of clay in the soil, which lends the wine both breadth and freshness. It's a cuvée that's only made in the warmest years – the last vintage to be bottled was the 2022 – and it's rich and dark-fruited, with a wonderfully plush texture and a fine-grained drag of tannins on the finish.

Yohan Lardy

www.yohan-lardy.com

Like many producers in Beaujolais, Yohan Lardy's family has been in-volved in the wine industry for many generations. His grandfather and father were both winemakers (father Lucien still is, see p. 118), and his uncle made oak barrels. It was perhaps inevitable, then, that Yohan would go on to university in Beaune and then Mâcon to study viticulture and oenology, after which he decamped to Chile for a year, where he worked for the biodynamic producer Odfjell. Although most of his work in-volved technical aspects of winemaking, from working on bottling lines to running chemical analyses, Lardy was given the opportunity to play with a number of experimental barrels and make his own wines.

By the time he returned home, what really fired him up was the idea of working in the vineyards, but not alongside his father. Lardy senior wanted – perhaps understandably – to retain control over the way that wines marketed under his own label were vinified, which didn't leave Yohan Lardy much room for manoeuvre. In 2011 he was offered the chance to take over a couple of hectares of vineyards in Moulin-à-Vent and jumped at the chance. Over the intervening years, Lardy has taken on more vineyards, and he now manages around 7.5 hectares, most-ly in Moulin-à-Vent, but with another half a hectare of whites in the Beaujolais Villages hills and a couple of hectares of Chénas, a *cru* he loves. Indeed, so keen is Lardy on Chénas's wild landscapes and 'excep-tional' terroir, that he hopes to expand his holdings in the *cru* in future.

For the moment, though, the *lieu-dit* of Au Michelon, which lies up on the northern limit of Moulin-à-Vent, is at the heart of his pro-duction, and is the source of both his main cuvée, Les Michelons, and his top-of-the-line 1903. The latter, as the name suggests, is based on a small 70-are parcel of ancient vines planted at the top of the slope.

Lardy farms these vineyards – and the others – organically, having worked hard to convert them from conventional agriculture right at the start of his tenure, a transformative process that took around five years. He ploughs as much of his land as possible by horse, with the rest worked either by tractor or by hand, and is slowly replanting some of the older vineyards. Lardy is keen to ensure that he – and other producers in the region – starts working on gathering as wide as possible a sample of massal selections from Beaujolais's old vineyards. 'We need to reproduce the wealth of genetic material we have here before all these wonderful vineyards are ripped out,' he says.

His winemaking is as gentle as possible, with only one or two scant *remontages* at the start of the fermentation process to ensure the cap is kept wet, and then he hand plunges once or twice towards the end of fermentation, which typically lasts 15–20 days. This last extraction is used to give him richness and weight on the mid-palate of his wines – he says that he doesn't want to make simple 'strawberry juice'.

His wines all have great precision and elegance. The Beaujolais Villages Blanc, which comes from vineyards near Lancié, sees a little bit of oak to lend weight on the mid-palate, but it's barely noticeable. Instead, the hallmark is a pleasing brightness and a savoury, celery salt aromatic character. Les Michelons is a lovely, pure-fruited, floral wine with focus and tension, extremely fine tannins, and a little twist of Moulin-à-Vent's characteristic pepper note. The Chénas Au Buchonet bears the name of Lardy's wife, Pauline, on the label. Lardy says that she loves the wine from the *cru* so much that she vinifies it, under his supervision. It's slightly more robust than Les Michelons in terms of structure, but there's good balance and lots of freshness, as well as an intensely floral nose that also shows the *cru*'s typical note of white pepper. The 1903 from the top of the Michelon vineyard in Moulin-à-Vent is a wine that needs some serious time in bottle – even though it's surprisingly approachable in its youth. Dense, plush and concentrated, the palate blends dark cherries, pepper, orange zest and blackberry fruit with a meaty edge that throws the rich fruit into sharp relief.

Thibault Liger-Belair

m.thibaultligerbelair.com/2525D1Y5XP

I've mentioned elsewhere in this book that I have a theory that wines take on something of the personality of the people who make them. People who are precise and slightly stern tend to make precise, slightly stern wines, while those with more outgoing personalities tend to make vivacious, hedonistic bottlings. If my theory is correct, it's unsurprising that Thibault Liger-Belair's cuvées are as expansive and generous as the man himself.

Liger-Belair is well known as a producer of top-notch Burgundian wines, some of them from among the foremost appellations in the region, but since 2009 he's also made wines from grapes grown in the vineyards he owns in Moulin-à-Vent. He first fell in love with the region when he was a student based in Belleville, attracted by both the landscapes of Beaujolais and its potential to produce wines of high quality. However, it wasn't until 2008 that he fulfilled a promise he'd made to himself all those years ago and bought his first parcel of Beaujolais vines.

His initial purchase of three hectares of vineyards has now grown to 12 hectares, all in Moulin-à-Vent. He cites the *cru*'s free-draining soils and the lure of its old vine material as part of the attraction, but also eulogizes its winds, channelled down across the vineyards by the surrounding hills, for their ability to keep the vines disease-free. It's clear he also celebrates the sense of freedom he feels in Beaujolais, released from the constraints of meeting the expectations of the customers for his highly priced Burgundies. Here, he says, he can experiment and adapt, take risks he would never be able to take when creating *grand cru* Pinot Noir. One of the key risks is his decision to plant a small parcel of young vines on their own rootstocks. Liger-Belair believes that the sandy granitic soils, which contain less than 3 per cent clay, may be inimical to the phylloxera louse, and so protect the vines from infestation.

When it comes to winemaking, Liger-Belair's philosophy has changed somewhat since his earliest experiments in Moulin-à-Vent. He has given up a quest for extraction and now seeks a more gentle style of infusion to create wines of subtlety and nuance. He uses a mix of de-stemmed grapes and whole bunches, layered in what he refers to as his '*mille-feuille*', always with whole bunches at the bottom to allow for free drainage of the juice expressed from the grapes, and then another five or six alternating layers on top. He sparges the top of the tank with a little carbon dioxide to protect the wines from the action of *Acetobacter*, and then lets the fermentation proceed at its own pace. He's not too worried about temperature control, either, allowing his ferments to climb up to 35°C to capture, he says, a wider array of aromas, referring to the process as a '*mijotage*', a slow cooking. The wines are then aged in old oak *foudres* and barrels for around 20 months, to allow for fuller integration of the tannins, prior to bottling.

The end results yield six different cuvées, of which two are blends from various vineyards and the remainder are single-parcel expressions. The Vieilles Vignes is a generous, full-bodied blend with a savoury edge that's based on vines of 65–105 years old. Les Perrelles comes from grapes grown in deep soils and shows an intensely floral character and a stony minerality. La Roche and La Rochelle provide an interesting contrast, and reveal subtle terroir differences in wines made from vines grown in close proximity to each other. La Roche is a cool, east-facing site with shallow granite soils that give a linear, taut wine with a kick of bright acidity and an intensely perfumed finish, while the south-facing La Rochelle is more opulent and generous in style, with darker fruit and a distinctively spicy character. Champ de Cour sits in a shallow depression that protects it from the most searing winds, and the result is a bold, rounded wine with tannins that sit towards the front of the palate. The final wine in the line-up is another blend, a cuvée known as Centenaire, which is only bottled in magnum and released at six years of age. Made from grapes grown in the oldest of Liger-Belair's vineyards, some of which date back to 1878, this is a rich, powerful wine that nevertheless shows plenty of grace as well as seamless balance.

Château du Moulin-à-Vent

chateaudumoulinavent.com

The Château du Moulin-à-Vent has been one of the *cru*'s foremost estates since its foundation in the early part of the eighteenth century. International recognition came early – the wines won a gold medal at the Universal Exhibition in London in 1862, although the property was known at the time as the Château des Thorins. When the *cru* was formally recognized as an appellation in 1936, the property changed its name to the Château du Moulin-à-Vent in recognition of the zone's new status.

In 2009, the property changed hands for only the third time in its long history, when it was acquired by the Parinet family. It is now run on a day-to-day basis by Edouard Parinet, who works closely with oenologist Brice Laffond. Over the course of the past 15 years, the two men have presided over a renaissance of the domaine's vineyards, which have been farmed organically since 2013. One of the key aims here is to preserve the property's wealth of old vines – the average age of

Harvesting in Moulin-à-Vent is done by hand, as it is in all the crus
(photo © Château du Moulin-à-Vent)

which is around 60 years, but some vineyards are heading towards their
one-hundredth birthday. These vines, which were in fairly poor condition when the Parinets purchased the property, have gently been nursed
back to health, although in the interests of long-term survival they are
gradually being replaced via a process of replantation based on massal
selection.

The Château owns six different parcels, all situated within sight of
the famous windmill. Of these, five – Le Moulin-à-Vent, Les Thorins,
Aux Caves, Les Verillats and La Rochelle – are based on granite soils
of varying depth and decomposition. The last parcel, the Champ de
Cour, is situated on stony alluvial soils. There are a couple of blended
wines – the zesty, fruity Couvent des Thorins and the estate wine. Both
are good reference points for the *cru*, but it's the characterful, elegant
single-vineyard wines and the micro-cuvées that really up the ante.

Of these, the Champ de Cour tends towards fleshiness, an artefact
of its clay-rich terroir, while Les Verillats and La Rochelle both have the
focus and finesse of wines derived from granite soils. Les Verillats is typically more approachable in its youth, while the savoury, intense, focused
La Rochelle repays long-term ageing. The plot of land dedicated to the
production of the Grands Savarins is situated in Aux Caves, which lies
on the western fringes of the *cru*, near the border with Fleurie. This

cuvée tends to be bright, crunchy and fine-boned, with a nervous tension that takes time to unwind. The Clos de Londres, a plot located just below the windmill's arms, is broad and weighty, with spicy dark fruit and fine, grippy tannins.

Domaine de Rochegrès

www.albert-bichot.com/fr/domaine-de-rochegres_24.html

Albert Bichot, a Burgundian négociant, had always had some Beaujolais wines in its portfolio, but in a vote of confidence for the region's prospects decided to invest in a stand-alone property in Moulin-à-Vent in 2014.

In truth, says Matthieu Mangenot, Bichot's technical director, the négociant could have ended up buying a property in any one of Beaujolais's *crus*, so firm was their intention to commit to the region. As it happened, purely by coincidence, they found a property that suited their needs in a *cru* that has proven to be a magnet for other Burgundian investors.

The Domaine de Rochegrès is spread out over slightly more than 5 hectares of Moulin-à-Vent vineyards, with a 1.9-hectare parcel of vines of between 80 and 100 years of age in Rochegrès itself, a larger 3-hectare vineyard in Le Mont, and a smaller holding in the *lieu-dit* of Les Caves. Vinification follows a protocol similar to that used for the house's Pinots, which is based on an average of 20 per cent whole bunches, which are placed in the bottom of concrete tanks in order to allow for free drainage of the juices, with the rest of the bunches destemmed. The ferment is allowed to build to temperatures that top out at around 26–7°C, with the aim of creating relatively long macerations of 18–21 days to extract both texture and a certain amount of structure. Mangenot warns, however, that Gamay needs to be handled more delicately than Pinot as it's easy to over-extract from the southern grape and end up with an undesirable vegetal character in the finished wines. Around 15 per cent of the wines are then aged in large *futs* of 350–500 litres, with the rest maturing in concrete tanks.

The domaine makes two Moulin-à-Vent wines. The Rochegrès is a selection of wines made from the best parcels and the best barrels. It's a blend notable for its silky elegance, dense, rather sinewy tannins and layered, spicy dark fruit, but it's a wine that can appear somewhat closed in its youth, benefiting from at least two or three years of bottle age. Le Roc is a blend of all the other Moulin-à-Vent parcels, and although it lacks the great density of the Rochegrès, it's still a generous, powerful wine with a stony, almost ferrous minerality and a long finish.

Bichot supplements its Beaujolais offering with some négoce cuvées, including a Fleurie La Madone. This warm site on the crest of Fleurie's granite hills produces a wine in which you can feel the sunshine in its perfumed palate of liquorice-dusted blood plums and the ripeness of its fine, powdery tannins. A Brouilly Roche Rose is rounder, more fleshy and generous, with slightly more discrete tannins and a burst of juicy raspberries. The Morgon Les Charmes is altogether a more brooding beast of a wine with a bloody, feral note on the palate and grippy, bold tannins.

Mangenot, who spends most of his professional life working with Pinot Noir, is firmly convinced that Gamay is a grape that has just as much potential as its northern cousin to make world-class wines. 'If you plant the grape in the right place and make the wines in the right way it makes wines whose finesse and elegance speak for themselves,' he says.

Domaine Richard Rottiers

domainerichardrottiers.com

Moulin-à-Vent is often seen as being the most aristocratic of the Beaujolais *crus*, and it's true that many of its most iconic wineries have their roots in the deep soils and even deeper pockets of some of Burgundy's foremost families. Richard Rottiers is part of this lineage, and yet a man apart. To begin with, his viticultural roots lie in Chablis, rather than the Côte d'Or, which is where most of Beaujolais's Burgundians hail from. And while many of his fellow Burgundians would not look out of place in a posh gentleman's club in London, Rottiers' informal clothing and long curly hair, worn tied back in a ponytail, make him look as if he might be more at home on a Bondi surfboard than in a boardroom.

It would be a mistake, though, to take Rottiers' lack of formality as a sign of a laid-back outlook when it comes to oenology. The casual exterior belies his approach to his work, which is thoughtful and studied in both the vineyard and the cellar, although like many good winemakers, Rottiers places the emphasis firmly on the importance of the viticultural aspect of his craft. Rottiers discovered Beaujolais almost by accident, after returning to France after having travelled and worked in New Zealand. It was while he was employed at Château Thivin in Brouilly that he fell in love with Gamay. Not wanting to compete with his former employers for land in the southernmost of the *crus*, Rottiers headed north and ended up in Moulin-à-Vent, where his initial 3 hectares of vines eventually turned into 12.

He's worked organically for the past decade, but is heavily influenced by the biodynamic movement, whose practices help him maintain his treasured old vines. Nevertheless, he's replanting bit by bit, with plenty of consideration being given to the kinds of rootstocks and plant selections that will allow his vineyards to thrive under the constraints imposed by global warming. 'If I didn't do that, I reckon I'd be starting harvest in July before too many years are out,' he jokes wryly.

Rottiers likes to get his fermentations started quickly – believing that an efficient start to the process helps to eliminate the risk of rogue yeasts getting to work – so he uses a *pied de cuve*. Once fermentation is underway, he uses a metal grille to submerge the cap, a traditionally Beaujolais way of managing the extraction. Most of his wines are aged in the same cement tanks used for fermentation, although some of his more structured cuvées spend at least some time in large seasoned oak barrels.

With the exception of a Brouilly made from bought-in grapes, a rounded, juicy wine with a pronounced floral character, all of Rottiers' bottlings are made from grapes grown in Moulin-à-Vent. The Mortperay is the roundest and spiciest of these, somewhat reminiscent of a Northern Rhône Syrah, particularly in warm years. The Dernier Souffle ('the last breath', a bit of a macabre joke based on the fact that the grapes come from a vineyard located near the local cemetery) is poised and fresh, with Moulin-à-Vent's typical peppery note. The Champ de Cour is a tense, focused wine that doesn't reveal much of its personality until it has opened up a bit, at which point it blossoms into a thoroughly elegant, charming wine with a distinctive floral and spice character. Les Thorins is the densest and most brooding of the cuvées, with firm but fine tannins.

10

FLEURIE

> **Year in which *cru* status was awarded**: 1936
> **Total vineyard area**: 790 hectares
> **Altitude**: 225–475 metres
> **Average altitude**: 340 metres
> **Notable *lieux-dits***: Grille-Midi, La Madone, La Chapelle des Bois, Les Moriers, Poncié, Les Labourons, La Roilette, Grand'Cour, Grand Pré, Les Garants

The Chapel of the Madonna sits atop one of the highest hills in Fleurie, and the lookout point situated immediately beneath it is a splendid place from which to enjoy views across the entire region and out towards Mont Blanc. It's odd to think that no one seems really sure why the chapel was built in the first place. One legend has it that it was built in the hope that the Madonna would intercede on behalf of the local grape growers and prevent the surrounding vineyards from succumbing to fungal diseases. The other story told is that the Madonna's chapel was erected on the hillside in thanks for her having protected Fleurie from being invaded by the Prussian army during the Franco-Prussian War of 1870–71. Either way, for growers and visitors alike, the Madonna and her chapel have now become a visual shorthand for the entire region.

The hill on which the chapel perches is far from the only one in Fleurie; the *cru* is among the most precipitous in Beaujolais. Most of its slopes are extremely steep, their gradients ranging from tricky to climb to head-spinningly vertiginous. In the main, these slopes are made up of pink granite, some of which is very shallow and stony, while other locations have a much greater depth of decomposed granite sands. And

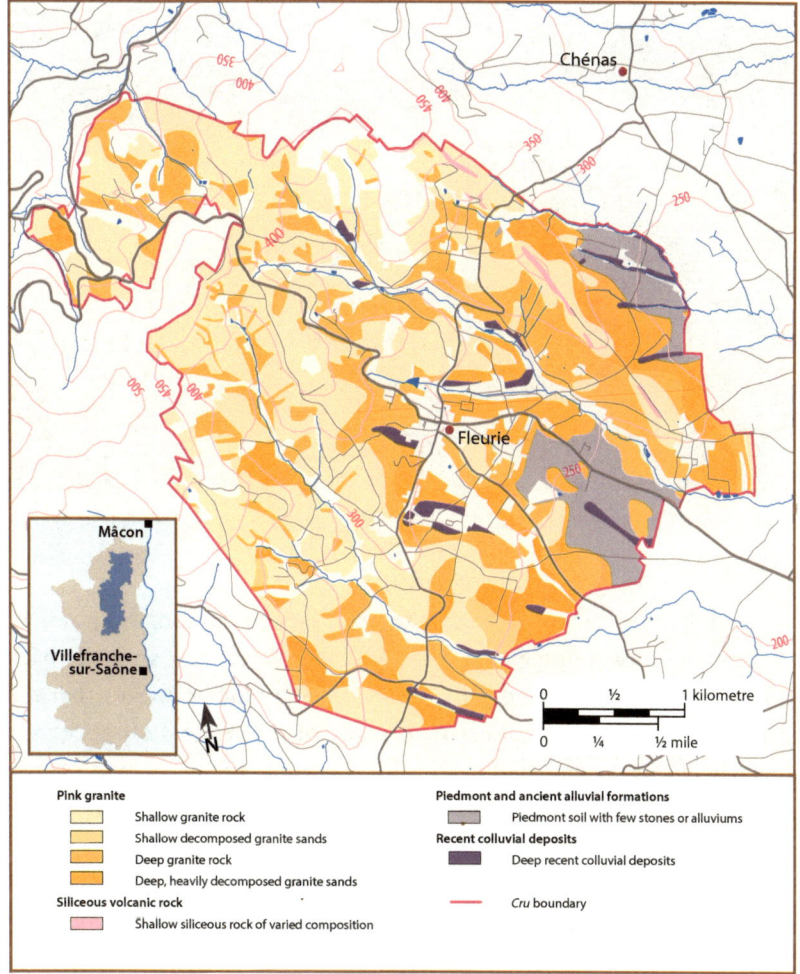

Map 6: The geology of Fleurie

while most of Fleurie's vineyards are planted on these stony soils, there are two tongues of alluvial deposits extending out from the east of the appellation towards the plain of the Saône River. The granitic sands are incredibly free draining; so much so that you can drive a tractor through the vineyards the day after heavy rains with no fear that it will get bogged down in sticky mud. This is great news if you're a grape grower in a very rainy year, less so in hot, dry years, when those sands can wick moisture away from the roots of the vines with deadly efficiency. Furthermore, it's difficult to develop humus on steep, rocky slopes, so Fleurie's terroir can make organic farming a challenge, especially when your vineyard is full of fragile elderly bush vines.

The Chapelle de la Madone looks out over the vineyards of Fleurie (iStock.com/Gael Fontaine)

Luckily for producers based in the *cru*, Fleurie has long been one of Beaujolais's most popular appellations, a popularity that stretches back to the Renaissance period. This long-standing renown means that the *cru*'s wines fetch better prices than many of the region's other equally steep, challenging appellations. It's little wonder, therefore, that Fleurie has a long list of top-notch producers; a far greater number than its surface area might initially suggest.

Those granite soils typically produce wines that most people would think of as being classic expressions of Fleurie: fine-boned, elegant wines with zesty red fruits on the palate and a distinctly floral perfume. However, it's important to remember that some of Fleurie's terroir affords considerable exposure to the sun, so some wines can show a more opulent, ripe expression than might be expected. And those wines derived from the alluvial deposits are often denser and more firmly structured than 'typical' Fleuries.

While Fleurie doesn't have a single, iconic *lieu-dit* that drives perceptions of the *cru* in the same way as the Côte du Py has become Morgon's emblematic *climat* (see p. 144), it has many highly prized *lieux-dits*. So much so that the *cru* is leading the race to have some of its best terroirs recognized by the INAO as *premiers crus* (see p. 14). Whether or not this application will be successful – and whether the apotheosis of its *lieux-dits* will be universally popular with local growers – remains to be seen. As ever in Beaujolais, *c'est compliqué.*

Producers

Château des Bachelards

chateau-bachelards.com

The links between the medieval monasteries of Burgundy and the refined understanding of the region's terroir are well documented. The influence of ecclesiastics on viticulture and winemaking in Beaujolais is less well understood. The Château des Bachelards is a bit of an oddity in this respect as it is located on a site established in the twelfth century by Benedictine monks. In the aftermath of the French Revolution, the property was acquired by the Platet family, who held it for more than two centuries before it passed into the hands of a new owner, who converted the vineyards to organic viticulture – one of the first to espouse these practices in Fleurie – and then pushed things further to become one of the few properties in Beaujolais to farm biodynamically. The property was then acquired in 2022 by Matthieu Gufflet, who owns a group called Terres de Natures, a collection of hotels, vineyards and restaurants spread across France, most notably Lyon's famous Mère Brazier restaurant and Sauternes's Château Guiraud.

The heart of the Château des Bachelards lies in its clos, whose walls were first built by those monks nearly a millennium ago. The Château's holdings now include 6.5 hectares of vineyards in Fleurie, nearly 5 hectares of Beaujolais Villages and a couple of hectares in the northern *cru* of Saint-Amour. Since at least the turn of the century, the Château des Bachelards has followed the Burgundian model of winemaking, destemming bunches on arrival at the winery then allowing the grapes a pre-fermentation cold soak for just under a week in order to extract both colour and aroma before allowing temperatures to rise steadily, triggering alcoholic fermentation. Although tannin extraction is carefully managed, this style of winemaking results in the creation of a more structured style than is typical of most Beaujolais, and these are wines that are designed for the long haul, although most are still approachable in their youth. Of the range, the best bottlings are the rich, liquorice-tinged Saint-Amour, the Fleurie Les Bachelards, a rounded, red-fruited wine with fine, grippy tannins that sit at the front of the palate, and the top cuvée, the Comtesse de Vazeilles. Named in honour of the woman who converted the estate to biodynamics and based on the fruit grown in the walled clos, this is a complex, elegant wine with fine tannins, good concentration and strawberry-scented fruit.

Yann Bertrand

les-bertrand.com

Yann Bertrand almost didn't make it to our scheduled meeting. While out on his tractor, working one of Fleurie's typically steeply sloping vineyards, his brakes failed and he was lucky not to end up in hospital. Such are the risks taken by Beaujolais producers on an almost daily basis, and may have been among the reasons that Bertrand's father, Guy, who farmed the vineyards before him, was not keen for his son to join the family business, although the struggle for financial survival had a large part to play as well.

In his early twenties Yann seemed destined for a career in banking and insurance, when he found himself with a difficult decision to make. His mother fell seriously ill, and Guy Bertrand was considering selling the vineyards off so that he could devote more time to taking care of her. Faced with an existential threat to the domaine, Yann decided to return home and take over the reins. He says he's never regretted the decision, and given the enthusiasm – and profound knowledge – with which he discusses various aspects of his work, from massal selections and the advantages and disadvantages of regenerative viticulture to microbiological assays, it would appear that finance's loss is winemaking's gain.

By the time Bertrand took over the property, in 2012, it was already in the process of conversion to organics, and although the wines are not certified as such, they are managed along green principles, inflected by biodynamics. Bertrand farms 6 hectares in Fleurie, with a further 1.2 hectares in Morgon and 1.7 hectares located in the Morgon zone but declassified as Beaujolais – although he hastens to specify that this old patch of vineyard stands on its own merits, regardless of which appellation he puts on the label. He's keen to maintain the region's typical bush vines, even when replanting. It is, he says, a structure that's uniquely suited to helping his Gamays deal with the increasingly hot, dry summers in the region, especially given that the free-draining granite soils have limited water-carrying capacity.

One of the most important steps, he says, in his winemaking is the triage he and his team of pickers perform in the vineyard at harvest. It's a meticulous process in which bunches are picked by hand, then examined in minute detail for damaged or shrivelled berries, which are removed individually. He employs winemaking techniques that are adapted to the needs of the vintage and each individual parcel. In some cases this means full 'dry' carbonic maceration, at other times it's more along the lines of a classic semi-carbonic maceration. In some vintages, says Bertrand, he doesn't even need to make a choice between the two as the skins of the grapes are so thick that even the bunches at the bottom don't get squashed. In order to preserve the character of his wines and ensure a healthy fermentation, he employs all his senses – as well as lots of work with a microscope when he deems it necessary. The aim is to use no sulphites at all, but he's prepared to add judicious amounts to a tank if he feels that the fermentation is headed in the wrong direction. Finally most of the wines are matured in a variety of oak barrels, which Bertrand sources from different regions as he believes that the grapes they once contained impart some of their personality to the wines he matures in them.

The end result is a series of wines that are notable for their perfume and vibrant freshness, with subtle, fine-boned tannins. Of the Fleuries, the Coup de Foudre is slightly peppery, with a long, precise finish. The Cuvée du Chaos comes from a vineyard with a small amount of clay in the soil, which lends a little more structure on the mid-palate, although it retains the bright red fruit and floral character of the Coup de Foudre. One of the most interesting wines is Cuvée Emilie – not made every year, this is based on a new vineyard Bertrand has planted to foster Gamay's extraordinary genetic diversity. He's collected plant material from every region in France in which the grape is grown to ensure not only a wide variety of phenotypes, but also as an insurance policy against weather extremes. As he explains, the late-ripening vines bring freshness in hot years, while the early ripeners cope better with cool, rainy vintages. The resulting wine – in 2023 at least – lacks some of the mid-palate concentration of the older vines, but it has a deliciously perfumed wild strawberry character. Alice is another one-off, this time made to celebrate Bertrand's tenth anniversary as a winemaker. The ripe 2022 vintage gave it a richer, riper fruit character than most of Bertrand's wines, and firmer tannins, but there's still a kick of bright acidity that lifts the finish. If I had to pick one bottling as my favourite it would be a tough decision, but I think I'd have to opt for Phénix, made from grapes grown on hard granitic rocks in La Madone, a wine of great finesse with a heady, incredibly floral nose and a distinct streak of stony minerality.

Anne-Sophie Dubois and Sylvain Martel/Domaine Cabissou

Instagram @annesophiefleurie/@domainecabissou

Anne-Sophie Dubois and Sylvain Martel share both a house and a philosophy of viticulture and winemaking, but work in two different *crus*.

Dubois, a native of Champagne, trained in Burgundy, but fell in love with Gamay. She arrived in Beaujolais in 2007 and moved into her property on the amphitheatre of Fleurie's Les Labourons, at the time an unfashionable *lieu-dit* whose high altitude and west-facing vineyards meant that it had a reputation as a site where grapes struggled to ripen. At the time, the fruit was sold to a cooperative, which in turn sold much of its production to négociants. Dubois decided to reclaim at least part of her 8-hectare harvest and to make wines for herself. As her reputation grew, so too did the proportion of the grapes destined for her own bottlings.

Martel grew up in Montelimar and worked in the Rhône before moving north to work in Beaujolais with the Domaine de Fa (see p. 64) in 2014. He began investing in his own vineyards in Juliénas five years later, in 2019.

Dubois and Martel take their role as grape growers seriously, and both of their vineyards are certified as organic, although in reality they farm along biodynamic principles. 'You can go from conventional farming to organic farming without changing the way you work,' explains Martel, 'but biodynamics is all about prevention rather than cure. It's also a very sensorial way of working, which requires a completely different level of observation. It's about not being in your mind all the time, and paying attention to what's going on around us instead.'

Martel and Dubois clearly revel in their relative isolation and their closeness to nature, explaining that they feel they really belong to their little corner of the countryside. When it comes to harvesting decisions, judgements are made by hand, by eye and by mouth. 'We judge by tasting,' explains Martel. 'The pips need to be ripe and the grapes need to have flavour. It's better if the stems are ripe, but if they're not, it's not a deal breaker. And when you rub the skins of the grapes you should be able to extract a bit of colour.'

Once the grapes are picked, they're chilled right down to around 8–10°C to allow for the extraction of both fruit and structure. Some of the bunches are de-stemmed, and small grapes are placed at the bottom of the tanks, which allows for a greater degree of structural extraction. Big grapes go in the middle and then they top off the tanks by placing their healthiest whole bunches in by hand. The tanks are then saturated in carbon dioxide and left to their own devices for three or four days, then they perform a gentle *remontage* to bring some oxygenation to the tank. The amount of *remontage* that takes place afterwards will depend on the vintage – the bunches are handled more gently in cooler years, like 2024, when the stems aren't ripe enough to deal with too much vigorous extraction. After pressing and the end of fermentation, the wines are aged in a mix of old oak – never very much – and tank. Some wines are bottled in the following spring, while the rest are bottled shortly before harvest the next year.

Dubois's wines are all from Fleurie. Les Cocottes is fresh and floral, with notes of juicy blood oranges and a gentle rumble of tannin beneath. L'Alchimiste, named after a Paulo Coelho novel, is a bit more closed and tight, with firmer tannins on the palate and a little smoky reduction that gives way to notes of irises and violets. Les Labourons, which is vinified in large oak vats, is composed of the best bunches of the domaine. It's an absolutely delicious, complex wine with very fine, grippy tannins and a silkiness of texture that puts many Pinots to shame. One to age, perhaps – if you can resist drinking it in its perfumed, floral youth.

Martel's Juliénas Les Fouillouses comes from a parcel of grapes grown on a mid-slope mix of alluvial deposits and diorite. It has oodles of slight wild red fruit, a peppery, salty finish and firm, pleasantly chewy tannins. His Bessay cuvée comes from vines planted at an altitude of 450 metres. It's a big, powerful wine with concentrated dark fruit, liquorice and spice, with suggestions of tobacco leaves and smoke on the long finish. The raspy tannins and sheer weight and power of the wine presage a long life to come.

Domaine de la Grand'Cour, Justin Dutraive and Ophélie Dutraive

domainedelagrandcour.fr

Like many winemaking families in Beaujolais, the Dutraive family's roots run deep, although their time in Fleurie – the *cru* with which they're most closely associated – only goes back three generations, to a time when Jean Dutraive purchased the Domaine de la Grand'Cour. Jean came from the village of Charentay, where his family not only grew vines and wheat, but also raised cattle. As a younger son, Dutraive knew he wouldn't inherit the family holdings, so moved north in 1969. His grandchildren say that he wasn't particularly fixed on buying land in Fleurie, it was just that the property was affordable and was already set up to bottle its own wines (which was fairly unusual at the time). Dutraive had decided that he'd had enough of being a polyculturist and wanted to focus on wine, so the 200-year-old property was the right place at the right time at the right price.

Grandpa Dutraive farmed his land sustainably well before these practices were labelled as such, and when his son, Jean-Louis, took over the domaine in 1989, he carried his father's work further, becoming well known as a pioneer of organic viticulture in the *cru*, although certification only followed in 2009. His three children – Justin, Ophélie and Lucas – are following in their father's footsteps. Together they produce wines from the domaine's vineyards under the Domaine de la Grand'Cour label. There's also a négociant activity that accounts for around 20 per cent of their annual production, although the proportion varies from year to year. The buying of grapes – mostly from friends and friends of friends, all of whom farm organically – began fairly recently, a pragmatic response to a significant loss of production from the family's own vineyards due to hail damage a few years back. In addition, they all make wines under their own labels – although Lucas, the youngest, has only just embarked on his venture. It may be a while before he bottles anything under his own name because the parcel of vines he's working with is in such a bad state of repair that he's about to replant from scratch.

Justin's wines, bottled under his own name, are paler in colour and lighter in style than the family wines, with less focus on structure and extraction thanks to shorter macerations of less than a week for his Beaujolais Les Bulands, a very approachable, strawberry-scented glugger with barely perceptible levels of tannin. The Régnié Les Bulliats, made from grapes grown on a soil that mixes granite and loam, is similarly supple in structure, with a savoury tobacco leaf note. The Beaujolais Villages comes from a vineyard near St Etienne-la-Varenne, south of Brouilly. A relatively high altitude of 250–300 metres, an east-facing exposure and decomposed granite soils serve to create a wine with a fine, chalky grip and a palate of dark fruits tinged with spice and iris. The longest macerations, lasting 15–20 days, are reserved for the Fleurie La Madone, and this is the only cuvée to be aged entirely in old oak barrels and *demi-muids*. It's an elegant, poised wine with the tension and finesse typical of the *cru*.

Ophélie's focus is on Moulin-à-Vent, where she has two plots. The oldest vineyard is in the process of replanting. The cuvée made from very young vines in the *lieu-dit* of Les Thorins may lack a bit of mid-palate concentration, but it shows off her winemaking skills in its poised, juicy palate that offsets a little stemmy character with juicy red berry fruit notes.

The family's vineyards are still mostly based in Fleurie, but the Dutraives own 1.7 hectares of land in Brouilly. The vineyards are planted on soils rich in clay and limestone, so careful extraction is needed to ensure that the tannins are not too robust. While it's true that they exert a little chalky grip, the wine is nicely balanced, with a richer, more rounded mid-palate than the Fleuries. There are four Fleurie cuvées. La Chapelle des Bois is approachable in its youth, thanks to its bright red cherry and blood orange fruit, enlivened with a hint of fresh mint on the finish, and its discreet tannins. The Clos de la Grand'Cour is a walled vineyard held by the Dutraives as a *monopole*. There's a generous amount of fruit on the mid-palate, but this is very much held in check by gravelly tannins in the wine's youth, suggesting an ability to age over time. In almost any other region of France, the 40-year-old vines that go into the Clos cuvée would be labelled as Vieilles Vignes, but in the case of the Dutraives that specification is reserved for a parcel of 50- to 80-year-old vines growing within the Clos. Unlike the first two bottlings, which are aged in 50 per cent old oak and 50 per cent stainless steel (in the case of La Chapelle) or 50 per cent cement (the Clos), this wine spends seven months in old oak barrels, which nevertheless inflect a trace of their character on this rich, dense wine. One to age – as is the Vieilles Vignes Lieu-Dit Champ*gne (the asterisk is deliberate – although Fleurie has a *lieu-dit* called Champagne, there are administrative issues surrounding the use of this name on labels). This is an astonishing wine of great tension and complexity, as well as extraordinary length.

The négoce wines, made from bought-in grapes, are labelled as Famille Dutraive. The line-up includes a lovely bright Chénas; a slightly wild, broad-shouldered St-Amour; and a focused, rather shy Chiroubles that takes time to unwind in the bottle.

Domaine de Grand Pré/Romain Zordan

Romain Zordan is a great big genial bear of a man who makes nuanced, precise wines from the grapes he grows on his 8 hectares of vineyards, most of which are located in Fleurie. Back when Zordan was at the start of his career as a winemaker he thought he was going to end up working a few kilometres further north. He'd almost agreed to manage a property in Moulin-à-Vent on behalf of Vincent Girardin, a well-known Burgundian producer, until his father's decision to retire in 2012 changed his mind. Instead Zordan returned home to the family domaine.

Romain Zordan laughs off some unexpected rainfall in his vineyards

The Domaine de Grand Pré (sometimes cited as the Château de Grand Pré) was bought by Zordan's grandfather in 1968, although at the time the grapes grown there were sold in bulk to négociants. The domaine was eventually split in two, and Zordan took one half of the vineyards, with the remaining half being handed over to his cousin, Yann Bertrand (see p. 108). Currently his vines are mostly old bush vines, which he says are 'great if you want to work conventionally, but incredibly complicated to farm if you want to work organically'. As a result, Zordan is restructuring his vineyards, with the ultimate aim of lifting the trunks – and the fruiting zone – off the ground to make his work both easier and more effective.

Like Bertrand, Zordan farms organically, and he espouses a similarly hands-off approach to winemaking. He likes to chill the grapes down on reception at the winery in order to allow for a gentle pre-ferment infusion, then allows the temperature in the tank to rise slowly. It's rare for the bunches to top out at more than 25°C, though, which helps to preserve fruit. For Zordan, the defining characteristic of his winemaking is the lack of *remontage*. For him, the act of drawing off juices from the bottom of the tank to sprinkle over the cap is where the borderline between full carbonic and semi-carbonic maceration lies, and he knows which side of the border he wants to inhabit. The decision about when to press the bunches off can take a week or a month, he says, but is ultimately determined by tasting. 'The minute I start to feel the presence of any tannins or greenness in the wine is when I take the decision to press,' he says, adding that he prefers his wines to be fruit-driven. In order to retain this bright fruit character, he only adds a little prophylactic sulphite to his cuvées, around the time of bottling.

Zordan buys in some grapes from a friend to make his Beaujolais Blanc, a rounded wine with good balance, some smoky minerality and a little textural grip. The Beaujolais Villages, also made from purchased grapes, comes from the village of Lancié and a vineyard based on a mixed clay and granite soil. It gets barely ten days of maceration before relatively brief ageing in cement tanks, a regime that produces a super juicy, violet- and strawberry-scented glugger for immediate drinking pleasure. The name of Zordan's Fleurie Cuvée Spaciale is a play on the 'special cuvées' produced elsewhere (and when Zordan says 'special', one gets the feeling that he thinks many of them are anything but). It's also a reference to the 'sputnik', the rounded fibreglass tank in which he originally made this wine. These days Spaciale is made in a more conventional tank, then aged in a mix of cement tanks and old barrels, and bottled without sulphites. It's based on a parcel of vines with an average age of 80 years, and the rounded palate layers mulberries, rhubarb, incense and a refreshing hint of mint, while the chalky tannins exert gentle grip. The Morgon comes from a small parcel of 100(ish)-year-old vines in Douby owned by Zordan. Here the tannins are broader and fleshier than those seen in the Fleurie, and the palate is rounder and richer, although still showing the layers of bright fruit so typical of his wines. Zordan also makes a Côte de Brouilly from grapes grown by his friend Jonathan Buisson at the Domaine les Roches Bleues (see p. 189). This dense, dark-fruited cuvée is given shape by compact, deep-pile tannins.

Domaine Grégoire Hoppenot

www.domainehoppenot.com/

Grégoire Hoppenot is a relative newcomer to winemaking, having spent much of his professional life working on the commercial side of the wine trade, initially for a cooperative in southern Beaujolais and then for Trenel, a Mâcon-based négociant company owned by the Chapoutier family. Nevertheless, Hoppenot had a winemaking itch he wanted to scratch, so in 2018 he decided to go for it, and took over

9 hectares of vineyards on long-term leases, many of them parcels of prime land in Fleurie.

The vineyards, which are located in the prime *lieux-dits* of Les Moriers, Les Garands, Poncié and La Roilette, were converted to organic farming, a process that took five years. The plan is to move on to an eventual restructuring of the vineyards, with wider rows to allow for mechanization and the use of cover crops, but all this will take time. In the interim, Hoppenot is also working on the plots that surround his house and winery in the *Bas Beaujolais*, where he's planted some Chardonnay and a little bit of Chenin Blanc and Pinot Noir, taking advantage of the very varied local geology by matching variety to the appropriate soil type.

When it comes to the vinification of his Gamays, he always works with whole bunches, fermenting at temperatures that he aims to cap at around 27°C. The macerations take between six and 20 days, depending on the vintage and the progress of each tank. He tastes two or three times a day to monitor the progress of the extraction, although he varies the amount of *remontage* or *délestage* used in response to what he perceives to be the needs of each wine. After pressing and blending, he matures the wines in a mix of cement tanks and old barrels as he doesn't like the impact of wood on Gamay.

He makes a Fleurie under the label Famille Hoppenot, signalling the fact that he buys in some of the grapes. It's not a particularly dense or concentrated wine, but it is perfumed and delicious, a wine for purely hedonistic consumption. The Clos de l'Amandier comes from the bottom of Poncié. It's the Volnay of Beaujolais, all peony, iris and wild strawberries, with fine but present tannins and vertical acidity helping to stretch out the long finish. Les Garants comes from a parcel situated higher up on the same hill. It's rounder and riper, with a draggy grip of tannins and herb-tinged red and black plum fruits. The Les Moriers comes from a parcel that was once situated in Moulin-à-Vent, but is now on the Fleurie side of the border between the two appellations. This is the most serious and rigorous of the cuvées, one whose firm tannins suggest the possibility of a long life for this dark-fruited wine.

Domaine Lafarge-Vial

Instagram @domaine_lafarge_vial

Volnay's Lafarge family has a long and illustrious history as Burgundian wine producers, so it may have raised a few eyebrows when Fréderic Lafarge and his wife, Chantal, decided to invest in a winery in Fleurie, followed by a few hectares of the surrounding vineyards. The truth is that Chantal (whose maiden name is Vial) grew up not too far from Beaujolais, so the region had always had a strong hold on her, and the couple fell in love with the region, and with Fleurie and its vineyards in particular. Perhaps, speculates their son Maxime-Henri, it's because they saw similarities between the wines that could be made in the *cru* and those of Volnay in terms of both structure and perfume.

The initial purchase in 2014 was 2.5 hectares of vineyards that straddle the border between Fleurie and Chiroubles in the *lieux-dits* of Bel Air and Cercillon, but their holdings have been further expanded with plots in the steep Joie du Palais and the high-altitude Clos Vernay, which lies at over 400 metres on the northern limits of Fleurie, just before the *cru* flows into Moulin-à-Vent. To ring the changes a little, the family have also invested in a vineyard in Brulhié, a *lieu-dit* situated on the southern flanks of Mont Brouilly. All the vineyards are farmed both organically and biodynamically (the Lafarges are among a very small handful of producers in Beaujolais to be certified biodynamic), and soils in the steepest of the vineyards are either hand ploughed or ploughed by horse.

Winemaking here has no truck with Beaujolais's typical semi-carbonic maceration. Instead the members of the Lafarge family, who share responsibility for all aspects of the business, from winemaking through to marketing, follow their Burgundian model. All bunches are de-stemmed on arrival – with the exception of the occasional use of up to 20 per cent whole bunches to add lift and freshness in warmer vintages. Indigenous yeasts then get to work on fermenting the grapes, and temperatures are allowed to rise up to an average of 25–28°C, peaking at around 30°C on occasion. Tannins are gently extracted, although this method of winemaking inevitably results in the creation of more structure than is typical in Beaujolais. Once fermentation is concluded, the wines are pressed off and run into a mixed suite of barrels of various sizes and ages. The gentle oxygenation the wines are exposed to on their way into barrel acts to counterbalance Gamay's reductive tendencies.

For wines made from vineyards that lie within metres of each other, it's astounding how different the personality of the linear, perfumed Chiroubles is from the more restrained and textural Fleurie. The Côte de Brouilly is altogether a bigger, bolder wine, with firm, almost chalky tannins and a vivid sour cherry and elderberry character. La Joie du Palais has real density, with as much black as red fruit, and an almost glycerolic richness to the mid-palate. Le Clos Vernay has a grippy seam of tannin that runs right through it, like lettering in a stick of rock, as well as a complex, layered palate of mineral-tinged red fruit. All the wines will repay ageing, but both La Joie du Palais and Le Clos Vernay actively need a few years in bottle to show at their best.

Domaine Lucien Lardy

www.lucien-lardy.com/

Lucien Lardy, a bluff man with the solid build of a man who's performed hard manual labour for all his life, has opinions, and he's not afraid to voice them. To be fair, he's had some 50 years of making wine year in and year out, so he's earned the right to have a point of view on the way wines are made and sold in his home region. Unlike his children, Yohan Lardy (see p. 96) and Laura Lardy, Lardy senior doesn't work organically – at least not systematically, although he has a small organic Chardonnay vineyard. Instead he works within the framework of HVE certification, which provides a set of principles growers are meant to adhere to, rather than the stipulations and constraints of rigorous or-ganic certification. Lardy believes that elements of the organic approach espoused by many growers in the region these days are performative rather than of any real significance.

Perhaps surprisingly, however, Lardy conducts much of his work in the vineyard and the *cuvage* according to phases of the moon, and pulls out the biodynamic calendar on his mobile phone to demonstrate the general principles. If you're training vines and you want more wood, he explains, you need to do it during a waxing moon, while if you want less wood and more fruit, you do the work with a waning moon. A waning moon is also the best time to rack wines from the barrel and bottle them because when the moon waxes, you'll find more solid matter – lees and other solids – floating in suspension.

When it comes to winemaking, though, Lardy insists that it's not a recipe. A good winemaker needs to be able to adapt their work to the exigencies of the vineyard and the vintage. Sometimes he de-stems, particularly in rainy years when he has concerns about the ripeness of the stems. Those are also the years when he tends to do a lot of *pigeage*, mainly towards the end of fermentation, largely to ensure colour extrac-tion rather than extraction of tannins (although, of necessity, the tech-nique will also increase these). In warmer, richer years there's less need for extraction, and a far greater use of whole bunches. At the end of the fermentation, the wines are aged in large old oak *foudres*, which helps to integrate the tannins and give the wine roundness.

Lardy used to farm 30 hectares of vineyards, but as he heads towards retirement he now only looks after 3 hectares in Fleurie and another 1 hectare each of Moulin-à-Vent and Morgon's Côte du Py. The latter is a surprisingly delicate take on a *climat* that often gives robust, hedonistically rich wines, with peppery red berry and cherry fruit and a bright finish. The Moulin-à-Vent comes from the *lieu-dit* of Thorins and shows a bit more dark fruit and a sprinkling of baking spice. It's a fleshy wine, with generosity and length. Les Roches is a fine-boned Fleurie, with elegant tannins and a slightly bloody, ferrous tinge to its pretty floral palate. The final Fleurie cuvée is Les Moriers, based on a small parcel of vines planted in 1911. It is opulent and dense, with ripe fruit and firm, chewy tannins that suggest a need for a few years in bottle in order to integrate fully.

Domaine de la Madone

www.domaine-de-la-madone.com

The Domaine de la Madone is situated, as the name suggests, within close proximity of the Chapel of the Madonna, a small church perched high on a hill atop the Fleurie vineyards, and visible from miles around. There's some debate as to why the chapel was built (see p. 104), but Arnaud Despres was among the band of grape growers who managed the team of oxen that hauled the statue of the Madonna to the summit of the hill and her home on the roof of the chapel. Arnaud's namesake, the current Arnaud Despres, is a member of the sixth generation of his family to make wine in Fleurie.

The family's holdings now extend out over 18 hectares of vineyards, all in Fleurie, which makes the Domaine de la Madone the largest family-owned vineyard proprietor in the *cru*. Most of the domaine's vineyards are located in the *lieu-dit* of La Madone, which lies on the slopes just below the chapel. The family also owns land in another of Fleurie's most famous *lieux-dits*, Grille-Midi, and, when Despres's cousin decided not to become involved in the wine industry, the domaine took on his vineyards, which are situated in Charbonnière, the highest *lieu-dit* in the *cru*. The latter is bottled under the label of the Domaine du Niagara, but it is made in the same winery as the Domaine de la Madone's eight cuvées; a rosé, six reds and, rather surprisingly, a Viognier.

The latter, which is bottled as an IGP Collines Rhodaniennes, came about because Despres wanted to make a white, but felt that his granitic soils were unsuited to the more widely planted Chardonnay. Taking inspiration from the geology of Condrieu, which lies less than 100km to the south, Despres planted a small parcel of Viognier in La Madone in 2015 (as far as he knows it's the only parcel of white grapes grown in the *cru*), and feels that the resulting wine has been so successful that he's recently doubled plantings (although the entire area amounts to less than a hectare).

The reds are largely made in a fairly classical fashion, with semi-carbonic maceration used for the majority of the cuvées. Extraction is, perhaps, more vigorous here than it is in many domaines, with two *remontages* of the juice from the bottom of the tank conducted every day. The entry-level cuvée, Dame Nature, enjoys a brief fermentation and is then bottled without any sulphur. Despres intends it to be what the French refer to as a '*vin glouglou*', a simple, refreshing wine that can be served lightly chilled in summer. It's a juicy, enjoyable wine that's clearly not intended for the long haul but gives a hit of immediate pleasure. Of the remaining cuvées, the Domaine du Niagara, based on grapes from the cool Charbonnière site, is nicely framed by plush tannins and juicy acidity, while the Dame de la Pétoche, which spends a year in old oak barrels, has a rounded mid-palate and a smooth, velvety texture. The domaine's showpiece is the 1889 bottling, made, as the name suggests, from vines planted in 1889, which Despres believes to be from one of the first vineyards in the region to be planted on American rootstocks in the aftermath of the phylloxera crisis. Despite the relatively high levels of alcohol (14.5% abv in 2022, a warm year), the wine is well balanced, with its firm structure well cloaked in fruit.

Despres, whose undergraduate degree included courses in business studies, claims that marketing and sales are not his strong point, yet he's turned his family domaine into one of the slickest wine tourism operations in the region. The tasting room, which overlooks some of Fleurie's steepest slopes, is slick and modern. It features not only the entire range produced by Despres, but also wines made by friends and colleagues and a whole range of local food products – not just the usual jams and biscuits, but also cheeses and charcuterie. A couple of years ago, Despres also opened an on-site restaurant, and lunch and dinner are served five days a week. The set menu changes every month, but the à la carte offerings always include the local andouillette as well as *gauffres*, waffles, served with a hearty side of sausage and salad, a homage to the meals the domaine serves its pickers at harvest-time every year.

Domaine des Marrans and Domaine Camille Mélinand

www.domainedesmarrans.com

Brothers Mathieu and Camille Mélinand are, in many respects, typical of the new generation of winemakers revitalizing the Beaujolais region. They grew up on the family domaine, purchased by their father in 1970, which they now farm together. Mathieu followed a conventional path into winemaking by taking on formal studies in viticulture and winemaking, while his younger brother Camille worked in an office-based environment before returning to the family property. Both brothers have worked overseas, Mathieu in Australia and New Zealand, Camille in Oregon's Willamette Valley, and although they haven't necessarily brought new oenological ideas home with them, they have returned with a good appreciation of the wider world of wine.

The property, which lies right on the border between the *crus* of Morgon and Fleurie, obtained its organic certification in 2024 (a tricky year for anyone espousing these practices given the copious amounts of rain and attendant risks of fungal disease). Like many of the most forward-thinking domaines in the region, the Mélinand brothers use a horse-drawn plough in some of their vineyards to work the soil, a technique which carries less risk of soil compaction than the use of heavy farm tractors.

The Domaine owns around 20 hectares of vineyards, with just over half in Fleurie, and the remainder dotted around Chiroubles, Morgon and Lancié, one of the foremost villages in the Beaujolais Villages zone. In addition, Camille farms another hectare of Chiroubles and 1.5 hectares in Fleurie, and the grapes grown there are used to create wines he bottles under his own label, Domaine Camille Mélinand.

The winemaking at the Domaine des Marrans is classically Beaujolais in style, which is to say that semi-carbonic maceration is largely the order of the day, although bunches that show evidence of unripe stems are de-stemmed and diseased berries removed to allow for a more rigorous selection. Selection is a key issue for the brothers, and two triages take place, one by hand in the vineyards to remove leaves and obviously damaged berries, then the bunches are placed on a vibrating table on arrival at the winery, and this helps to get rid of any shrivelled, raisined berries. The Mélinands want to ensure fermentation gets off to a good start, so they don't chill the bunches down but aim to kick things off at an ambient temperature of around 15–18°C, with the aim of topping out at around 25–28°C by the end of the process. Somewhere around 10 to 15 days after the start of the intracellular phase of fermentation (depending on the vintage and the cuvée), they drain off the free run juice and press the whole bunches before reuniting them to continue the alcoholic phase of the fermentation. They give the whole process a helping hand by adding a *pied de cuve* to the tank, a yeast starter culture based on grapes picked slightly ahead of the main harvest and whose alcoholic fermentation is closely followed to ensure that it is populated by desirable, healthy strains of yeast. The Beaujolais Villages are aged in cement tanks for six or seven months while the Crus spend up to 18 months in large old oak *foudres*.

The only exception to the winemaking process cited above is that used to make the domaine's Beaujolais Blanc. After a conventional alcoholic fermentation, 20 per cent of the wine is aged in Burgundian *pieces*, while the remainder is matured in tank to retain freshness. The result is one of the most poised, bright-fruited whites made in the region, a wine with impressive balance. The Beaujolais AOP Vieilles Vignes makes a good introduction to the range, with its zippy, refreshing red cherry-scented palate, while the Fleurie Les Marrans, which accounts for 40 per cent of the domaine's production, is a very pretty take on the *cru*, with detailed, precise wild strawberry and red cherry fruit and fine-boned tannins. There are a couple of other Fleuries in the range. The Lieu-dit Ch*mpagne cuvée, whose name is asterisked as the result of a wrangle with customs over the rights to use the designation in full, is a richer, more structured wine with layered flavours and precise balance. The Fleurie Clos du Pavillon is the only cuvée with an overt oak influence, although Mathieu says future vintages will be less marked by oak as the barrel they use ages. Their Morgon cuvée comes from the *climat* of Corcelette, a vineyard with deep soils and very little stony material. It's rounder and weightier than the Fleuries, with layers of pepper and aniseed spice and a bracing kick of orange zest. The Chiroubles Aux Côtes is made from grapes grown on poor, very stony soils and steep slopes. The altitude of these vineyards, at around 400 metres above sea level, lends the wine a taut, tense structure that provides an element of restraint to the generous palate, which is layered with bright red pomegranate and cherry fruit tinged with notes of summer flowers. An altogether exceptional example of a wine from this little-known *cru*.

The wines Camille bottles under his own label walk slightly closer to the wild side than those bearing the name of the family domaine. There's a little less sulphite added here – not that the Domaine des Marrans uses much in the way of sulphites, other than a minimal dose at bottling – and extraction is even gentler in Camille's wines than in those of the Domaine des Marrans. The result is a peppery, spicy, bright-fruited Chiroubles and slightly weightier, chewier Fleurie.

Jules Métras

Jules Métras would probably laugh in your face if you described him as having an aristocratic pedigree, and yet, in the context of natural winemaking in the Beaujolais Cru, Métras is about as close to royalty as you can get. His father, Yvon, was a member of the band of brothers erroneously described as the Gang of Four (see p. 11) who pioneered organic viticulture and minimalist vinification in Beaujolais from the 1970s onwards. But while Lapierre and most of the Gang were based in Morgon, the Métras focus has always been on the vineyards of Fleurie.

Yvon was joined in the winery in 2010 by his son, Jules, who launched his own label with the 2014 vintage. By this time Jules had spent some time working in different wineries around the world, gathering up experience and insights during *stages* in the Ardèche, Jura, Chile and New Zealand. For a decade, Jules farmed his own vineyards, but with the 2024 vintage, and Yvon's retirement, Jules has taken on responsibility for 4.5 hectares of vineyards, most of them in Fleurie. With great regret, he's given up the plots in Chiroubles, saying that he loves the terroir but isn't going to miss the hard physical graft of working on the steep slopes. 'My parents always wanted to keep the domaine on a small scale,' he says, 'and given how challenging the market is for wine at the moment, I'm really glad.'

The small scale of the Métras domaine means that Jules can lavish detailed attention on his organic vineyards, many of them planted at some of the highest altitudes in the *cru*. Winemaking is, as you might expect, based on whole-bunch fermentations, with no additions made, other than remedial amounts of sulphites on bottling (and then only if Métras feels it's necessary).

His pale-coloured, bright-fruited Vin de France, Chica, is a homage to his Spanish mother, who passed away in 2023 and who, he says, could drink only the lightest of wines during her final illness. It's almost a rosé, albeit a deeply coloured one, juicy, floral and low in tannin. The

Cercillon, which comes from one of Fleurie's highest sites, is simply labelled as a Beaujolais. It exceeds anyone's expectations for this appellation, with its fine, focused palate, redolent with notes of dried rose petals and a dusting of pepper. There's a Moulin-à-Vent in the range, made from a parcel of grapes grown just beneath the *lieu-dit* of Champ de Cour. It has a broad, silky palate with intermingled notes of spice, cigars and peonies framed by very fine tannins. The Vieilles Vignes cuvée is made from vines aged between 60 and 90 years old grown in the sunny *lieux-dits* of Grille-Midi and La Madone. One month of maceration in tank before pressing gives the wine dense, rounded tannins to complement the fleshy, concentrated fruit on the palate. It's a complex wine with great length that merits some bottle age to allow it to unfold fully. The 2024 vintage was Métras's last in Chiroubles. The straight Chiroubles was partially de-stemmed – a response to a challenging vintage in the *cru* – but still shows the appellation's typical focused, fine-boned structure, while La Montagne is an incredibly fine, elegant wine with great perfume and precision, as well as astounding length.

As I leave Métras's winery at the end of my tasting, he thanks me for my support of Beaujolais in general and my enthusiasm for Chiroubles in particular, then hands me a bottle of La Montagne to take with me on my travels. It feels like a valedictory gesture, although I'm not sure whether he's saying farewell to me or to his beloved *cru*.

Clos de Mez

www.closdemez.com/

Marie-Elodie Zighera-Confuron comes from a distaff branch of the Thévenet family that's very well represented among the winemakers of the Beaujolais, but she grew up in Paris, far from the vineyards. Nevertheless, she visited her grandmother most years, and developed a deep love for the rolling hills she could see from the house in Fleurie. At the age of 15, she announced that she wanted to become a winemaker, and take over the running of her grandmother's 20-hectare property, whose grapes had been sent to the local cooperative for many years.

Her parents, who weren't convinced that this was the right career for their daughter, agreed on condition that she complete a course of studies in viticulture and oenology. A basic diploma was followed up with two years at Dijon University, where she studied viticulture, then a further two years in Montpellier, working on a diploma in oenology. Having finished the academic phase of her education she then decided to get some hands-on training in Burgundy, which is where she met her husband, Jean-Pierre Confuron, of Vosne-Romanée's Domaine Confuron-Cotetidot. Finally, in 2006, she felt ready, and officially took over the reins at the Fleurie estate on 1 April, which she says makes this one of the region's longest-running April Fool's Day jokes ever.

But Zighera-Confuron's work is no laughing matter. She alternates her time between teaching oenology at Beaune's agricultural college and managing 5.3 hectares of organic vineyards in Fleurie and Morgon, a figure which is due to rise to over 8 hectares in 2026. When it comes to winemaking, work at the Clos de Mez (the name is derived from the first three initials of her name) is as thorough and thought-through as you would expect from someone who teaches the science and practice of oenology. She never de-stems grapes – she likes whole-bunch wines, which was one of the reasons she went to Burgundy for hands-on experience in the first place. Nevertheless, she says she learned the hard way that you can't expect to treat Gamay in the same way as you would Pinot Noir and get the same results. 'Gamay is a very austere grape,' she says, 'and after the first couple of vintages I realized that the amount of extraction I was doing meant that the wines would take at least a decade in bottle to come round.'

She doesn't believe that this need for ageing in the wines she made in those first years is necessarily a bad thing, but points out that while people expect great Burgundies to age for years, the assumption is that wines from Beaujolais will be drinkable in their youth. She doesn't want to make simple fruity gluggers, though, so when making her main Fleurie and Morgon cuvées she derives inspiration from techniques used in Burgundy and gently treads the bunches at the top of her tanks so that they release their juices. The level of extraction she allows depends on the quality of the vintage, but she says that it is a matter of judgement – based on frequent tastings and common sense – rather than a recipe. The wines are aged for three years prior to release, one year of which is split between older barrels and tanks, then a further year (right after blending) in tank, followed by a year in bottle.

The resulting wines both have a distinctive richness and plushness. The Fleurie La Dot is named in honour of her grandmother as the parcel of vines this comes from was part of her dowry (the French word for dowry is a *dot*). It's more rounded and fleshy than many Fleuries, with a very pretty, dark-berried character, stony minerality and a long, focused finish. The Morgon Château Gaillard bears the name of the *lieu-dit* of the vineyard where the grapes are grown. Planted on granitic soils on the northern limit of the *cru*, where it abuts Fleurie, the wine shows more grace and finesse than many Morgons, although it's denser and broader than the Fleurie, with rounded tannins that exert a gentle grip. There's one more wine in the line-up. Mademoiselle M is a Fleurie based on a more conventional – for Beaujolais – semi-carbonic maceration, with little in the way of *remontage*. It's an early-drinking take on the grape with an exuberant, fruit-focused palate.

Château de Poncié

www.chateaudeponcie.fr

The Château de Poncié is situated on a prime hillside site that overlooks a good portion of the *cru* of Fleurie and the village, with its pretty steepled church. The advantages of the location were recognized early on by the monks of Cluny, and the earliest written records of winemaking on the site date back to 949 CE – a date recognized and echoed in the property's contemporary branding. After the French Revolution, the property was taken over by a Burgundian négociant, but after a couple of hundred years in their hands, it was purchased by the current owner, a Lyon-based businessman, in 2020.

Of the 100 hectares belonging to the Château, only around 30 are planted with vines, with much of the area dedicated to fostering biodiversity, so the property is surrounded by woodland and meadows. Some 4 kilometres of hedges have been planted by the new owners, and these not only protect the vineyards from winds, but also provide a home for a diverse range of bird and insect species. Sheep graze the vineyards in winter, and hens are moved around the property so that they can scratch the soil, limiting the growth of undesirable weeds.

The vineyards – which are mainly located in Fleurie, with a couple of hectares of Côte de Brouilly – are all certified organic and are in the process of conversion to biodynamics. The winery itself is a state-of-the-art, spare-no-expense number, with a pristine array of cement tanks, eggs, terracotta amphorae and barrels in a variety of shapes and sizes, all emblazoned with the Château's logo.

Wine tourism is a strong focus here, and the Château offers bike hire for rides round the vineyards and family-friendly treasure hunts, as well as the more standard cellar tours and tastings. There are plans for further development in future, and high-end accommodation may even be on the cards, although this is a few years off yet.

The wines are not, yet, quite as exciting as the scale of the project suggests. The main cuvée, the Fleurie 949, has some pretty floral character, but lacks a bit of focus and depth. The single-vineyard wines are more interesting. Les Moriers, a Fleurie made from 80-year-old vines, has more concentration on the mid-palate and a bit of gentle tannic bite, while the Côte de Brouilly, Le Pavé, is slightly richer, with some juicy dark fruit and rounded tannins.

Clos de la Roilette

www.laroilette.com

There can't be all that many winemaking domaines named after a racehorse, but the Clos de Roilette is a little different in a number of respects. The property, which is based in Fleurie, got its name after the original owner, a Monsieur Croizet, threw a fit of pique on learning that his vineyards had been excluded from the appellation of Moulin-à-Vent when its boundaries were drawn up in the 1920s. Rather than settle for labelling his wines as coming from Fleurie, which didn't have quite the same cachet back then as it does now, he decided to create his own brand, and named it after his favourite thoroughbred mare. Fast forward a few decades to the 1960s and Croizet's descendants sold up to the Coudert family, having lost interest in making wines entirely.

The property is now managed by the second and third generations of the Coudert family, Alain and his son, Alexis. Together they own 14 hectares of vineyards, of which 12 hectares are located in Fleurie. But while almost all of Fleurie's vineyards are planted on the *cru*'s distinctive pink granite soils, the Couderts' holdings are focused on the clay-rich *lieu-dit* of La Roilette, situated on the eastern fringes of the appellation. The resulting wine, simply labelled as Fleurie, accounts for around 60 per cent of the Clos's annual production. It's bolder and more generously framed than most Fleuries, with a smoky, meaty nose, although the palate is much fresher than the aromas suggest. The tannins exert some real grip, and the wine repays ageing for at least a couple of years after release.

The Clos releases three more Fleuries. The Cuvée Christie is made from grapes grown in the cooler granitic terroir of the Champagne *lieu-dit*. Largely destined for the US market, this is much more in the style of a classic, bright-fruited and delicate Fleurie, with a vibrant floral character. The Cuvée Tardive is made from the property's older parcels in La Roilette. It has big, bold tannins, albeit ones cloaked in a generous amount of pepper-tinged dark fruit, making this another wine to repay a bit of bottle age. La Griffe du Marquis is based on the same fruit as the Cuvée Tardive, but this time the wines are aged in Burgundian *pieces* rather than the large-format tuns the Clos typically uses to mature its wines. The barrels for the Griffe are seldom new, but there's still a clear oak-derived character to the cuvée. The final pair of wines in the line-up are derived from small single-hectare plots the Couderts inherited from other branches of the family. The Brouilly is a delicate, fruit-forward wine that is best enjoyed in its youth. The Moulin-à-Vent, although it comes from a parcel located a scant 500 metres from La Roilette, is an altogether different character, with rounded, rich, mouth-coating tannins and darker fruit.

Julien Sunier

julien-sunier.com

If you believe, as I do, that wines – or at least the wines made in a fairly small scale, artisanal way – share some of the personality of the men and women who make them, it's easy to understand why there's a vitality to Julien Sunier's wines. Sunier is a man who radiates energy. Even when he's sitting still, he gives the impression that he's on his way from one place to the next, from one idea to another. He talks fast, one thought tumbling over the next. One suspects that he doesn't suffer fools gladly, if at all. Some of the brightest rising stars of the region have learned their winemaking skills at his side ('What's the point of learning if you can't share it?' he asks). And yet Sunier ended up making wine in Beaujolais almost by accident.

Although he grew up in Burgundy, his parents were hairdressers, not winemakers. Sunier quit school, drifted from one part-time job to another, and ended up working in wine sales. He badgered the UK-based wine merchant Jasper Morris MW for a job, and worked with him for a few months, then he travelled from France to New Zealand and on to Portugal, juggling jobs in the wine industry with weekends on a surfboard. It was pure chance that he stumbled into a job in Beaujolais, working for a large négociant that had decided to invest in quality winemaking at a time when the region was in the viticultural doldrums. Sunier spent months building them a new vinification cellar that was never used. Depressed and disheartened, he almost didn't stay, and he was on the verge of leaving the region when he stumbled across a property that was for sale.

'I never really meant to buy it,' he says, but he believes fate forced his hand. In 2008 he found himself with a derelict farmhouse and 2 hectares of Morgon vineyards on a long-term lease. The rest, as they say, is history – but when people say that, it's a way of gliding over the many years of sheer hard graft that it takes to set old vineyards to rights, to build a working cellar, to establish a reputation and a solid base of importers in key markets around the world. That Sunier has managed to do so and has risen to become one of the leading lights of Beaujolais's new wave of producers is testament to the sheer force of both his personality and his determination.

His approach to viticulture and winemaking ticks many of the boxes associated with the current generation of rising stars in the region – organic viticulture, minimal intervention in the winery – but there's a pleasing lightness of touch to all four of the cuvées he makes. Wild Soul, his Beaujolais Villages, is lively and fresh (albeit not always as fresh as Sunier would like, given the warmth of recent vintages). It is what the French refer to a *vin glouglou* (a delightful piece of onomatopoeia that suggests its sheer gluggability, even in English). The Régnié is juicy and rounded, while the Morgon shows the density and breadth so typical of the appellation. The linear, focused Fleurie is the most delicate of Sunier's *crus*, with fine-boned tannins and a heady, perfumed nose.

Domaine Valma

When Stéphane Mathieu was a teenager growing up in Lyon he spent time in the Beaujolais countryside, and at the age of 15, he told a woman living there that he would buy her vineyards when he was grown up. It's rare that such adolescent pronouncements come true, but in Mathieu's case he made good on his promise, buying the small vineyard plot in La Madone from the 98-year-old previous owner.

Stéphane and his wife, Valentine, met while studying wine commerce in Bordeaux, then went on to have careers for big companies. She worked in marketing for Domaines Rothschild and Cointreau, while he gained experience as a buyer. But throughout it all they secretly hankered for life on the farm – to be specific, life on a wine farm in the Beaujolais, a region they refer to as *la belle endormie*, the sleeping beauty. They took the courses necessary to allow them to manage a viticultural property, then Valentine did some *stages*, one in Champagne and a more formative one at Château Thivin on Mont Brouilly in 2020. As they had no track record, the Mathieus figured that they'd be best off finding land in a *cru* that was reasonably well known, and managed to find vines, a *cuvage* and a house in Fleurie, the appellation of their dreams.

That was in 2021, and they immediately set to work converting their 5.5 hectares of vineyards, all in Fleurie, to organics. 'The link between viticulture and the quality of wine is something we don't talk about often enough,' insists Stéphane. He's been lucky enough to taste Beaujolais *crus* dating right back to the 1950s and 1960s, and says that many of these wines hold out much better in the long term than those of the 1980s through to the early 2000s. He puts the longevity of the older wines down to the fact that in those days people used far fewer products in the vineyards than they began to do in the 1970s, and that, over time, this wore out the soils and weakened the quality of the grapes grown there.

Valentine is responsible for the day-to-day running of the domaine, while Stéphane works part-time in order to ensure Valma's financial stability while the couple build their reputation. In 2021, Valentine got a bit of a break when she had the opportunity to train with consultant winemaker Jacques Néauport, who himself trained with Jules Chauvet (see p. 12) and worked alongside the Gang of Four and their friends. She was clearly a quick study as the four cuvées she and Stéphane make together show great precision and perfume.

The couple farm two parcels on Les Labourons, and the straight Les Labourons is a very pretty, pure-fruited wine with lots of crunch and a lovely bright finish. Les Labourons, Face B, is their old-vine cuvée, aged in old wood barrels for eight months, which rounds the palate out and helps to integrate the grippy tannins. It's an altogether more complex, elegant wine with a long finish. Valentine describes the La Madone parcel they purchased from the old lady (who was still around to enjoy the wines at the time of writing) as 'powerful and wild', so they have to pay close attention to their picking date to get the wine right. It's a wine of tension and focus, with firm but fine tannins that give it a pleasing chewiness on the long finish. La Chapelle des Bois is a big wine, with great richness and weight on the mid-palate, and although it lacks the poise of the other three cuvées, it's still an impressive, well-built wine.

11

CHIROUBLES

Year in which *cru* status was awarded: 1936
Total vineyard area: 280 hectares
Altitude: 270–600 metres
Average altitude: 410 metres
Notable *lieux-dits*: Javernand, Bel-Air, Les Pontheux, Chatenay, Les Roches, Au Craz, Rochefort, Grille Midi, Les Bonnes

While I realize that it's unfair of me to play favourites, I have to admit that there is one *cru*, in particular, that has stolen my heart. Chiroubles, whose name derives from the Old French for a stack of stones, a *chirat* (see photo, p. 133), is one of the smallest of the *crus*. It's definitely the steepest, with bush vines that perch precariously on vertiginous slopes (more than a fifth of the *cru* is situated on slopes of more than 30 per cent). I feel dizzy with vertigo and breathless with exhaustion when I think about how hard it must be to hike up and down these hills in order to prune and harvest – work that must largely be done by hand and on foot. Chiroubles's vines are all planted on the shallowest of pink granite soils, the only *cru* for which this can be said, a terroir that brings its own challenges. Furthermore, the *cru* frequently finds itself in the path of the most viciously devastating of the hailstorms to sweep through the region.

Chiroubles is, without a doubt, a demanding, high-maintenance appellation. No wonder all but the most determined of *vignerons* are giving up their vineyards in this beautiful and wild *cru* in droves. To drive the point home, the total planted area given above was the figure for

2024. In 2022, 315 hectares were harvested. This represents a loss of 35 hectares of vineyards, more than ten per cent of all plantings, in just two years.

And yet the wines of Chiroubles are often stunningly, heartbreakingly beautiful. Those stony granite soils and high altitudes combine to lend the wines finesse, tension and a heady perfume. If the robust, structured cuvées of Morgon's Côte du Py or Mont Brouilly are Beaujolais's answer to those grown on the hill of Hermitage, 140 or so kilometres to the south, the wines of Chiroubles are analogous to the precise yet headily aromatic wines of Côte Rôtie. But while wine lovers around the world are more than happy to open their wallets and pay big bucks for the wines of Côte Rôtie, it's rare for even the most expensive bottles of Chiroubles to reach prices of more than about £25 (US$35). It's easy to understand the economic rationale behind the attrition of so many of this *cru*'s vineyards, but the potential loss of this jewel of a *cru* is a largely unrecognized tragedy for anyone who appreciates wines of perfume and precision.

Producers

Domaine Chapel

www.domainechapel.fr

Domaine Chapel's origin story reads like an alternative script for the film *Sliding Doors*. Michele Smith, wine director for a three-star restaurant in Brooklyn, turned up late for an appointment at Domaine Lapierre, only to find that the man she was supposed to meet (Mathieu Lapierre) had had to leave for another appointment. Before going, Lapierre delegated responsibility for the tasting to David Chapel, son of one of France's most famous chefs, Alain Chapel, who was working at the domaine at the time. The tasting turned into a conversation, and the conversation persisted when, a month later, Chapel moved to New York to continue the relationship.

Two years later, in 2015, the couple moved back to France to fulfil a dream they both had of growing grapes and making wine. Smith (now Smith-Chapel) says that there was never any question about where they were going to settle. They both loved the wines, the landscapes and the culture of Beaujolais, so they headed straight there and began searching for their vineyards.

Over the course of the intervening decade, the couple have made wine from grapes grown in a number of *crus*, much of it initially as négoce purchases, but now they're focusing on their own forever vineyards,

Chiroubles derives its name from chirat, *the Old French word for a stack of stones (iStock.com/Gael Fontaine).*

with 7 hectares in total, of which two are in Fleurie, two parcels of 1 hectare each on different sites in Chiroubles, and 3 hectares bottled as Beaujolais Villages (although, from 2024 onwards, the grapes used to make this wine will come from young vines grown within the *cru* of Régnié). The only négociant cuvée they plan to make, going forwards, is a brisk, stony Bourgogne Aligoté made from a parcel of vines they've sourced in the Mâconnais.

Before harvest the Chapels spend a lot of time sampling the grapes in order to determine the right picking dates. 'If our kids are eating the grapes,' laughs Smith-Chapel, 'it's a pretty good sign.' Winemaking proper begins with an intense triage in the vineyards and then again at the domaine. Everything that passes muster goes straight into vats, except in years when the stems aren't ripe, at which point the couple take a view on what proportion of the bunches need to be de-stemmed. Other than that, winemaking is a pretty hands-off affair. They might do a little *pigeage* to get some juice to make a *pied de cuve* if the yeasts are stressed, but otherwise fermentation is left to proceed at its own pace, albeit with regular monitoring of progress to spot any incipient problems before they develop.

The Beaujolais Villages, which shows a gently herbaceous stemmy character, has supple, well-handled tannins that blend seamlessly into the bright cherry fruit, an indication of the brief maceration time. The Chiroubles, a blend of grapes grown in the *lieux-dits* of Chatenay and Poullet, is fine-boned and complex, with layers of cola spice, strawberry and rosehips, supported by plush tannins. The Fleurie Charbonnière comes from one of the steepest vineyards in the *cru*, and shows great density and richness of spicy blueberry fruit and liquorice, along with a lick of stony minerality on the very persistent finish.

Domaine Damien Coquelet

www.domainedamiencoquelet.com

Where we in English might call someone 'a man of few words', the French get to the point far more efficiently with two quick syllables, *taiseux*. Damien Coquelet is *taiseux*, and yet he's got much to crow about.

The name Damien has chosen for himself and his 10-hectare domaine, 'Coquelet', means a young male chick, and was Coquelet's childhood nickname. It serves to conceal the fact that Damien is the stepson of Georges Descombes (see p. 153) and stepbrother to Kewin Descombes (see p. 154). Given this pedigree it's perhaps unsurprising that Damien decided to become a winemaker, but what is perhaps more astonishing is the age at which he made his first vintage in his own right. Coquelet was only 19 when he set up on his own, making wines that are notable for their wild naturalness. There are no additives used in his semi-carbonic macerations, which means not only no cultured yeasts but, if at all possible, no sulphites either (although he reserves the right to add a tiny dose in case of vinification emergencies).

The resulting wines can walk a fine line between funk and freshness, but the most successful of his wines have a lovely fresh vibrancy to them. The straight Chiroubles is light and juicy, with a briskness to the tannins and a stemmy, crunchy flavour profile. The Chiroubles Vieilles Vignes has altogether more power and intensity to it. The Morgon Côte du Py is rounded and rich, with gently grippy tannins, while the Vieilles Vignes Cuvée from the same *climat* is more complex, combining a funky undertow with stony minerality, a touch of spice and bright flavours of redcurrants and mulberries.

Domaine l'Epicurieux/Sébastien Congretel

Instagram @epicurieuxbojo

It's not long into my conversation with Sébastien Congretel before I start wondering who he reminds me of. It doesn't take me that much

longer before I come to the conclusion that the striking parallels between him and California's Randall Grahm, another restless, inventive
spirit, are unavoidable. Like his American counterpart, Congretel is easily bored by the routine and predictable, and is always in search of the
next interesting idea to capture his attention.

Congretel says he's a romantic who wants to make 'punk wines',
which is why, after eight or so years at the coalface of making interesting
but relatively conventional wines from grapes grown in the vineyards of
Lantignié, Morgon and Régnié, he's jacked it all in to pursue a path of
innovation with some grapes from Chiroubles. It's easy to understand
why his new vineyard inspires the romantic side of Congretel's nature.
Situated at some 500 metres above sea level and surrounded by a forest, his vineyard – left to run wild by its previous owner – appeals to
Congretel's desire for the unconventional. The fact that Chiroubles is
a *cru* that is largely ignored by many producers, who consider its steep
slopes to be largely unprofitable, is part of its allure.

Congretel has decided that winemaking is no longer about paying
his bills. Instead he's returned to his previous career working on international oil platforms as a way of subsidizing his desire to experiment
without the need to take financial constraints into consideration. Since

These young vines in Chiroubles are being trained en échalas, *a system typically
used on the steep hillsides of the northern Rhône*

the 2023 vintage he's been playing with a technique he calls '*flotaison*', in which he draws off the free-run juice from a tank and pipes it into a large terracotta amphora. This juice is infused for several months with some whole bunches, then when he deems the time is right, the result is pressed off into tank before bottling. The remainder of the initial tank from which the free-run juice has been extracted is allowed to continue its relatively conventional full carbonic maceration and is bottled separately. While the latter cuvée is full of the juicy, fruit-forward deliciousness that one might expect from this kind of style when made by the hands of a talented winemaker, the *flotaison* wine is both more challenging and more complex. Both wines will be available, in very limited quantities, mostly – if not exclusively – in France.

Congretel says he will continue to make both wines for as long as they still interest him, although he's already thinking ahead to the next stage in the evolution of his new concept. He's excited about the fact that his Chiroubles vineyard has a small plot of Aligoté grapes, and his plan is to create two new wines, one based on infusing whole bunches of black grapes in white wine, while the other will steep white bunches in red wine. At the moment he has no idea of what the final outcome of this experiment will be, but for Congretel that's beside the point: the joy of it all lies in the journey and not the destination.

Domaine de la Grosse Pierre/Domaine Pauline Passot

www.domainedelagrossepierre.fr

Pauline Passot's family were *métayers*, her grandparents having taken over the day-to-day management of the property she now runs in Chiroubles in 1953. Passot herself left Beaujolais in her twenties to go and work as a sommelier in nearby Lyon, and the wines she tasted on the restaurant floor filled her with the desire to travel overseas and see what she could learn elsewhere. The experience she gained while based at Marlborough's Seresin Estate gave her new insights into the world of both work and wine. 'France – and the restaurant world – is very hierarchical,' she says, 'but what I learned in New Zealand was that people need to be happy to work as a team, and everyone has to lend a hand. You can't stand on ceremony, and Mathieu [Mélinand, of Domaine des Marrans, see p. 121, to whom Passot is married] and I both roll up our sleeves and dig our vineyards by hand alongside our workers.'

Passot also learned a number of vinification techniques while overseas, of which, she says, the most valuable has been the confidence to work with indigenous yeasts. On her return to Beaujolais in 2016, Passot started her own label, Domaine Pauline Passot, with a small parcel of vines in Chiroubles's *lieu-dit* of Grille Midi, and in 2018, when her parents retired, she took over their property, the Domaine de la Grosse Pierre. Of the 9.5 hectares she now farms, all but two hectares are situated on the steep granitic slopes of Chiroubles. 'It's a *cru* that is difficult to farm and difficult to sell,' she says, 'but the terroir is absolutely magical. Slopes and altitude combine to create wines with great freshness and fruit.' She pauses briefly before adding, 'People may now be looking for easier terroirs to work with, but easy doesn't necessarily give you great wine.'

What does give you great wine, though, is painstaking attention to detail, and there's plenty of evidence of that at the Domaine de la Grosse Pierre. Passot's vineyards are all certified as organic – a way of farming that is aided by the fact that the wind that blows through her high-altitude vineyards helps reduce the pressure of fungal diseases. The key challenge for Passot has been hail, which strikes Chiroubles with both frequency and severity (in 2023 she lost 70 per cent of the crop in her main vineyard due to a storm that struck in early July). She's bought a vibrating table recently, and this helps to ensure that the bunches that go into her cement fermentation tanks are in perfect health.

Passot adapts her winemaking to the requirements of each vintage. In warm years she tends to use a higher proportion of whole bunches in her fermentations as the stems help create a sense of freshness in the wine and absorb some of the alcohol. In more challenging vintages – especially those in which the bunches have been damaged by hail – she de-stems far more. On the latter style of fermentation she does as little extraction as possible, preferring to allow the tannins and colour to infuse gradually. And in all instances where she does intervene to extract, she does so in the middle of the fermentation since she feels that the levels of alcohol present at the end of fermentation can extract too much, resulting in clumsy, bitter tannins. Passot says that she tried using old barrels for maturation and even these marked the wines too much for her taste, so she returned to the neutral impact of the cement tanks that her father and grandfather before her used.

Passot's wines all show the great purity of fruit she aims for. La Grosse Pierre, made from grapes grown in the vineyards that surround the family property, won't make old bones, but is a thoroughly delightful, perfumed cuvée for the short to medium term. Claudius is made from the oldest vines grown in the same vineyard as the Grosse Pierre, but vine age gives this bottling huge concentration, while remaining refined and precise. Au Craz comes from a high-altitude vineyard planted at 480 metres on very poor, stony granite soils. It shows less of the floral character present in the first two wines, with a ferrous, almost bloody character and very fine tannins. The Grille-Midi is the only wine bottled under the Domaine Pauline Passot label. It's an intensely perfumed wine whose floral aromas almost jump out of the glass at you, while the palate is poised and focused. Her two other cuvées come from outside Chiroubles. The Fleurie Bel Air lies just over the brow of the hill from one of her Chiroubles vineyards, but shows a little more roundness and richness on the mid-palate. Morgon Douby is the richest wine of the line-up, with slightly darker, riper fruit than the others, and slightly more tannic grip.

Château de Javernand

javernand.com

The Château de Javernand is a real family affair. Or, to be more precise, two families. Pierre Prost, the scion of a Mâconnais-based family, met Arthur Fourneau, whose family owned the Chiroubles-based Château de Javernand, while at college. Rather wonderfully, Prost fell in love with Fourneau's cousin, Mathilde Pénicaud, and married her. The trio now farm both properties together, having converted their vineyards to organics back in 2012. Since then, they've pushed their approach even further by focusing more closely on improving the biodiversity on their 55-hectare property. Only a third of the land they own is turned over to viticulture, with the rest split between meadows and woods. The vines, planted on the steepest, driest soils, are surrounded by hedges, which not only serve to break up the winds that sweep across the hillsides, but also form ecological corridors for local mammals and birds. Great emphasis is also placed on improving soil health at the Château, to the advantage of the microfauna that lives underground.

Vinification is as natural as possible, with around three-quarters of the grapes vinified in whole bunches. There's no recipe, though, Prost says, with decisions about fermentation styles taken on the basis of the ripeness of the bunches they harvest. Their four cuvées – all made from fruit grown on the property – are blends rather than parcel selections, and all show the luminous, perfumed fruit and bright acidity so typical of Chiroubles.

Les Gatilles is the most fruit-driven of the property's wines, vinified with a semi-carbonic maceration and very little *remontage*, then aged in concrete tanks for around nine months. The result is a fine-boned, crunchy wine with lively cherry and raspberry fruit. The Vieilles Vignes is partially de-stemmed and the greater level of extraction this affords results in a wine with focused and rather taut tannins that exert a pleasing grip on the palate. Indigène is only lightly dosed with sulphites prior to bottling. It has a layered, complex palate whose berry fruits are enlivened with notes of orange zest and summer flowers, all neatly balanced by fine, elegant tannins. Climax, which is aged in oak, is the richest, weightiest wine produced at Javernand. There's a lot of concentration here, but it retains its freshness, along with generous quantities of polished tannins.

Domaine du Long Nuage Blanc

Instagram @domainedulongnuageblanc

Winemaking domaines in Beaujolais come in all shapes and sizes, but few of them are as tiny as the 1-hectare Domaine du Long Nuage Blanc in Chiroubles. But, when you're working part-time – Alexia Koener as a speech therapist and Michaël Gilboux as a mobile bottler – a hectare of vineyards, and the 4,000 or so bottles that result in each year, (not to mention raising a young child) are probably about all any couple can comfortably manage. Besides, every wine producer has to start somewhere.

Gilboux trained as a biochemical engineer in his native Belgium, working for a major beer producer, before catching the wine bug. He decided to go and work a harvest in New Zealand (hence the name of his Beaujolais domaine, which translates as 'the domain of the long white cloud'). One trip to New Zealand turned into a second, which was followed in subsequent years by time spent working in Australia's Clare Valley, Bellarine Peninsula and Margaret River. On a few of these trips he was accompanied by Koener, and together they decided that they wanted to make their own wine.

Their choice of Beaujolais and Chiroubles as a venue for their enterprise was determined as much by pragmatics as by choice. They both loved the style of the wines made in the region, but the fact that it was in relatively easy driving distance of their families in Belgium, and perhaps more importantly, the affordability of housing and land in Chiroubles was integral to the decision. They moved into a farmhouse just outside the village in January 2020 and set to work transforming a steeply sloped vineyard to organic agriculture.

It's been a tough few years, not least because they're slap bang in the middle of the hail corridor, and most years they lose a significant volume of their already tiny production. In 2022 they lost 10 per cent, but 2023's hailstorm stripped them of half their grapes in one fell swoop. Things improved slightly in 2024, with only 15 per cent of the potential harvest lost to hail. It's not an easy life up there on the hills of Chiroubles.

Luckily their links to their home country have helped them to develop a strong market for their wines in Belgium, and that – along with smaller volumes sold here and there in France – is helping them to establish their brand. They currently make three wines. The Chiroubles Javernand is made from their younger vines. Relatively high yields in 2023 and the use of semi-carbonic maceration make for a bright, fruit-driven wine with modest levels of alcohol (12.5% abv) and crunchy, slightly stemmy tannins – it's all somewhat reminiscent of a light Cabernet Franc from the Loire. The Chiroubles from their older Rochefort vineyard is made of sterner, more structured stuff as well as riper fruit. It's a wine with a prominent floral character as well as a hint of pepper, and a sparky,

Winemakers in Beaujolais keep track of the progress of their fermentations on a daily basis, charting falling sugar levels and keeping an eye out for potential problems

vibrant freshness. Cuvée Victor, which is made from a small parcel of vines in Régnié's *lieu-dit* of Thulon, is named after the couple's son, who arrived on the day they first harvested the plot. It's the broadest, densest, grippiest wine of the three, and would repay a bit of ageing in bottle to allow it to open up. The couple also plan on planting a parcel of white grapes on some of their land. Not Chardonnay, which they don't believe can create great wines on their granitic soils, but Riesling, a grape they fell in love with while working in Australia, and which they think will thrive on the hills of Chiroubles. Watch this space.

Famille Morin

www.domainefamillemorin.fr

The Morin family moved into their hilltop property in 1926, although they farmed it as *métayers* rather than owners. It wasn't until the late 1990s that Eric and Pauline finally took possession of the domaine that their family had farmed for three generations. Theo, a member of the fourth generation, completed his academic studies in commerce and winemaking then took some time out to undergo some *stages* in Burgundy, the Languedoc and, more locally, at the Domaine de la Grand'Cour (see p. 111) before beginning work alongside his parents in 2022.

The 10-hectare property has long been farmed organically, but Theo has pushed for organic certification as he's keen to develop more exports, and believes that this will help with overseas sales. Of those 10 hectares, 7 are in Chiroubles, with the balance located in Morgon and in the nearby Beaujolais Villages zone of Lantignié, where the family have planted Chardonnay and Aligoté. Ten years ago, the Morins also decided to plant some experimental red grapes, and now have a half hectare each of Syrah, Gamaret and Marselan.

The Marselan is used to make a sunset-pink pét nat, which is off-dry and gently foaming, with slightly funky flavours of red apples and berries, and a little twist of phenolic bitterness on the finish. The Gamaret is intensely fruity, with a flavour profile reminiscent of wild strawberry jellies. The Syrah is less successful, to my mind, with a very green fruit profile and slightly astringent tannins. All of these cuvées are bottled as Vins de France, while all the Gamays – with the exception of a Morgon cuvée – are labelled as Chiroubles.

Vinification for these wines is semi-carbonic, and conducted at low temperatures so as not to extract much in the way of colour or tannin.

The wines are then aged in a mix of old oak vats and concrete tanks for around 10 months prior to bottling. The Morgon Terrain Rouge comes from a parcel of vines grown on flat red stones and clay. It's a juicy, fleshy wine with good levels of bright acidity and gently grippy tannins. The entry-level Chiroubles cuvée is light and crunchy, with a burst of cranberry and redcurrant fruit. The Javernand is altogether more serious in style, with a little stemmy whole-bunch character adding a trace of slightly bitter green tea to a palate packed with pepper, peonies and red cherries. The Vieilles Vignes comes from a parcel of vines planted in 1926, and shows both great concentration and precise balance. It's long and layered, with gently raspy tannins and heady floral notes.

12

MORGON

Year in which *cru* status was awarded: 1936
Total vineyard area: 1,060 hectares
Altitude: 200–500 metres
Average altitude: 310 metres
Notable *lieux-dits*: Côte du Py, Les Micouds, Douby, Corcelette, Aux Charmes, Le Grand Douby, Les Marcellins, Javernières, Grand Cras

Morgon vies with Fleurie for the title of Beaujolais's best-known *cru*. Part of its near-ubiquity on retail shelves and restaurant lists around the world is due to its size: Morgon is a large *cru*, second only to Brouilly. This means that whatever scale of production is desired – from high-volume supermarket own-label wines right down to small-scale artisanal cuvées – Morgon can deliver. Its strong associations with the Gang of Four (see p. 11), who were all based in the *cru*, has also helped to re-inforce its image as a source of high-quality wines. It doesn't hurt that Morgon is the source of many of Beaujolais's most long-lived wines. Marie-Elodie Zighera-Confuron (see p. 124) speaks of an eye-opening tasting in which a 1911 Morgon outshone all the similarly venerable Burgundies that had been opened alongside it.

The *cru* offers producers a range of soil types to play with when crafting their wines. The northern and western zone is dominated by the pink granites you'll find in the surrounding *crus* of Fleurie, Chiroubles and the northern tip of Régnié. These soils typically give a more delicate frame to the wines of Morgon, rather than showing the burliness and structure typically associated with the *cru*. Much of the west and south

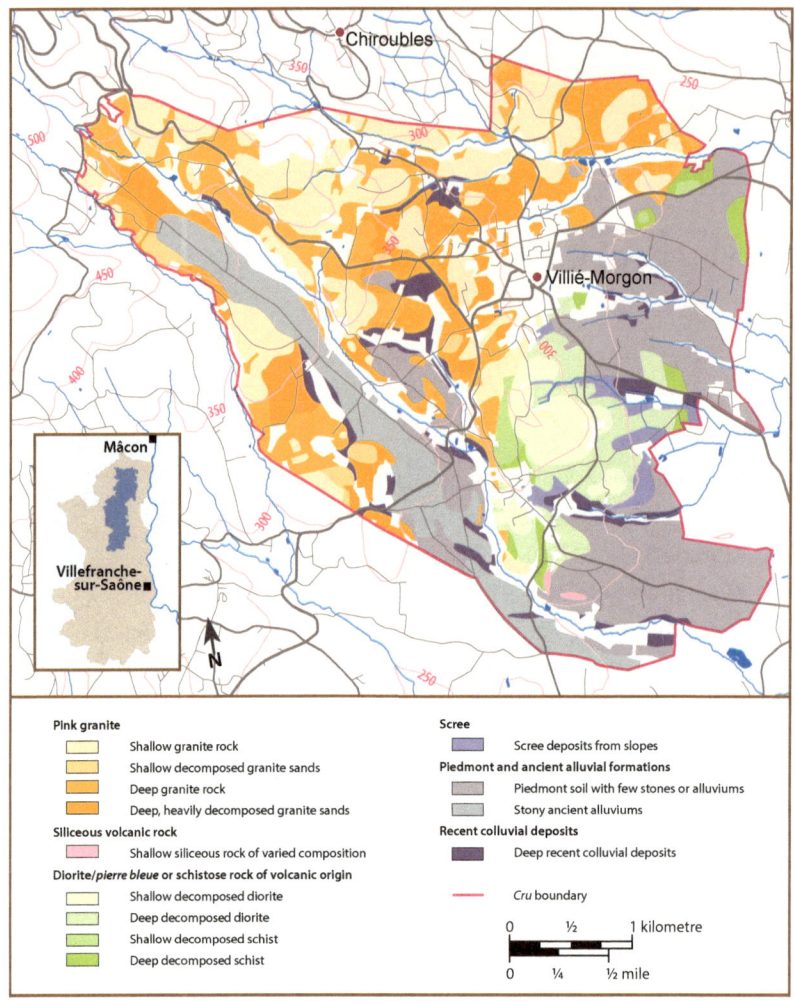

Map 7: The geology of Morgon

of the *cru* is planted on soils formed by piedmonts and alluvial deposits, with varying amounts of stones and deposits of clay. The wines produced here typically show a weighty, fleshy mid-palate. But the most famous of the *cru*'s *climats*, the Côte du Py, is largely formed of hard blue diorite, although there's also some schist on its western slopes.

The Côte du Py is a rounded hill situated on the eastern edge of the *cru*, just south of the village, Villié-Morgon, that gives Morgon its name. The Côte rises to an altitude of 358 metres and is topped by a cross commemorating the 1906 vintage (a hot, dry vintage renowned for its excellence in an era when achieving ripeness was an issue). Although

From the top of the Côte du Py, you can look out over the vineyards of Morgon and its neighbouring crus

local legend suggests that the Côte is the eroded stub of a long-extinct volcano, it is far more likely that it was created from extruded volcanic material thrust up by subterranean geological forces. The hard blue stones of the Côte often bear a rusty reddish tinge, testament to the presence of iron oxides. This is the soil that gives many of Morgon's most iconic wines their density and richness of fruit as well as their firm tannins, although this ripeness is enhanced by the exposure to the sun afforded to the vineyards situated on the top of the hill.

The Côte du Py is just one of the six *climats* that have played such a key part in creating the renown of Morgon – the other five are Corcelette, Les Charmes, Douby, Grand Cras and Les Micouds. All the other *crus* have long focused on the smaller parcels, the *lieux-dits* (see p. 19). And therein lies a huge bone of contention that, at the time of writing (spring 2025) was exercising the time, attention and opinions of every grower in Morgon. Soon after most of the *crus* were created, in 1936, Morgon opted to subdivide itself into six large *climats*, as had always been the local tradition. Until recently, these *climats* were widely used to communicate about the *cru*'s terroirs and its wines. Not only have they been recognized by the consumers who buy Morgon's wines for the best part of a century, they were also used by professionals and referenced on the INAO's own website. However, in 2023, a government department charged with monitoring fraud took a closer look at some of the vintage declarations, both current and historic, filed by producers based in Morgon and realized that the *climats* being claimed on the label had never been officially validated. As a result, from the 2024 vintage onwards, it has become illegal for Morgon's domaines to cite the name of a *climat* on their wine labels unless the grapes were actually grown in the (much smaller, more specific) *lieu-dit* after which the larger *climat* had been named. As a result, many winemakers are going to have to change the names of long-standing, often historic cuvées. Wines that had once been labelled Corcelette, for instance, may have to become Bellevue or Fond Long, while a Côte du Py might be renamed La Chaponne or Aux Pierres. Growers who had made wines from a blend of different *lieux-dits* within a *climat* might have to come up with a totally original name for a cuvée that was once known simply as Les Charmes (one more instance where *c'est compliqué* in Beaujolais). For some producers – those whose renown is already well established – this may not pose too much of a problem. The guarantee of quality offered by their name on a bottle will probably trump any hesitancy their clients may feel when faced with a 'different' wine on the shelves of a shop or a restaurant's list. For those relying on the fame of the Côte du Py or Corcelette to sell their wine, the consequences of this bureaucratic decision may well be more severe.

As a final aside, it should be noted that, as a result of this large-scale change in the nomenclature of many of Morgon's wines from the 2024 vintage onwards, some of the wines referred to in this chapter (and Morgons cited elsewhere in this book) may end up being called something completely different by the time you read this.

Producers

Vignoble Arnaud Aucoeur

vignobleaucoeur.com

It's not all that rare for viticultural families to pass the winemaking baton on from father to son (or, these days, daughter). Nevertheless, a producer who can boast that he's a member of the thirteenth generation to make wines in the same *cru* is rare. (The fourteenth generation is currently engaged in studies and *stages* that will allow them to manage the domaine when their turn comes.) Arnaud Aucoeur's ancestors arrived in Morgon in 1825 and began farming their land, initially as polyculturists – the norm in those days – but before long they became specialist grape growers.

Despite his deep viticultural roots, Aucoeur is not as firmly wedded to local tradition as you might expect. 'I've worked as a grower for 25 years,' he says, 'but I'm always open to new ideas. Every vintage is different, so you need to be flexible in the way you think about things.'

Aucoeur's readiness to adapt is amply demonstrated both in the vineyard and in the cellar. Much as he'd like to farm organically, he recognizes that the system imposes a certain inflexibility that he feels might lead to a loss of quality in challenging vintages. For Aucoeur, quality is paramount, so in 2021 (for instance), when persistent rain led to high levels of fungal disease pressure, he sprayed his vines with antifungals as frequently as he felt necessary. Similarly, confronted with the increasing challenge of flavescence dorée (see p. 46), he's happy to use pesticides to keep the insect vectors of the disease under control. Aucoeur feels that a small dose of prevention is far better than a more drastic cure.

Prescriptive practices are not the order of the day when it comes to harvesting either. Aucoeur used to pick his 16 hectares of vineyards in strict rotation, but for the past few years he's been paying closer attention to the needs of each parcel. Analyses are performed frequently in the run-up to the big day, and picking order is decided on the basis of the results the laboratories provide.

Similarly, while most producers have pretty set ideas as to how they plan to vinify the grapes once they arrive at the winery, Aucoeur likes to adapt his practices according to the character of each plot in each vintage. Thermovinification (or at least an adapted version of thermovinification that involves initial heating, rapid chilling and then a long fermentation), semi-carbonic maceration and Burgundy-style destemming and extraction are all grist to his vinificatory mill. Some cuvées even employ a blend of winemaking techniques, with a dash of thermovinification adding fruitiness to a wine that would otherwise be more structured, for instance.

Aucoeur makes wines in all of Beaujolais's ten *crus*, as well as Beaujolais Villages and Beaujolais (in white, pink and red) and in the Mâconnais, some of it as part of a négoce business (from bought-in grapes), but the heart of the Aucoeur family holdings remain in Morgon, home to around two-thirds of their production. The Morgon Terre d'Origine is worth keeping in bottle for a couple of years at least, as over the course of time it acquires weight and roundness to balance Morgon's typically firm tannins. The Morgon Côte du Py is even weightier and richer, with lashings of dark fruit and a brooding deep spice character. Even away from the home turf of Morgon, the wines Aucoeur makes all show great freshness and balance – his Juliénas has the gravity and density so typical of the appellation, but the firm tannins have been judiciously extracted and there's still a delightful vibrancy to the dark fruit. Saint-Amour's clay soils give its cuvée some serious weight, but it's hidden away behind an almost translucent veil of pretty red cherry fruit.

Daniel Bouland

Officially, Daniel Bouland is retired. However, he points out that the state pension he gets isn't going to pay for his twin passions – skiing and his motorbike – so he keeps toiling in his vineyards, producing fantastically dense wines that continue to thrill.

Bouland, whose ancestors had been making wines in Morgon for at least four generations, took over the family vineyards in 1982, around the time the Gang of Four were beginning to achieve worldwide recognition. But despite being located in the same village as them, Bouland has always travelled a little apart, eschewing the natural winemaking path forged by his contemporaries.

This doesn't mean that Bouland is any less conscientious than them, either in the vineyard or in the cellar, he just prefers to do things his way – and his way is often the hard way. He's devoted to his old vines – many of his parcels are close to 100 years old – and he tends to them with dedication. He won't work organically, as he feels this would require him to restructure his vineyards in a way that would shock his ancient plants and cause them to die off. Instead he treats as little as possible, walking through his vines on foot, with a hand-spray attached to a backpack full of whatever liquid remedy he deems necessary. Bouland says that his old vines deal better with diseases like esca than younger vines might, but he's prepared to help them along by delaying pruning on vines that he feels are susceptible until the sap is rising, a protective measure that adds pressure on him to prune as late as possible.

Bouland has a parcel or two in Chiroubles and the Côte de Brouilly, but his main holdings lie in Morgon, where he makes a suite of parcel selections based not only on *lieux-dits*, but also on variables like whether or not the soil is composed of stones or granitic sands. He says he finds it more interesting to do this than to make the region's more traditional blends.

In terms of winemaking, he's a classicist, believing that Beaujolais's semi-carbonic maceration technique brings out the best in Gamay, although he tends to ferment at temperatures of up to 33–34°C, which is higher than most. This allows him to extract structure, while he maintains that the presence of the stems in the ferment gives his wines freshness. Rather unusually, he takes great care to expose his wines to oxygen prior to bottling, in order to ensure that they lose the austerity and reductive character to which Gamay can be prone in youth. He does this via a process reminiscent of double decanting, in which the wines are piped from their maturation vessels into an open-topped epoxy tank, allowing the wine to splash around in the tank as it's fed in. He then cleans the maturation vessels thoroughly before piping the wines back in from the epoxy tanks. Bouland says that it takes him a good eight days to conduct this process for the entire vintage, but feels it's worth it in terms of the generosity and openness this allows his wines right from the start.

Even though Bouland is at pains to help his wines open up by means of gentle oxygenation, all his Morgon bottlings are structured wines with a long life ahead of them. Typically the cuvées made from grapes grown on stony soils, the 'Cailloux' wines, are riper and more generously fruited than those made on sandy terrain, the 'Sable' bottlings. The only exception to this alternation between sand and stone comes from the Les Delys wines, whose two bottlings are the lighter, more floral Les Delys and the Les Delys 1926, which is as dense and rich as you might expect from a wine made from centenarian vines.

Domaine Guy Breton

Guy Breton – known to all his friends as Max – is a member of Beaujolais's famous Gang of Four (see p. 11). He inherited his grandfather's vineyards and, along with the other Gang members, wanted to create wines that reflected a sense of place.

Key to that was bringing the soil of the vineyards back to life, as Breton felt strongly that the use of chemicals in the vineyards would kill the yeasts that live on the skins of the grapes, with the result that you would have to add cultured yeasts to your tanks to ensure that fermentation could finish. There's no organic certification at Domaine Guy Breton, though. Certification means that certain processes must be followed and regulations must be obeyed, and Breton is not a man who is content to have rules foisted upon him.

The grapes that arrive at the winery are chilled overnight, then piled into tanks for a slow, gentle intracellular fermentation at temperatures of around 17–18°C. Any juice that gets expressed by the grapes at the bottom of the tank is drawn off and fermented separately, then blended back into the main cuvée after it has been pressed off. This approach is designed to create wines that are extremely pale in colour, with minimal amounts of tannin, and plenty of bright, pure fruit and good amounts of acidity. These are characteristics present in all the wines, whether it's Marylou, a Beaujolais Villages named after Breton's daughter, or the parcel selections from Fleurie, Morgon, the Côte de Brouilly and Chiroubles. The P'tit Max, a Morgon made from 120-year-old vines still on their own roots and aged in second-hand barrels sourced from the Domaine de la Romanée-Conti, is perhaps the most dense and dark-fruited of all Breton's wines, but it still has a transparency of fruit that seems to be a hallmark here, shot through with vivid acidity and a little tea-leaf character that gives the wine a refreshing twist of bitterness on the finish.

Jean-Marc Burgaud

jean-marc-burgaud.com

When Jean-Marc Burgaud first set up in Villié-Morgon, back in 1989, few people would have put money on him to become one of the *cru*'s most important producers. After all, he only had 1 hectare of vineyards in Morgon, with a further hectare each in Régnié and Lantignié, the village in which he grew up, and these were rented. These days, Burgaud farms some 17.5 hectares of vineyards, of which 5 hectares are in Lantignié and the remainder are all in Morgon. He even has 7 prized hectares of vines on the Côte du Py, of which more than half are in pole position on the sun-bathed summit of the hill. Furthermore, his wines regularly attract plaudits from some of the world's most respected wine critics. In other words, Burgaud is very much a force to be reckoned with.

He's got to the top through a combination of talent and sheer hard graft, both in the vineyards and in the *cuvage*. Burgaud's vineyards are all his own. He believes that in order to make quality wines, you need to know your grapes intimately, so he spends much of his time in the field, with his shirtsleeves rolled up, working alongside his employees.

With the exception of the Les Grands Cras cuvée, which includes a little de-stemmed fruit, Burgaud works entirely with whole bunches in the winery. His approach to the semi-carbonic maceration he practises is nuanced, with pre-press fermentation times ranging from about a week for wines that are intended to be enjoyed in their fruity, youthful pomp, to around twice that for cuvées that are destined for longer age-ing. Either way, he tastes his wines at least once a day during the course of the ferments to ensure that he doesn't push the extractions so hard that the wines become bitter. He's not a great fan of the combination of oak and Gamay, so the wines – even his Côte du Py – are all aged in concrete tanks.

His Beaujolais Lantignié is a great introduction to the range, a lovely pure-fruited wine with supple tannins and far more concentration than you might expect at its very affordable price point. Burgaud is insistent, however, that you should judge a producer on the quality of their entry-level wine, saying he devotes as much love and attention to this bottling as he does to his top Morgons. He makes four individual bottlings from this *cru*, of which Les Charmes is probably the most approachable in its youth thanks to its fine tannins, silky texture and attractive, elderberry-scented fruit. Les Grands Cras comes from a clay-rich parcel located in the southern part of the *cru*. There's a plumpness and weight to the wine, with ripe plum and chocolate fruit draped over plush tannins. Corcelette comes from a parcel planted on shallow granitic soils, and it shows all the linear precision typical of this terroir, along with slightly crunchy, fine tannins and tea-leaf and aniseed-tinged raspberry fruits. The Côte du Py, as you might expect, is a wild, dark-fruited, brooding beast of a wine that takes its time to open up in the glass. It evolves really well in bottle, developing a character that's more reminiscent of a fine Barbaresco than the Pinots to which mature Gamay is frequently compared.

Domaine Chamonard

Instagram @domainechamonard

Beaujolais's famous Gang of Four (see p. 11) has always, on closer in-spection, had higher membership numbers than the name might sug-gest, and Jean-Claude Chanudet has a better claim than many to have been a founding member of the group. Chanudet and Marcel Lapierre, the fulcrum around which the gang largely turned, had been best friends since their schooldays, and their relationship remained strong over the years. In many ways, the Chanudet family might even have been said to pre-empt the central tenets the Gang held dear. Chanudet's father had long been of the belief that chemical treatments or supplements should not be used in the vineyard and that winemaking was a hands-on process that required a flexible approach rather than a recipe.

Jeanne Chanudet, Jean-Claude's daughter, is the latest to take over the reins at the family domaine, and her philosophy is largely in line with that of her father and her grandfather before him. Jeanne, who trained as a vet, says that the only way in which her approach is different to that of the previous generations is that winemaking gives her an opportunity to indulge her fascination with microbiology, and she therefore tends to conduct more tests in-house than they would. She still takes advice from her father when necessary, and both Jean-Claude Chanudet (known locally as '*le chat*', the cat) and Jeanne's grandfather lend their expertise to the final blending sessions prior to bottling each year.

Otherwise, the house style is to put in the hard work in the vineyard and then stand back and let the wines make themselves, with the minimum amount of intervention possible. Jeanne makes it sound so easy when she talks about gently stacking grapes into the fermentation tanks – she likes them as cool as possible beforehand so that the fermentations start slowly, allowing plenty of time for the aromatic profile of the wine to develop. Carbon dioxide is piped into the top of the tank to form a protective blanket, but as the vineyards aren't treated, Jeanne says it doesn't take long before fermentation kicks off, and the juices from the crushed grapes at the bottom of the tank start to ferment, releasing enough carbon dioxide to protect the tank through to the end of the first stage of fermentation, which usually takes two or three weeks. What Jeanne almost forgets to mention is the need for constant vigilance on behalf of the winemaker to ensure that these fermentations remain clean. This style of winemaking – especially when it proceeds at a measured pace – runs the risk of a wide range of microbial life developing in the tank. Jeanne checks her tanks two or three times a day, smelling, tasting, listening, using all her senses to ensure that the fermentations are proceeding smoothly. If she has any doubts, she samples the wines or the cap, runs analyses, views slides under a microscope, and takes whatever measures she deems necessary to protect the purity of the juice.

It's a process that fascinates her, and she says that looking down the barrel of her microscope at a snapshot of her fermentations makes her realize that every cuvée is its own different microbiological universe. Her goal, as far as possible, is to allow each of these universes its full range of expression – to do otherwise would be to impose a false identity on the wine. Jeanne makes three different bottlings, and they really do all have their own unique character. The Fleurie is focused, with delicate, perfumed red fruit and gently raspy tannins, while the Morgon has more concentration and weight, with deeper, darker, spicier fruit and a rasp of tannin. She's also introduced a new cuvée to the range, Le Droit de Véto (a pun that plays on the idea of the right to veto – a reference to her insistence that she be allowed to make this cuvée against her father's protests – and her training as a vet). This is another Fleurie, but the vineyard is located right up against the Morgon boundary of that *cru*. It's richer in style than the family's standard Fleurie, with a fuller body and rounder tannins, as well as more fruit concentration. Oh, and the label further reinforces the pun, with a cartoon of a vet wearing a stethoscope whose listening tube leads to a glass of wine held by a cartoon cat. Clearly, *le chat* has come round to the idea …

Domaine Georges Descombes

Although Georges Descombes is not a member of Beaujolais's famous Gang of Four, in the eyes of many, he's their plus one. In other words, he's almost as closely associated with the movement to reinvigorate the region's wines as any member of the original group. Descombes grew up in a family with holdings in the vineyards of Morgon, but was working in a wine bottling plant at the time he first got to know Marcel Lapierre. The two men became firm friends, and it wasn't long before Descombes set up on his own, farming a small plot of vines on a long lease.

Like many of the original wild men of Beaujolais, Descombes had vineyards that were organically certified for a while, but he ended up turning his back on the rigours of certification. There was one particular parcel of vines on a steep slope in Brouilly that was hard to farm according to the strict regulations imposed by the certifying body, and producers were either fully certified – for all their vineyards – or they weren't. Descombes's response was to walk away – 'the people who care know how I work,' he shrugs.

They know how he makes his wines, too. Descombes works along similar lines to his friends: triage in the vineyards, intracellular fermentations under a blanket of carbon dioxide. He doesn't much care for the notion of drawing off the liquid from the bottom of the tank, saying that there's usually precious little of it expressed by his thick-skinned grapes in any case. He prefers slightly more structured wines than some of his old friends, so he typically allows the musts to ferment at temperatures of up to around 25–26°C. He says that there's no recipe, every year is different and his job is to let the wine do its own thing so that it can speak for itself.

He's concerned about the challenges imposed by the recent run of warm years. 'Our grape, Gamay, isn't one that makes good wine at 15% abv,' he says, 'but the challenge is that you need to let the grapes develop their full phenolic ripeness before you pick. The trouble is that if you do, the sugar levels can spiral upwards.'

On the evidence of a recent tasting, Descombes doesn't need to worry about a lack of freshness in his wines, which all show a tangy upkick of acidity on the finish. His range, sourced from 15 hectares of vineyards and some bought-in grapes, comprises around a dozen or so cuvées, although the total varies from year to year. Most *crus* have a 'standard' cuvée, aged in tank, and a *vieilles vignes* cuvée that matures in older oak barrels. The contrast between the standard Morgon and the *vieilles vignes* is illustrative, with the former showing some of Morgon's weight and breadth, but in the context of Morgon the fruit is relatively delicate and bright, lacking some of the brooding quality often found in the *cru*. The *vieilles vignes*, however, is dense and rich, and will take some time to unpack fully to reveal its layered, complex palate; this is the typical difference between Descombes's standard cuvées and those made from older vines.

Kewin Descombes

Kewin Descombes, like his father before him (see Georges Descombes, above), isn't afraid to take the path less travelled. He farms organically, but doesn't believe in seeking certification, which he sees as being largely a box-ticking enterprise, and he ferments his wines at temperatures normally associated with the production of white wines rather than reds. He's not aggressive in the way he expresses his sometimes controversial outlook, but carries himself with the confidence of a man who doesn't much care whether others share his opinions or not.

Although Descombes learned how to tend vines and make wine at his father's side, he also did some formal studies at the Lycée Viticole in Belleville, less than 10 kilometres from home, but quickly returned to his home turf in the hinterlands of the Morgon appellation. He set up shop a few hundred metres away from his father in 2013 and began creating wines in his own image (he's at pains to say that although he shares much of the same viticultural philosophy as his father, his wine-making style is different).

The first parcel he bottled under his own name came from some old vines in the Morgon *climat* of Corcelette. The vines had been pretty much abandoned by a neighbour and, in Descombes's words, 'the parcel was in a right old state'. It took a couple of years of rigorous pruning for the sprawling plants to be restored to a manageable state, and a further three years of hard work for the soil to begin to come back to life (having previously been depleted by years of chemical sprays).

In terms of winemaking, Descombes favours a light-handed approach. Grapes are chilled down to 8–10°C overnight after harvest, which allows for the semi-carbonic fermentations to start gently. He never really allows the yeasts (indigenous, of course) to pick up too much pace as he aims to cap temperatures at around 16–18°C, levels more closely associated with white winemaking than red. The aim is to prolong the fermentations for as long as possible, with top cuvées remaining in tank for up to a month. Some are then aged in old oak barrels for a further few months before bottling (no fining or filtering, and only homeopathic doses of sulphur at the last possible minute). The final result is wines with a distinctive freshness and bright fruit, with fine tannins.

Descombes makes a couple of white wines, a savoury, honeyed Beaujolais Blanc and a surprisingly delicate orange wine, with just a hint of grippy tannins on the finish. He considers his Beaujolais, Kéké (his childhood nickname), to be his hallmark wine in many ways, and although it's not complex, it's deliciously gluggable, with a zesty sour cherry character. There's a slightly sterner Beaujolais Villages in the range and a tightly wound Moulin-à-Vent, but the heart of Descombes's production lies in Morgon, with a blended parcel from 'younger' vines (actually, at 50–60 years old, these vines are veterans) and a densely fruited Morgon Vieilles Vignes, made from a parcel of 85-year-old vines in Corcelette. This last wine is not marketed until the fine but structured tannins have been given a bit of time to integrate, leaving an overall impression of a layered, complex wine that's accessible in its youth, but should age well for a decade or more.

Louis-Claude Desvignes

louis-claude-desvignes.com

Taking up the reins of a domaine as the latest scion of a highly regarded family of wine producers is not always the easy ride it might seem. Sure, the gig often comes with holdings in some of the better vineyards of the region and a cast-iron introduction to some of the world's top importers, but the burden of expectations can weigh heavy on young shoulders, and any attempt to make changes, however slight, comes with a virtual guarantee of opprobrium.

Nevertheless, Louis-Benoit Desvignes wears the family mantle well. 'I grew up with someone who loved what he was doing,' he says, speaking of his father, 'and he passed that love on to me.' The Desvignes family have been making wine in Morgon for generations, and Louis-Benoit and his sister Claude-Emmanuelle have succeeded in adapting the family's ancient practices to the challenges imposed by the modern world and the demands of contemporary consumers. 'Take wines from Morgon, for instance,' he says. 'These have always been wines for the long-term. But we've adapted the way we used to work and we're looking for refinement and elegance as well as structure.'

The family vineyards are managed organically. More, says Desvignes, as a way of showing their customers that they're serious about their environmental commitments than out of any desire to follow the sometimes convoluted requirements of the certifying bodies. Desvignes is not wedded to convention when it comes to winemaking, either. He eschews 'pure' carbonic maceration as he believes that the manner of vinification can dominate the expression of the wine, and claims that he's still not really sure what semi-carbonic fermentation is, despite having supervised some 20 vintages since he took over the reins at the property. (Nevertheless, whole bunch fermentation, with a small amount of destemmed grapes, is at the heart of the domaine's winemaking.)

The overall aim is to optimize freshness and tension in the wines, and modern and traditional tools are co-opted in an attempt to ensure this result. The wines all show great freshness, but there's a density and structure to them as well. Even the simplest cuvée – l'Aube à Javernières, a Beaujolais – has greater depth and textural richness than is generally found. The parcel selections from Morgon all have distinctive characters. Javernières is one of my favourites – it's taut and focused in its youth, but it opens up in the glass to reveal layers of dark fruit tinged with blood oranges and summer flowers, all supported by fine, grainy tannins. Les Impénitents comes from the same terroir, but is made from a parcel of vines planted over a century ago; it shows great concentration and depth, while the Montpelain, based on a massal selection of 1931, has a firmness of tannin and a dark savouriness reminiscent of Nebbiolo.

Thibault Ducroux

www.thibault-ducroux.com

Although this property is named after the winemaker Thibault Ducroux, in reality the domaine is a two-hander, in which Thibault's brother, Dmitri, handles all aspects of sales and marketing. The brothers are members of the fourth generation of the Ducroux family to make wines in Morgon – their father still makes wine under his own label in the same winery.

Dmitri learned his trade working for a big négociant, travelling the world and selling wines, and refined his knowledge by taking a course at the UK's Plumpton College. Thibault stayed at home, and worked with Julien Sunier (a key figure in terms of training and inspiring a whole new generation of winemakers in the region, especially those with an interest in organic viticulture and minimal intervention winemaking, see p. 128). Together, the *frères* Ducroux set up shop in 2019, and now work 4 hectares of vines in the Charmes and Corcelette *climats* of Morgon, 3 hectares on the broad plains of Beaujolais and a further 0.78 hectares in Fleurie. Most of these parcels belong to a neighbour, who leased the plots to the brothers on a long-term basis. Thibault says that they've been lucky enough to end up with vines that are planted at high altitudes in the *crus*, which allows them to retain freshness in the finished wines, even in the recent run of very warm vintages.

Their approach to both viticulture and winemaking can be roughly summarized as being as hands off as possible in terms of the use of additives and chemicals. They use no treatments in the vineyard, other than sulphur and copper, when necessary, to help combat fungal diseases, and sulphur isn't used until bottling, when a minimal dose is used to ensure the wines remain fault-free. The brothers say that their father, who grew up in an era when sprays and treatments were the norm, is frankly horrified by their approach, and even though father and sons vinify in the same cellar, there's a clear delineation between Ducroux senior's approach (temperature-controlled stainless steel tanks and cultured yeasts) and the tack followed by the younger generation (cement tanks whose porosity allows for gentle oxygen exchange and indigenous yeasts, supported by a *pied de cuve*).

All the wines show a great purity of style, from the joyfully juicy *En Roue Libre* Beaujolais to the two Morgons (one a blend from the two vineyards, the other derived solely from Corcelette fruit) and the linear, perfumed Fleurie. The Corcelette cuvée, which is aged in second-hand barrels (a mix of 228-litre Burgundian barrels and larger barrels sourced from the Rhône) is the most densely structured wine of the line-up, and its firm but fine tannins and great depth of fruit promise great longevity to come.

Jean Foillard and Alex Foillard

Although the wines made by Jean Foillard (a member of the Gang of Four, see p. 11) and those made by Alex Foillard have their own separate identities, with different labels and different vineyard origins, the truth is that father Jean and son Alex now work closely together on Jean Foillard's own range and the two labels might, effectively, be considered to belong to the same producer. Alex's chief responsibilities at his father's property lie in a focus on viticulture, but he assists Jean in the cellar too. Having said that, all wines sold under the Alex Foillard brand are Alex's sole responsibility.

Jean's focus is – as it has always been – on the vineyards of Morgon, while Alex's range includes a Beaujolais Villages, a Brouilly and a Côte de Brouilly. Ultimately, however, the philosophy that guides both properties is a unified one that focuses on environmental sustainability (Jean's vineyards are certified organic, while those of Alex are not). The health of the soil is considered vital to the creation of quality wines, so a good deal of effort in all parcels is directed towards ensuring that the earth into which the vines plunge their roots is vibrant with microbiological life. Hard physical labour is supplemented by the usual range of non-interventionist treatments, but rather unusually Alex espouses the use of orange rind as protection against downy mildew.

Winemaking for both follows a semi-carbonic pathway, and scrupulous attention is paid to daily tastings of the juices at the bottom of the tank and inspection of the cap, with regular samples sent off to the lab for chemical analyses and microscopy. The Foillards believe firmly in chilling the grapes on reception, and the pressed juice is also cold settled in former milk tanks at 12°C prior to the start of fermentation – in both cases, the aim is to slow the activity of the yeasts and enzymes responsible for fermentation in order to retain as much fresh fruit character as possible.

The finished wines, whether bottled under Alex's label or Jean's, show real finesse and a truly vivid fruit character, as well as a characteristic weight. Rather unusually, Alex's Brouilly comes from grapes grown on the hard blue granite most typical of the Côte de Brouilly, while the Côte de Brouilly is made from a vineyard based on the pink granites most frequently seen in Brouilly. This role reversal results in a very floral, perfumed style of Côte de Brouilly and a more restrained, darker-fruited Brouilly, with fine, raspy tannins and a bit more concentration on the finish. Jean's hallmark cuvée is the Morgon Côte du Py, which takes its time to unfurl its dense, dark-fruited palate from the taut, stony tannins which enclose it in its youth. In exceptional years, the Foillards also produce the 3.14 cuvée (a play on the homophonic relationship between the mathematical term 'pi' and the Côte du Py). This full-bodied, oak-aged wine is not only rare, but also the closest Beaujolais gets to an expensive, prestige cuvée (although it still costs far less than many Burgundian *premiers crus*).

Domaine Mee Godard

meegodard.com

There still aren't all that many women making wine in Beaujolais, and fewer still are women of Asian origin. Mee Godard breaks all kinds of moulds. Born in South Korea but adopted by a French family at an early age, Godard grew up far away from daily life in the vineyards. Nevertheless, when she went to Oregon to study an undergraduate degree in biochemistry, she inflected it with a minor in wine science. She continued her academic career with a Masters, where her research led her to investigate polyphenols and plant physiology, after which she returned to France, where she sat for the Diplome National d'Oenologue in Montpellier, a winemaking qualification.

After gathering her academic laurels, Godard gained some real-life experience in wineries in Burgundy and Champagne, but her main gig was selling oenological products. Somewhere along the line, she fell in love with the wines of Beaujolais, so she was thrilled to be able to buy around 5 hectares of vines in Morgon towards the end of 2012. These days Godard has just over 8 hectares in production, still based around her original purchases in the Morgon *climats* of Corcelette, Grand Cras and the Côte du Py, and supplemented by some Moulin-à-Vent and Beaujolais Blanc.

Initially her approach to farming was to work along environmentally sustainable lines, but the more involved she became, the more rigorous her viticultural practices became too. Now the vineyards are either fully certified as organic or in conversion, and she inflects her work with biodynamics too.

Her approach to winemaking is not dogmatic. Depending on the character of the vintage and of the parcel, she may use a small proportion of de-stemmed grapes. Mostly, though, her grapes undergo a whole-bunch semi-carbonic maceration in concrete tanks for some two to three weeks. She's not too concerned if temperatures rise into the high twenties Celsius, rather than insisting on cool fermentations to drive towards brighter fruit and less structure.

There's a potency and depth to Godard's wines, although somehow she manages to combine this with an ethereal delicacy and refinement. The wines from Morgon and Moulin-à-Vent all tend to take a bit of time to unwind and reveal themselves fully, but even in their youth they hint at their potential elegance and complexity. The Moulin-à-Vent tends to be more linear and taut than the more robust Morgons, and its aromas tend towards oolong tea leaves and spring blossom. Of the Morgons, Grand Cras has darker fruit than the Corcelette, but both have the tension of a coiled spring. The Côte du Py and the Passerelle 577 both come from vineyards planted on the *cru*'s hard blue volcanic rocks, with the Passerelle coming from a specific sub-plot within the vineyards that Godard says always shows incredibly well when young, but which can also age for years. Both have grippy, stony, fine-boned tannins, although – as Godard suggests – the Passerelle shows a generosity in its youth that's largely absent from the tightly wound Côte du Py.

Domaine Lapierre

www.marcel-lapierre.com

It's no exaggeration to say that, for many wine lovers, Domaine Lapierre *is* Beaujolais. Marcel Lapierre, founder member of the Gang of Four (see p. 11), put his stamp on what it was to be an artisanal winemaker in Beaujolais in an indelible manner, becoming inextricably linked with organic viticulture, the use of indigenous yeasts and minimal additions of sulphites. His pace-setting work in the 1980s and 1990s helped to redefine the region, both for wine lovers and for the generations of winemakers who were to follow in his footsteps.

A tough act to follow, in other words. And yet Marcel's children, Mathieu and Camille, have done a pretty good job of not only being seen as worthy successors to their father, but also becoming a source of inspiration to other young winemakers in Beaujolais. By the time Marcel died in 2010, Mathieu – who had trained as a chef – had already spent some six years working at his father's side. Mathieu was joined in the family business in 2013 by Camille. The two work together, carrying on the family traditions, albeit with a light touch and a sense of independence that one feels sure would have pleased their father. The Lapierres of the current generation aren't didactic about their approach to viticulture. 'Conventional agriculture leaves you with a smaller population of yeasts and therefore a less healthy fermentation,' says Mathieu, adding that 'The best results aren't necessarily from organic grapes, however. In difficult years [like 2024], organic isn't always useful due to the reaction between copper and the soils.' Nevertheless, the domaine's vineyards are certified organic (and have been for more than 20 years).

Mathieu's discourse – and the reference points he checks along the way – ranges widely, segueing effortlessly from the pros and cons of horse-drawn ploughing to the eighteenth-century *piqueurs-buveurs* of Lyon, who took care of the *élevage* of the wines that were shipped, still fermenting in barrels, southwards from Beaujolais and the importance of the canal system built by Napoleon III, to the distribution of the *crus* of the Victorian era. From there he moves on to an analysis of the importance of microscopy in natural winemaking and the need to manage the timing of various key moments during the course of the fermentation precisely in order to achieve the desired outcome. All this within the space of a brief quarter of an hour, an insight into the mercurial mindset that is clearly a Lapierre family trait.

The Raisins Gaulois, a Vin de France, is made from the domaine's youngest vines (which average out at 15 years old, so would be considered middle-aged almost anywhere else in France). Depending on the year, it might also contain declassified grapes that had originally been destined for other cuvées. It's incredibly pale in colour, and bright and refreshing in character, with a little hint of green tea bitterness on the finish helping to bring everything into focus. The Morgon – the bulk of the Lapierre production – comes in two styles. There's an unsulphited bottling, denoted by an N on the label, and a wine that receives a light dose of sulphites, whose label carries an S. In the young wines, the N cuvée is slightly brighter and fresher, with a delicate raspberry and pomegranate character, while the S is slightly more muted on the palate, with a smoky, focused finish. As the wines age, the N develops tertiary characters earlier and to a greater extent than the S, which retains its linear structure, but is far more perfumed and layered than it is in its reticent youth. The markets for S and N can vary from one year to the next, but there's a consistent preference for N from about a third of the Lapierre clientele – who have also, apparently, taken to purchasing jeroboams of the wine in a big way, while demand for magnums has fallen. The jewel in the domaine's crown may well be the Marcel Lapierre bottling, made in exceptional years from centenarian vines grown in Douby and the Côte du Py. It's a wine of great density and weight, with real focus and length.

Domaine du Petit Perou

www.petitperou.com

There's no shortage of Thévenets in Morgon, and family relationships are complex. Laurent and Hugo Thévenet are members of the fourth and fifth generations to work on the family's domaine, which is named after the nearby *lieu-dit* of Perou and which is situated right next door to Jean-Paul and Charly's property (yes, they are related, but at a generational remove).

The number of vineyards owned by this branch of the family has ranged widely over the years. Jean Thévenet started the domaine in 1902 with 8.5 hectares, which rose to 12 hectares under the management of Jean's son Henri. The next generation was led by Roger, who only inherited 3.5 hectares of vineyards (the remainder was parcelled out among his siblings), but his success meant that he was able to pass on 10 hectares to his son, Laurent. By the time Covid hit in 2020, Laurent's son Hugo had joined the family business, which owned 20 hectares of vineyards, spread out across various *crus* and the *villages* zone. Lockdown prompted a reappraisal, and the family now farms 14 hectares of vineyards and makes nine wines. It's a fairly typical snapshot of the fluctuations in vineyard holdings of a successful domaine in Beaujolais over the course of a number of generations.

There are two whites, one of which is bottled as a Beaujolais, the other as a Bourgogne Blanc, a rosé and an edgy little Beaujolais, Tu M'Tiens au Jus (which can be roughly translated as 'keep me posted'), which is pleasantly stemmy, crunchy and very zesty. There are four *cru* bottlings, including one from Brouilly's Pisse Vieille, a generous, rounded wine whose palate is packed with strawberry fruit and spice, with a refreshing twist of Campari-like bitterness on the finish.

The remaining three *cru* bottlings all come from Morgon. There's Les Dryades, a blend of grapes grown in nine different parcels spread across the *cru*. It's surprisingly fine and fresh for a wine made in this often weighty *cru*, with both red and black berry fruits and tea-leaf character. The vines that go into the Morgon Vieilles Vignes were planted by Hugo's grandfather and have now reached a truly venerable age of 90–110 years. It's a big, bold wine with the richness and density that is so typical of the old vine bottlings made in the region, although it doesn't lack freshness, even in warm vintages. The Morgon Côte du Py is also made from a parcel of ancient vines. Aged in 500-litre oak barrels, this is a tightly wound wine that needs time in bottle to open up and show at its best.

The Thévenets continue to experiment, and they now bottle a Syrah, the Désir, as an IGP Comtés Rhodaniens. The vines were planted in 2012 and the Thévenets have realized that they need to limit the yields afforded by this generous variety in order to get it to show at its best, but current bottlings are nicely balanced, showing Syrah's typically peppery cool-climate character, as well as some lively red fruit. Not content to rest there, Hugo has a new Morgon in the pipeline. The wine will be aged in amphorae, and he plans for this to be a structured, firm cuvée for long-term cellaring.

Anthony Thévenet

It is, perhaps, entirely understandable, given that one of his grandparents died as a result of exposure to the kinds of chemicals that were once routinely sprayed on vineyards, that Anthony Thévenet has chosen to aim for organic certification and a total absence of chemicals (other than sulphur and copper) in his own. The irony is that the very same vineyards that he farms as naturally as possible are those his grandfather once owned.

Thévenet (no relation of the better-known Charly and Jean Paul) says that it took almost five years of patient work on the land, and much soil turning and use of mulches, for these two hectares of Morgon vineyards to show signs of life, for the worms to return to the soil and for the inter-row grasses to grow anew. He took over the land in 2013, while he was still working with Jean Foillard, and in 2014 he acquired a further hectare of vines in Corcelette and another parcel on the Côte du Py. These were followed by vines in Chénas, Beaujolais Villages and, most recently, Moulin-à-Vent.

Work in both the vineyard and the cellar is conducted, as far as possible, in harmony with the lunar phases, and – like many of the more naturally inclined producers in the region – Thévenet only doses his wines with a light sulphiting around the time of bottling. Fermentation is conducted under a blanket of carbon dioxide, and any juice expressed from the grapes is collected from the bottom of the tank and poured gently over the cap on a regular basis during fermentation. This carbonic maceration phase takes between 5 and 20 days, depending on the cuvée (more ageworthy cuvées are allowed a greater degree of extraction), and the temperature isn't permitted to spiral above 25°C, in order to preserve the fruit.

Thévenet's wines are more dark-fruited and robust than many, and the tannins of some of his wines are perhaps a little rustic. The Beaujolais Villages is gluggable and fresh; just the kind of thing you might want to drink, lightly chilled, at a summer barbecue. Of the *cru*-based wines, the standouts are the Morgon Centenaire, made (as the name suggests) from 100-year-old vines, and the Chénas. The Morgon, despite the sheer intensity of fruit and firmness of tannin, shows enviable freshness, while the Chénas is in an altogether more linear and taut style, with a seam of lively acidity.

Jean-Paul et Charly Thévenet

It's not easy to find the way into the Thévenets's winery – the GPS directions lead you to a wall with a blank, closed door – but once you slip round the back, the welcome is warm, and the sign over the cellar proudly proclaims 'Jean Paul & Charly Thévenet Winery, Gang of Four Member'. Jean-Paul (Thévenet senior) is, of course, a member of the group that changed the face of Beaujolais. Perhaps, instead of referring to them as the Gang of Four, with all those connotations of the cabal that sought to rule China after Mao's death, they should be referred to as the Beaujolais Beatles.

Although Charly officially took the reins at the domaine a few years ago, Jean-Paul likes to keep his hand in, and on the day I visited he was shinning up and down ladders to draw off samples from the concrete tanks for tasting. While these small pours were largely for my benefit, regular sampling and supervision is key to the style of natural winemaking Jean-Paul helped to usher into the region back in the seventies and eighties. The Thévenet approach to both viticulture and winemaking is that you should allow the vines (and the wines) plenty of room to do their own thing, but you've also got to monitor them closely and be ready to intervene, where necessary, if things look as if they might go astray.

This regime has stood the Thévenets in good stead as they farm their vineyards – Thévenet *père*'s original Morgon vineyards have been supplemented by some holdings in Régnié since 2007, bringing the grand total up to around 7 hectares of vines. These are farmed more or less organically, with little inflection points where biodynamics are brought to bear, but certification is not in the Thévenet game plan. The hands-off approach in the winery results in the creation of wines that are notable for their freshness and brightness. Rather surprisingly, it's the Morgon Vieilles Vignes – which combines the concentration of old vines with a terroir that usually lends weight and power – that appears to be the most delicate of the wines, almost Pinot-like in its ethereal grace. The Régnié Grain et Granite is bold and rich, with rounded tannins and plenty of spice, while the lighter Régnié, En Voiture Simone, shows the focus and linearity so typical of the wines grown on granite sands.

13
RÉGNIÉ

Year in which *cru* status was awarded: 1988
Total vineyard area: 380 hectares
Altitude: 250–500 metres
Average altitude: 350 metres
Notable *lieux-dits*: Montmerand, La Haute Ronze, Les Braves, Les Chastys, Thulon, Vallières, Oeillat

The twin steeples of the church in the village of Régnié-Durette are as inextricably linked to the built landscape of Beaujolais as is the windmill of Moulin-à-Vent or Fleurie's Chapel of the Madonna. The village is located in the wedge-shaped, gently sloping southern part of the *cru*. If you look northwards, though, you'll see steeper slopes, crowned with forests, in the background.

Régnié is the most recent appellation in Beaujolais to graduate from named village (one of the many villages in the Beaujolais Villages zone) to official *cru*. This doesn't happen with any great frequency – in fact, since the initial flurry of *cru* creation in the 1930s, Régnié is the only village, so far, to have broken through the glass ceiling (although winemakers in Lantignié and Blacé have high hopes that it will not be the last, see p. 195). In order to mount a case for its promotion, Régnié would have had to argue, persuasively and forcefully, that its terroirs were already recognized as the source of wines of high quality. And yet, since its apotheosis, the *cru* has struggled to make good on its early promise, and much of its annual production is sold off in bulk and declassified to *village* status.

The twin towers of Régnié-Durette's church are instantly recognizable
(photo courtesy of Fabrice Ferrer/Beaujolais Wines)

However, there's much to admire about Régnié's terroir. Despite the fact that, on average, Régnié is not one of the most sloping *crus* in Beaujolais, there are a number of scarped granitic hillsides here, with a range of altitudes and exposures. Where granite doesn't dominate, you'll find soils derived from sandstones, schists and, particularly in the south, richer alluvial deposits and piedmont formations. All of this allows for a range of fruit expression and structure in the wines made here, although most Régniés are notable for their plush, juicy character rather than their firmness of structure.

There is one other thing that's worth mentioning in the context of Régnié and its capacity to make high-quality wines. The relative afford-ability of its vineyards seems to have attracted an increasing number of newcomers in recent years, many of whom have brought a new spirit of dynamic optimism to bear on their winemaking. It may not be all that long before Régnié becomes as famous for the quality of its wines as it is for its twin-steepled church.

Producers

Domaine les Capréoles

capreoles.com

After years spent working as an agronomist for Gérard Bertrand, a major producer based in the Languedoc, Cédric Lecareux could have

stayed put when he decided to make his own wine. He quickly elimi-
nated the region from his search, however, despite his familiarity with it.
His interest in climate science led him to believe that the region might
not be a good long-term bet. He was leaning towards Beaujolais – his
wife is from the region, he had friends there and he had a soft spot for
Gamay – but it was by pure chance that the ideal property came up in
Régnié soon after he started looking.

The house, its surrounding vineyards and the winery that went with
them was sold to him by a family who'd lived there for four centuries.
The property's viticultural fortunes had waxed and waned over the years
– at one point there were around 30 hectares of vines linked to it, but
by the time Lecareux took possession, there were only three.

Ten years later, in 2024, the domaine farms 8 hectares of vines, of
which 5 are located in Régnié and most of the rest in Lantignié, one of
the top communes in the Beaujolais Villages appellation (he also makes
a Morgon cuvée). The initial idea was to get to a total of 10 hectares,
but, says the softly spoken Lecareux, he'd rather spend his energies ensuring that the 8 hectares he owns perform at their best. One of his key
projects, on taking over the property, was to transition the vineyards
from conventional viticulture, with its reliance on chemical sprays, to
organic. It took a couple of years to bring the Régnié vineyards back to
life, but the more badly damaged Lantignié vineyards took five years to
begin to thrive. The vineyards have been certified organic since 2018
and Lecareux has now moved beyond simple organics and has been
awarded full biodynamic certification by Biodyvin.

At the start, says Lecareux, he vinified his Gamay in the same way
he'd learned when working in the Languedoc, allowing temperatures to
climb to 26°C for his semi-carbonic fermentations. But he found that
these temperatures meant that the alcohol levels climbed quickly, leading to the extraction of bitter notes from the stems. He experimented by
removing the juice from the bottom of the tanks for a day or two and
then using the liquid to top up the tanks, but that didn't give him the
results he was looking for. Now he seeks to keep temperatures as low as
possible, while using a *pied de cuve* to help kick-start the fermentation.
He tastes constantly, and as soon as he sees alcohol levels start to rise –
which usually takes two to four days, depending on the vintage – he re-
moves the juice and allows it to ferment in a second tank, ensuring that
the first tank continues its largely intracellular fermentation. The two
tanks are only blended together after the first tank has been pressed off.

Lecareux believes that Beaujolais producers are currently experiencing a golden age, one in which growers no longer need to struggle to ensure adequate levels of ripeness in their grapes (as they did in the past). 'But,' he warns, 'within ten years or so we will have to deal with climates similar to those in Valence, 150 kilometres further south, where Gamay is routinely harvested at 15–16% abv. In the end, Beaujolais will no longer be able to continue as a region dedicated to Gamay – we'll need to have other grapes here.'

In the meantime, there's little doubt that Lecareux's wines will continue to impress. The entry-level Régnié cuvée, the Chamodère, is a truly attractive easy-drinking wine for youthful consumption. His Sous la Croix (another Régnié) is made from grapes grown in very poor, shallow granitic soils. Lecareux says that this parcel of old vines (averaging around 50 years) always shows the same silkiness of tannins, regardless of the vintage. L'Impermanence, his Morgon, is dense and rich, but has an almost Italianate sour cherry character and fine, grippy tannins.

Domaine Raphaël Chopin

Raphaël Chopin farms eight hectares of vineyards in total, of which half are in Régnié, with a further 3 hectares in Lantignié, and another hectare in Morgon. With several generations of growers in his family background – his mother's family were making wines in Beaujolais back in the late eighteenth century – Chopin's career was never really in doubt. After the usual academic studies – viticulture, oenology, business studies, albeit in the southern region of the Ardèche rather than the more usual Beaune or Macon – Chopin headed off to Forester Estate in Western Australia for some hands-on experience overseas. What he brought back home with him was a greater appreciation of the influence of temperature control – in particular the use of cool temperatures – on the flavour and texture of wines.

He uses these insights every year when making both red and white wines at the domaine he launched in 2009. Unlike many producers, he kicks off his fermentations at the high end of his temperatures scale (up to 20°C for the whites, up to around 25° for reds), then gradually chills them down over time. The cool temperatures are a source of stress for the yeasts, and as a result they boost their production of glycerol, improving the texture and weight on the mid-palate of the finished wines. Most reds are fermented semi-carbonically, although one cuvée – the Gaia – is produced using a 'dry' fully carbonic maceration. Chopin uses a specifically designed spherical tank of moderate size to conduct this intra-cellular fermentation as the shape of the vessel means that bunches are less likely to get crushed by the weight of the other grapes, thus remaining intact.

Tannin extraction is hardly vigorous, with a couple of minutes a day on the semi-carbonic ferments just to ensure that the cap remains wet, and a bit more *remontage* during the alcoholic fermentation phase to help keep the fermentations bubbling along vigorously and to lend structure to the wines. Mostly the wines are aged in cement tanks, although the two top bottlings spend time in large old oak barrels which hold around 500–600 hectolitres, a size he believes is far better suited to his wines than the smaller barrels he used in the past.

His white wine, Theia, named after one of the Titans of Greek mythology, is bright and fresh thanks to Chopin's practice of blocking malo-lactic conversion as he believes Chardonnay in Beaujolais tends towards too much ripeness to lose any of its innate acidity. His reds, on the other hand, tend towards richness and weight, partly due to the terroirs with which he works, but also due to his focus on texture and structure. La Savoye is a smoky, spicy, cherry-scented Beaujolais Villages from Lantignié. Les Braves comes from a parcel planted on Régnié's pink granites, which gives the wine its pretty, perfumed character. The *lieu-dit* of La Ronze in Régnié is the source of the majority of Chopin's wines, and it lends all of them its characteristic heft. The simplest of these bottlings is La Ronze, a fleshy, generous wine with good levels of acidity and a ferrous, almost bloody note on the finish. Archambault, his old-vines cuvée, is aged in *demi-muids* and is a complex, dense wine with a rounded mid-palate and plush tannins. The same parcel of 80- to 90-year-old vines is also used to make Gaia. Here, carbonic maceration gives the wine heady aromas of wild strawberry, iris and dried herbs. The tannins are supple and fine, with a bit of gentle grip on the finish, which serves to give the wine some focus.

Domaine de Colette

domainedecolette.com

There are a lot of hands-on grape growers in Beaujolais who talk about their respect for nature and the way they hark back to traditional methods of working, but there are still very few who use horses to work their soil rather than tractors. At Domaine de Colette, though, a fine palomino horse may be the first friendly face to greet visitors, closely followed by its companion, a donkey. Working in harmony with the environment is important for Pierre-Alexandre Gauthier, who took over the property from his parents after returning from working at a contract winery in New Zealand. Gauthier says he didn't learn much in terms of winemaking technique while he was out there, but the sheer volume of liquid that he was handling on a day-to-day basis made him very aware of the importance of being organized in terms of workflow.

Since his return, he's moving towards the conversion of the 18 hectares of vineyards he manages to organic certification. Of these, most are in Régnié and the Beaujolais Villages zone, although there's a little bit of Moulin-à-Vent and slightly less Fleurie in the portfolio. There's also a scant hectare of Chardonnay, bottled as Beaujolais Villages Blanc, made from grapes grown on the clay soils of Emeringes, on the northern fringes of the Beaujolais zone.

Gauthier points out that most of his vineyards lie at altitude. Back in the day, he says, it may well have been tricky to make wines of depth and concentration from these vines, but now that climate change has become a big issue, he welcomes the freshness inherent in his terroirs. There's no recipe to his winemaking – Gauthier prefers to adapt his techniques according to the constraints of the vintage. Generally speaking, though, the foundation of his style is semi-carbonic maceration, in order to make the fruit-driven wines he loves, but he might de-stem up to around 50 per cent of a cuvée for wines that are destined for longer ageing, and *pigeage* is often used towards the end of fermentation to ensure that there's enough rounded tannin to lend the wines sufficient structure.

The white is zesty and concentrated, full of character and tangy fruit. There are a couple of Beaujolais Villages made from Gamay, of which the pick of the bunch is the very pretty Lantignié, with its notes of summer flowers and oolong tea. There are four Régniés, including a Coteaux de Vallière that is so sinewy, savoury and spicy that it's quite reminiscent of a Syrah from the Northern Rhône, and the Clos des Buyats, made from grapes grown on the richer alluvial soils of the *cru*. The latter is structured and rich, but retains freshness and balance, even in warm years. Definitely one for the long haul.

Domaine Ducroux/Christian et Thibault Ducroux

As noted in the Preface to this book, in some cases working out which chapter a producer belongs in is pretty easy. But when I considered where to place this profile of Christian Ducroux (now aided in both the vineyards and the winery by his son Thibault), the question arose: how on earth could I categorize a producer whose vineyards are split more or less equally between the *villages* zone and that of the *cru* of Régnié, but who, furthermore, eschews any notion of using the standard classification system adhered to by most producers in the region and instead opts to bottle his wines as Vins de France? (The answer is that any chapter I might choose for this entry is, of necessity, an arbitrary selection.)

There is little doubt that Christian Ducroux zigs where others zag. When I visited in early May it was easy to see which of the nearby vineyards were being farmed conventionally, using herbicides. Their vines, whether neatly tended or not, were planted in bare soils, the green of the leaves starkly contrasting with the pink- or yellow-tinged sands. Organic producers tend to encourage grasses to grow between the rows and under the vines, but normally these hug the earth, rarely rising above a few centimetres in height, and their vines are easy to pick out, even though it's green on green. Ducroux's vineyards are a thing apart: wild, untamed gardens in which grasses and wildflowers grow rampantly, in some cases completely obscuring the vines from view. Fruit trees are dotted around the vineyard, occupying valuable agricultural real estate, a complete contrast to the monoculture that largely dominates the landscape.

Ducroux has farmed biodynamically for a while, but in the last ten years or so he's adopted a radically different style of vineyard management from that of even his most ardently organic neighbours and now practises permaculture. He changed his approach as a result of a combination of exposure to new ideas at seminars and salons, and his participation a decade ago in a trial of new viticultural techniques. In view of the results of the experiment, which resurrected a vineyard he'd written off as a bad lot, Ducroux now wants to encourage biodiversity at all levels in his vineyards, from the visible plants that share space with his vines above ground to the fungi, unicellular organisms and earthworms that live within the soil.

He says that the period when he does the least work in his vineyards is in spring, when all his neighbours are busy ploughing and spraying, but in summer, when many growers take a bit of a break, Ducroux is out in his vineyards, attending to his sprawling canopy and cutting back all those grasses. By returning the organic matter contained in the grasses to the soil, he boosts the level of nutrients available to the vines when they need them the most, and prevents them from competing for water at what is generally the driest time of the year. He does no more or less work than other growers, he says, he just does it all at a different time of year.

And, unlike most producers in the region, he doesn't bottle a blend of all his Beaujolais Villages or his Régniés, nor does he bottle parcel selections bearing the names of the *lieux-dits* he farms. Instead Ducroux blends all his juices together, and after fermentation and a brief maturation bottles the light, fruity free-run juices as a cuvée called Prologue. The juices from the first press are used to make Exspectatia, a wine whose palate is notable for its dark cherry fruit and intense violet character, while the fine tannins remain resolutely in the background, creating a framework around which the lush fruit is draped. Those tannins also add a little hint of stemmy greenness at the end, which helps refresh the palate. Patience is his *vin de rébéche*, the result of a final firmer pressing of the *marc*, and a year's ageing in old casks. Ducroux calls it Patience because it is the most structured of his wines, one which repays a bit of time in bottle in order for the slightly denser tannins to integrate into the body of the wine. In addition, Ducroux – aided by his son, Thibault, who has ostensibly taken over management of the domaine from the 2024 vintage onwards – makes a white. As one might expect, they've bypassed the obvious option – Chardonnay – and chosen instead to plant vineyards full of grapes that they've trialled, with the more successful ones incorporated into a white blend, the Cuvée Thibault. Melon and Aligoté haven't made the cut, and they're wary of using too much of their Muscat as it marks the wine so strongly with its perfume, even when used in small quantities. A small quantity of PIWI grapes like Muscaris and Souvignier Gris have been used, but the basis of the wine is a blend of Pinot Gris and Riesling, inflected by smaller amounts of mountain grapes like Savagnin (from the Jura) and Jacquère (from Savoie). The result is a white with a vibrant, focused structure, lively acidity, smoky minerality and a blend of lemon zest, pineapple, stone fruit and gentian flower flavours.

Thomas Rivier

Although Thomas Rivier's childhood was peripatetic, with many of his formative years spent in the Middle East, paths inevitably led to Régnié, where his grandparents lived. The vineyards that fringed their house were always a part of Rivier's life. Learning how to prune, or how to harvest a healthy bunch of grapes, became a fun part of family holidays.

By the time his parents took over the domaine, Rivier was working as a landscape gardener. They handed the property on to him in 2019 on a long-term lease. Rivier knew that if he wanted to make wine, this was a now-or-never proposition.

Rivier's vineyard holdings are relatively rare in the context of Beaujolais in that they consist of a single contiguous parcel of vines spread out across 5 hectares that lie below Régnié's twin bell towers. Of these, 3.5 hectares are currently planted, and many of the older vines are gradually being replaced with newer plantings that are a mix of massal and clonal selections, all with the aim of improving diversity and resistance within the Rivier vineyards. Soils here are all underpinned by hard granitic rock topped with varying depths of free-draining granitic sands.

Rivier, a member of the Vignerons du Vivant group (see p. 202), is certified organic, but his aim is to expand the parameters of his environmental credentials by increasing his land's biodiversity. He's currently planting hedging in and around his vineyards, and believes this will not only create a haven for animals, but also help to shade the vineyards and channel breezes towards hotspots at the height of summer. The roots of these hedges – and those of the trees that he's hoping to dot around the property – will also promote microbial and fungal life in the soil, and help to capture carbon.

His hard work in the vineyards is counterbalanced by a relatively non-interventionist approach in the cellars. He doesn't control temperature too much, unless the ferment starts to head towards the high twenties Celsius, as he believes the pre-fermentation chilling technique used by many growers is artificial.

Rivier only makes two cuvées, the lighter, less structured Tomix and the richer, denser Thomas Rivier. The former is intended to be the entry-level cuvée, and often feels a bit more fun than the slightly ponderous top wine, whose tannins can seem somewhat bitter in some vintages.

Antoine Sunier

antoinesunier.fr

For once, a shared surname in Beaujolais does actually signify a close family relationship. Antoine Sunier is Julien Sunier's (see p. 128) younger brother. This Sunier never really intended to follow in his brother's footsteps, but, frustrated and rather bored by his job in the telecoms industry, he decided he wanted to work outdoors, surrounded by nature. Visits to Julien's property in Beaujolais had made him realize how much he loved the area for its landscapes, its people and its wines. He enrolled at agricultural college in Burgundy and found himself studying alongside the scions of some of Beaujolais's most venerated domaines. On graduating, they all returned to the family properties, while Sunier began his search for his own vineyards in the region.

He stumbled across a parcel of vines in Régnié in 2014, at a time when the *cru* had few takers, and now he farms a total of just over 5 hectares of vines, most of which are on Régnié's most prized granitic soils, although he has a small parcel of vines on Morgon's alluvial soils.

This Sunier has proven to have a delicate touch in the winery, as well as a steady hand in the (organic) vineyard, and all the wines show great purity of fruit and bright acidity. The first of his four wines, the light, juicy Gamay Poursuite, is a Beaujolais Villages made from declassified Régnié grapes. As he says, this is a '*vin sans chichi*' – a wine without pretentions. A short maceration period, followed by a brief *élevage* in cement tanks, results in a light-bodied, totally smashable wine that begs to be lightly chilled in summer, ahead of a picnic or a barbecue. In addition, there's a trio of *cru* wines. The Morgon is rounded and rich-fruited, while a Régnié has supple tannins and bright red-berry fruit that point to gentle maceration and extraction in the cellar. The most ageworthy of the cuvées is the more structured Régnié Montmerond, made from grapes grown on shallow, poor granitic soils at one of the highest elevations in the appellation. While the tannins are fine, they exert a gentle grip that suggests a potential for long development and even greater complexity to come.

Domaine de Vernus

domainedevernus.com

Frédéric Jametton decided that, after 30 years spent working as an insurance broker, it was time to invest in his real passion, wine. In 2017 he set out to find a property he could call his own, and found an estate located slightly to the north of the village of Régnié-Durette. In 2019 he hired a consultant winemaker, Guillaume Rouget, whose day job is running the family property, Burgundy's Domaine Emmanuel Rouget, and together they set about making plans for the new domaine.

The Domaine de Vernus now owns around 12 hectares of vineyards, with bush vines that clock in at an average age of around 60 years. Although these vineyards are not farmed organically, little in the way of chemical products is used on a systematic basis, and close attention is paid to biodiversity, with the plans to plant hedges around the vineyards and trees within them already well under way. The health of the soil is also deemed to be important at Vernus, and some of its plots are ploughed by horse rather than by machine. Vinification is adapted to the requirements of both individual plots, vintage conditions and the desired outcome, with most bunches being fully or partially de-stemmed prior to fermentation in stainless steel vats and maturation in Burgundian oak barrels, the exception being the Beaujolais Villages, which is vinified using semi-carbonic maceration.

There are ten cuvées made at the Domaine de Vernus, of which five are designated 'Characterful' wines, either blends from one of four *crus* (Chiroubles, Fleurie, Régnié and Morgon) or a Beaujolais Villages, while the 'Exceptional' wines are parcel selections, two from Régnié, and one each from Morgon, Fleurie and Moulin-à-Vent. The cuvées I tasted all showed some real density of structure and concentration of fruit. The Beaujolais Villages has formidable concentration for a wine that is, effectively, the domaine's entry-level bottling. The Régnié is pretty, delicate and fresh, made in a perfumed, floral style somewhat reminiscent of a Volnay. La Cadole, the 'Exceptional' Régnié cuvée, is incredibly deeply coloured, with equally deep concentration of dark, graphite-tinged fruit on the palate. It's well balanced – so much so that you have to be paying attention to notice the hefty amount of alcohol buried beneath all that ripe fruit. The Morgon Grands Cras shows really lively acidity and notes of red berries, stone fruit and baking spice, and the long finish is framed by firm, talcum powder-fine tannins.

Domaine Philippe Viet

domainephilippeviet.fr

Philippe Viet had always been a bit of a wine buff, but after 15 years of working in the banking industry and as an IT consultant, he decided to throw in the corporate towel and follow his passion.

A tasting of Eric Janin's wines (see p. 94) led to both a lifelong friendship and a growing interest in the wines of Beaujolais. Work experience in Janin's vineyards was followed by time in both the Loire and Australia, before Viet settled to his wine studies in Beaune, and finally put down roots on the outskirts of Morgon.

Most of his vineyards lie within the *cru* of Régnié, although Viet also makes a vibrant, refreshing Beaujolais Villages wine from grapes grown in Lantignié and an elegant Fleurie.

Viet, a thoughtful man who chooses his words carefully, has given much consideration to his approach to both viticulture and winemaking. His first step on taking control of his Régnié vineyards was to start the process of converting them to organic farming. He believes passionately in the duty that growers have to take care of the environment, saying that 'If you don't take care of the land, you're not taking care of people either'.

The process of conversion hasn't always been an easy one. Viet says that although some plots are easily convertible, others have been bashed around by the use of chemicals. With great regret, he's in the process of working out how best to replace a parcel of 100-year-old vines that he's planning to grub up in the near future. He's vacillating between planting a massal selection or opting for a mixed assortment of clones. Either way, he says, the key thing is the maintenance of diversity in a vineyard, otherwise there's a greater risk of the plants succumbing to maladies. He also wants to plant at high density, believing that inter-vine competition encourages the vines to work harder and produce more concentrated fruit.

Viet's ultimate winemaking goal is balance. Judging the right moment to pick, balancing off the competing claims of rising sugar levels, falling acidities and phenolic ripeness, is a challenge, but one he relishes.

Once the grapes are safely harvested, he prefers to start his semi-carbonic fermentations at around 20°C, with daily *remontages*, and then once the wines reach about 10% abv, he introduces punch-downs to the regime. Eventually, press and free-run juices are blended and matured in a hodgepodge of vessels that range from the conventional (stainless steel tanks and a 500-litre puncheon, which is used to mature a proportion of his savoury, ferrous Fleurie) to the unexpected (two large sandstone amphorae squat in a corner of the small winery).

Of the two Régnié cuvées, the Haute-Ronze is the lighter and fresher, with fine, elegant tannins and red fruit tinged with pepper and menthol. The Mosaique is richer and riper in style, with fleshy tannins that dominate the wine in its youth, before it opens up to reveal an opulently fruited palate.

14

BROUILLY AND THE CÔTE DE BROUILLY

Year in which *cru* status was awarded: 1938

Total vineyard area: 1,180 hectares (Brouilly); 300 hectares (Côte de Brouilly)

Altitude: 195–425 metres (Brouilly); 200–485 metres (Côte de Brouilly)

Average altitude: 290 metres (Brouilly); 300 metres (Côte de Brouilly)

Notable *lieux-dits*: Combiaty, Côte de Brouilly (Brulhié), Brouilly, Godefroy, La Chaise, Reverdon

It probably seems odd that I've chosen to run two different *crus* together in one single chapter, but there's method in my madness. Most producers based in the Brouilly zone also make wines from grapes grown in the Côte de Brouilly, and vice versa. So strong are the links between the two *crus* that growers in the two zones have decided to work together under the umbrella of an organization known as Terre des Brouilly to promote the two appellations together. There are significant differences between the two *crus*, however, one being scale and the other geology.

Brouilly, the most southerly of the *crus*, is also the largest, although only by a matter of 120 hectares. It is, however, far more dispersed and geologically diverse than Morgon, the second-biggest *cru*. Brouilly is spread out across six different communes: Cercié, Charentay, Odenas, Quincié-en-Beaujolais, Saint-Etienne-la-Varenne and Saint-Lager, and surrounds the *cru* of Côte de Brouilly almost entirely.

Geologically speaking, much of the south and west of Brouilly, along with the *lieu-dit* of La (sometimes Les) Bruyère(s), which lies on the north-west boundary of the *cru*, is based on granitic soils. Many of the vineyards here are situated on hilly escarpments. The eastern part of the *cru*, and much of its north, is far more varied in terms of soil structure, with a mix of ancient alluvial soils, limestones, marls, flints and even some outcrops of diorite. The slopes here are much gentler than they are in the western part of the appellation. As a result of this geological diversity, it is very difficult to generalize about the typicity of the wines made in Brouilly, although a significant number of the wines I've tasted are fruity and approachable, if not necessarily built for the long haul.

Rising above it all, and visible for miles around, is Mont Brouilly, the rounded nub that marks the remains of an extinct volcano that was active around 380 million years ago, and the seat of the Côte de Brouilly appellation. The western flanks of the hill are largely composed of pink granites, while the lowest part of its north-facing slope is composed of stony scree. The soil most typically associated with the Côte de Brouilly, however, is diorite, and the hard volcanic rock dominates a generous semi-circle of its slopes running clockwise from those facing north right through to the south-south-west. The influence of this geology means that many of the wines from the Côte de Brouilly are structured and full-bodied, with a ripe, dark-fruited character.

Producers

Domaine Bonnet-Cotton

bonnet-cotton.fr

The stone buildings that house Domaine Bonnet-Cotton have nestled on the slopes of the Côte de Brouilly since the middle of the nineteenth century, when they belonged to the nearby Château de Pierreux. Pierre Cotton's family have managed the property, initially in *métayage*, for five generations, but for much of the time they shared the cellars with up to four other growers. Cotton made his first wines under the watchful eye of his parents in 2014, and his first under his own label in 2017, but it wasn't until 2019, when he met his partner, Marine Bonnet, that the pair bought the house and the winery outright.

Even in Beaujolais, where agricultural land and buildings are relatively cheap, this was a stretch for a pair of young growers, but Bonnet and Cotton came up with an ingenious plan. They asked friends and colleagues to invest in shares in the property, with returns paid not in cash but in wine – every share owner is entitled to six bottles of wine per year. This show of tangible support allowed the couple to take ownership of the house they now live in, the winery and several hectares of vineyards. They now work around 11 hectares, of which some belong to the domaine and some are rented, spread out across the Côte de Brouilly (4 hectares), Brouilly (2 hectares), 1 hectare each of Fleurie, Régnié and Beaujolais, and another hectare on which they grow a number of grapes that fall outside of the Beaujolais classification system, along with a final hectare of vineyards due for imminent replantation.

These grapes in the vineyards outside of the Beaujolais classification are mainly hybrids, and the couple work with them in the interests of research and also with an eye on the possible future of the region in a time of warming temperatures. This desire for experimentation and a keen environmental awareness are themes that emerge in the way the couple work in the vineyards, where they combine organic certification with the more holistic approaches largely derived from regenerative viticulture (they are members of the Vignerons du Vivant group, see p. 202). Bit by bit, the once conventionally farmed land is being brought back to life, and the recently planted hedging that borders the property's vineyards is a promise of biodiversity to come.

The approach to winemaking is flexible, with variations between full dry carbonic maceration (with the removal of juices) in vintages where the stems haven't fully ripened, to semi-carbonic maceration, where

The volcanic slopes of Mont Brouilly, visible for miles around, rise out of the surrounding vineyards, most of which lie within the borders of the cru of Brouilly (iStock.com/Gael Fontaine)

fermenting juices are permitted to extract tannins from riper stems. One of the key techniques employed is the use of cool temperatures, which starts with the overnight chilling of grapes on reception to slow down the rate of fermentation right at the start, to limiting fermentation temperatures to a maximum of 20°C (a very low temperature for red grapes). The aim is to ensure a long, slow, steady fermentation that extracts gentle tannins without a trace of bitterness and maximizes the amount of bright fruit character in the wines. Wines that are intended for youthful consumption are fermented for a short period of around a week, then matured briefly in cement tanks, while the more structured *crus* ferment for longer and are then gently drained off into a mixture of old oak barrels and oxygen-permeable flexitanks for maturation.

The funky labels, designed by a local artist, are eye-catching, but are suggestive of a more brash winemaking style than the wines demonstrate. Instead, subtlety and sophistication are the order of the day. The Brouilly Les Mines is a pretty, approachable wine with supple, rounded tannins and lively acidity, while the Côte de Brouilly 100% Cotton shows the typical austerity of a wine made from grapes grown on the appellation's blue stone, albeit with the promise of much to come once the wine has had a few years in bottle to unwind. The wines produced under the Vin de France designation are, perhaps, a little looser – they are definitely less conventional. There's a skin-contact Chardonnay, whose name – Orange Carbonique – and label make a tongue-in-cheek reference to *A Clockwork Orange*, while the Piscine Olympique (Olympic Swimming Pool) is a rosé whose name was inspired by an old painted sign on the side of a now-demolished building, whose colours referenced the yellow, pink and red of the grapes that make up its blend. Muscaris and Souvignier Gris are both disease-resistant crosses, and they've been blended together with some Gamay to create a wine that is deep sunset pink in colour and whose nose is heady with grapes and flowers.

Château de la Chaize

www.chateaudelachaize.fr

What might you get if you crossed a fairy-tale French château and a working winery? The answer is the ultra-glamorous Château de la Chaize, a seventeenth-century castle whose main buildings and gardens were designed by Jules-Hardouin Mansart and André le Notre, the architect and the gardener of Versailles. Its purchase by the Gruy family, in 2017, is reputed to have been the most expensive in the history of

The glamorous Château de la Chaize, still in the process of renovation.

Beaujolais – and that's not counting the investments that have since been made in the refurbishment of the 450-hectare property.

The buildings themselves have been restored to their former glory under the supervision of Didier Repellin, chief architect of Monuments Historiques, which runs France's national heritage sites. The 150 hectares of vineyard, most of which lie in Brouilly and the Côte de Brouilly, have been restructured and converted to organic viticulture, and a programme of agroforestry has been implemented. The winery has been fully renovated, and its tanks – along with the rest of the property – are heated thanks to a small-scale geothermal plant that's been incorporated into the structure. An equally impressive programme of tourism and visits focused on both the Château's history and its wines is being rolled out, with large-scale events planned for the future.

It's all very ambitious, as is the approach to winemaking, which is supervised by Boris Gruy, with the help of an experienced team. Thirty people work full-time in the Château's vineyards and cellar, supplemented by a further 90 people at harvest so that the grapes can all be harvested by hand. They're sorted and, depending on the style of the wine, either de-stemmed on arrival or gently fed by gravity into concrete or wooden vats for fermentation. The wines are aged for anywhere between eight and 18 months in barrels that range in size from 30 to 90 hectolitres.

The wines are mostly built for the long haul, needing time to open up in bottle. Les Deux Amis, a Brouilly based on a blend of different vineyard parcels, is a good place to start exploring the range. It's pleasingly vibrant in style, with liquorice-tinged raspberry notes and supple tannins. Combiliaty, another Brouilly, is the result of 11 days of maceration and 15 months of ageing in oak casks. It's a dense, brooding wine with dark plum and cherry fruit on the palate, fine-grained but firm tannins and a long, deep, tar-inflected finish. La Chapelle des Bois comes from one of the Château's two Fleurie vineyards. It's got an unusually rich palate, with plush tannins and floral notes that provide a pleasing counterpoint to some dark berries. The Lieu-Dit La Chaize is another Brouilly, sourced from a sloping vineyard located right behind the Château. The bunches are 90 per cent de-stemmed to allow for a greater degree of extraction. There's great depth and weight to the fruit, and the finish is long and harmonious.

Domaine Chevalier-Métrat

Instagram @domainechevaliermetrat

The Domaine Chevalier-Métrat is at a crossroads right now, with Cyrielle Métrat, a member of the third generation, poised to take over the family's 10 hectares of vineyard holdings from her parents.

Métrat has been living and working on the foothills of Mont Brouilly since 2022, after several years spent working in the banking sector – an experience that only served to confirm her sense that life on the family farm was her destiny. A few years ago, though, she wasn't all that sure about the idea, having spent her childhood witnessing the hard work her parents put into managing a wine property at a time when Beaujolais's growers were struggling to make a living. Métrat faces the task ahead of her with the enthusiasm of the born-again convert, talking with quiet certainty of her readiness for the challenges in store, not least of which will be the restructuring of an ageing vineyard.

Her father began the replanting work a decade or so ago, adopting the cordon training that was all the rage back in the day. But although Métrat says this trellising system makes it easier to manage the vines, she believes that bush vines may have greater longevity in the long run, so she's thinking of adopting the popular practice of trellising the goblet vines she plans to plant.

She seems to favour a steady hand on the winemaking tiller at present, although there's a glint in her eye when she talks about the oenological practices she observed while working out her apprenticeship in the wine cellars of the Northern Rhône. There are probably few changes to come to the property's line-up of wines in the near future, although she's enthusiastic about the potential to make a second white cuvée, oaked in this instance. The current white, the Plaisir de l'Atelier, is made from Chardonnay grown on a small patch of limestone soils that lie on the borders of Brouilly and the Beaujolais Villages zone. It's more sophisticated than many Beaujolais Blancs, with a rich but vibrant palate of tropical and citrus fruits and a bit of mid-palate texture. The Brouilly Les Mines is a slightly old-fashioned style of wine, with a little of that confected bubble-gum character that was once widely found in the region. The Côte de Brouilly Les Grillés is an altogether more serious wine, with a real plushness of texture and generous amounts of dark fruit, enlivened by a refreshing hit of menthol on the finish. It's a shame that the zero sulphite Côte de Brouilly only seems to succeed in cooler years (given the run of recent warm vintages) as it has a real purity of blueberry and black cherry fruit, with some fine tannins for support. If you're after a wine for the long haul, though, you might prefer l'Heronde, a Côte de Brouilly matured for 12 months in *demi-muid* barrels. It's a big, ripe, potent wine with dark currant and damson fruit tinged with spice, its generosity of fruit and wealth of tannins a nod in the direction of Beaujolais's southern neighbour, the vineyards of the Northern Rhône.

Domaine Dupré-Goujon

www.dupregoujon.fr

It's a beautiful, clear late spring day when I drive up to meet Sebastien Dupré and Guillaume Goujon, and from the winery you can see the Alps in the distance, while the vine-covered slopes of the Côte de Brouilly spread out in the foreground. Dupré and Goujon, both too busy to spend much time admiring the view, met at agricultural school, and cemented their friendship by working together at a property in the Terrasses du Larzac, an appellation in the Languedoc. Goujon said that insights they gained in the south have helped them understand how best to manage their vineyards in an era of increasingly hot, dry summers.

Dupré returned to Beaujolais first, taking up the reins at the family domaine in 2015, and was joined three years later by Goujon. They began the process of conversion to organic farming, achieving certification in 2021, and are now well on the way to becoming fully biodynamic.

Restructuring the vineyards was also a priority, reducing the planting density from the traditional 10,000 plants per hectare down to around 6,500. They raised the trunks of their vines in order to allow them to extend the canopy onto a wire, and are currently in the process of identifying the best of their old vines to enable a massal selection for the next round of replanting. But the biggest task has been to introduce agroforestry to their landholdings, with the aim of improving both biodiversity and the vitality of their soils, likening the importance of a healthy subsoil microfaunal population to that of a healthy gut biome in humans.

Together they farm 10 hectares of vineyards in the Côte de Brouilly, with a further 4.5 hectares of Chardonnay planted in Blacé. They also recently planted just under a hectare of Aligoté in Blacé as well. Aligoté, like Gamay, they say, is a bit of an underdog – both can produce copiously and then be used to make dilute, forgettable wines, but when planted in the right spot and managed appropriately they can create wines of character and structure.

There's no lack of structure in the red wines they make from their Côte de Brouilly vineyards, a *cru* whose diorite soils tend to create dense, concentrated wines with bold tannins. They temper these by maturing their wines in large old oak barrels for a minimum of two years prior to release, even though they're careful not to extract too much from the wines during fermentation. The first wine they ever made together, a cuvée called 631, is still part of the range. A blend of all three of their parcels on the Mont Brouilly, and the only one of their Côte de Brouillys to be aged for a year in old barrels and a year in cement tanks, it's a tangy wine, with focused, slightly fuzzy tannins, and a palate full of salty red liquorice flavours. Le Pavé comes from east-facing slopes, and is the most delicate and precise of their parcel selections, with a lovely kick of freshness on the long finish. The Brulhié, as is often the case with this *lieu-dit*, shows great concentration of fruit, but its density is leavened by a floral note. The tannins are pretty firm, even in lighter years like 2021, but well integrated into the body of the wine, helping to channel the long finish. L'Héronde has the plushest texture of the three, along with great aromatic complexity, and deep-pile tannins. The Chardonnay bottling, a Beaujolais Villages known as Le Clos des Muriers, is an opulent wine with a lot of mid-palate texture. Although the acidity isn't very high, the wine is refreshing and balanced thanks to a little twist of bitterness on the finish and some stony minerality.

Jean-Claude Lapalu

Although Jean-Claude Lapalu grew up just over 10 kilometres away from Villié-Morgon, the epicentre of Beaujolais's natural wine revolution in the 1980s, he might as well have been on another planet in terms of the wine culture that surrounded him. His parents grew grapes for the local cooperative, so that's what Lapalu did too. But his restless intellect meant that he soon got bored with life on a treadmill of volume production, and he began to question the values of conventional agriculture and the style of the wines for which his grapes were destined.

An autodidact by instinct, he trained himself in a new approach to viticulture and winemaking by tasting wines from other producers, and it wasn't long before the world of natural wines began exerting a magnetic pull on his tastebuds and his thought processes. He began converting his rented vineyards to organic viticulture in 1999 – something the owners of those vineyards were not always all that keen on due to the lower volumes of production – and got to work selling the end product. It took him a while – and numerous trips to retailers and restaurateurs in nearby Lyon and in Paris (the latter proved to be far more open to him in the early days) – but slowly his reputation grew.

These days Lapalu is recognized as a master of Beaujolais's natural wine movement, on a par with the Morgon founding fathers. Most of his grapes are sourced from the 10 hectares of vineyards he owns in Varennes in Beaujolais Villages and nearby Brouilly, although he also buys in small volumes of grapes. Most of these come from friends and family whose vineyards are also located in the same areas, and are largely used to increase the volume of wine he's able to sell. He does make a small amount of Pinot Noir sourced from Igé in the Mâconnais (vinified in the same way as Gamay and labelled as a Vin de France), and an Aligoté cuvée will soon join the range. These last wines are made in small quantities and mainly serve to satisfy Lapalu's intellectual curiosity.

Lapalu may be a member of the fraternity of natural winemakers, but don't make the mistake of assuming that his wines, therefore, walk on the wilder side of the aromatic spectrum. His cuvées – of which there are 13 – are notable for their precision and brightness, and with a couple of notable exceptions, alcohol levels rarely rise above 12.5% abv. Clarisse, Lapalu's daughter, who has recently begun working at the family domaine, puts the wines' purity of fruit down to two factors, the health of the grapes they harvest and her father's scrupulous vigilance throughout the entire winemaking process. During the course of the semi-carbonic fermentations he's in the winery early each morning, monitoring the progress of each tank, sampling the wines to ensure that they aren't about to take a detour down an undesirable microbiological pathway.

One of the wines for which Lapalu is best known is his Beaujolais Villages Vieilles Vignes, a blend of grapes with an average age of 70 years, from a variety of parcels. It's a bright, tangy wine with gently raspy tannins and lots of perfume and freshness on the finish. The Brouilly Vieilles Vignes – another wine that is seen in most markets – is denser and richer, with a stony minerality that provides a pleasing counterpoint to the bright notes of red cherry and raspberry. Another Brouilly, La Croix des Rameaux, comes from a warm, south-west-facing parcel, and as a result shows riper, darker fruit with a hint of bitter liquorice and a generous, rounded mid-palate. The Cuvée des Fous, also from Brouilly, is made from a parcel of 120-year-old vines, which lend it great concentration and richness, as well as a layered, concentrated palate. The tannins are taut and, in the wine's youth, restrict the full expression of the fruit – this is a wine that really merits being laid aside to age for at least five years after bottling to allow it to unwind. If I had to pick one wine, though, to sip at slowly, pondering its nuanced complexities, it would be the Eau Forte, a Vin de France, in spite of the fact that it's eligible to be labelled and sold as a Beaujolais Villages. (The declassification stems from the fact that the first ever bottling of this wine, the 2012, didn't meet the requirements of the local *agrément* panel, who said it was atypical. Lapalu shrugged his shoulders and decided that he wouldn't bother to enter it for certification ever again.) The wine has a gorgeously perfumed, floral nose, while the elegant, poised palate blends cranberry juice and fresh mint with a gravelly minerality, all framed by fine, powdery tannins.

Domaine Robert Perroud

www.robert-perroud.com

To be quite honest, I wasn't expecting all that much from my visit to Robert Perroud, a producer who seems to have escaped the notice of most of my peers, despite the fact that he took over the family domaine some 35 years ago. It wasn't long into our meeting, though, that I began to sense that I'd stumbled across an exceptionally thoughtful man, one who actively enjoys the process of questioning his own beliefs in order to achieve positive change.

Perroud realized more than 20 years ago that although he knew how to take care of his vineyards and make good wine, the skills necessary to market them were not necessarily his strong point. Reasoning that what was true for him was probably also true for a number of other producers working on the same small scale as him, he launched Terroirs Originels, a company that employs a small sales team working on behalf of a diverse network of independent wine producers located in the Mâconnais and the Côteaux Lyonnais as well as in Beaujolais.

In 2007 he began converting his vineyards to organic farming – a challenge, he says, when dealing with old bush vines due to the difficulties they impose in terms of working the soil – and a quarter of his holdings are now certified organic. Perroud says that the remainder of the vineyards are largely farmed organically, but he reserves the right to be able to treat them in difficult years. 'In order to keep working, you need to be able to pay the bills,' he points out.

Perroud's approach to winemaking is equally flexible, and although he works along the lines of semi-carbonic maceration, he's prepared to adapt his practices to the needs of each vintage. He tries not to add sulphites early as he believes that this allows for more aromatic expression in the grapes, but says that it's vital for a winemaker to use all his or her senses to ensure that fermentation proceeds smoothly. He's not just talking about the sense of smell and taste, or even about the visual monitoring of the progress of each tank, he even mentions the need to listen closely to a fermentation to make sure that it's all bubbling along nicely. He pays close attention to the possibility of any off-aromas that might be developing, although he says he's relaxed about a little volatility early on in the process as it typically blows off around day four. But, if necessary, he has absolutely no compunction about adding sulphites to a tank if he feels it needs protective intervention. Juices are pressed off around eight days in for wines destined for early drinking, and these are then aged in a mixture of neutral containers – old casks, stainless steel and cement. Wines that will repay further ageing typically get another three or four days in tank to create a bit more structure before being racked off into mainly older barrels; Perroud isn't averse to the occasional new barrel, although he doesn't like high levels of toast.

The tasting, conducted towards the end of my visit, served only to confirm that Domaine Robert Perroud is a quiet force to be reckoned with. There's a couple of whites first, both Beaujolais Villages, of which the most exciting is the Pur Chardonnay, a wine inspired by the minimalist approach of some of the younger members of the Terroirs Originels group. It's quite deeply coloured, and has great texture, as well as flavours of orange peel and Golden Delicious apples, and a finish with an unusual note of toasted sesame seeds. Foudre No5, a Côte de Brouilly, is a lovely bright wine, with zesty red fruits and supple tannins. It doesn't have the concentration or complexity for long ageing, but is an absolute joy in its youth. L'Enfer des Balloquets is a Brouilly whose name refers to the warmth of the vineyard in which the grapes are grown. It's quite full-bodied and round, but again there are plenty of charming bright red fruit aromas. La Fournaise de Perou is a more serious, weighty Côte de Brouilly, based on vines planted in 1963. Twelve months in barrel helps create structure and heft on the mid-palate, while the vineyard provides ripe notes of plums, spice and a hit of liquorice on the finish. The remaining wines are all from Brouilly. Pollen, from the Saburin *lieu-dit*, is a tightly wound wine that needs time, but is fine, elegant and unforced. This taut structure must be a characteristic of the Saburin site, as Romain, also from Saburin, is similarly tense, but is even more layered and focused than Pollen, with pronounced minerality and a refreshing burst of menthol on the finish. La Pente – as the name suggests – comes from steep slopes, and has deep, dark fruit and firm, chalky tannins that will unwind over time.

Domaine Les Roches Bleues

domainelesrochesbleues.com

Jonathan Buisson took over his wife's family domaine, located on the slopes of Mont Brouilly, in 2019, and says he's been learning on the job ever since. He's clearly a quick study, as the property's vineyards are thriving and the wines he makes have both personality and polish. The 11 hectares of vineyards he farms are spread between the *crus* of Brouilly (4 hectares) and Côte de Brouilly.

Buisson's approach to both viticulture and winemaking is thoughtful and considered. The vineyards are all either certified organic or in conversion towards certification, but Buisson is pushing his environmental credentials even further. He's a member of the Vignerons du Vivant in Beaujolais, a group of producers who farm according to principles that place great emphasis on soil health and biodiversity (see p. 202), and he picks and chooses from a range of biodynamic treatments without allowing himself to be overwhelmed by dogma. He uses nettle teas, for instance, to promote soil health, but eschews the countless hours of stirring involved in 'dynamizing' the liquid according to biodynamic principles as he believes the jury's out on the effectiveness of the process.

In comparison to neighbouring plots where the land has been stripped bare by years of weedkillers and fungicides, Buisson's vineyards look lush and healthy. The proof of the pudding lies, however, in the glass. Buisson has had no formal winemaking training, apart from a year's worth of agricultural college. 'I would have liked to have gone and done a *stage* with a few producers in France and elsewhere,' he says, 'but my first child was two years old and my wife was pregnant again when we took over the property.' Instead, he's learned by experimenting and by careful observation of what he believes to be best winemaking practice elsewhere in the region.

His approach is carefully considered. Entry-level cuvées are allowed to ferment intracellularly for a relatively brief period before they're pressed and racked into tank to finish their alcoholic fermentation. This, he says, helps to preserve their fruit and freshness. La Croquante, his entry-level Brouilly, is a great example of this, with bright red berry fruit and gently rounded tannins. His more 'serious' parcel selections spend longer in the first phase of fermentation (up to around a fortnight) and are then racked into large oak barrels, where they remain on their lees for a year or even more. Buisson adjusts the amount of time all the wines spend in each of these phases according to regular tastings, and while he's keen to handle the wines as little as possible, he's prepared to step in should circumstances dictate: 'I even had to put one of my 2022s through a tangential filter,' he says in mock horror, 'when I saw that it was beginning to develop a little volatility.'

All three parcel selections come from vines grown on hard blue granite, even the Pierreux, which comes from Brouilly, where this kind of soil is relatively rare in comparison to the more friable pink granite. The Pierreux, Brulhié and l'Heronde bottlings share a similar nervous tension, but the Pierreux is the lightest and the most linear of the cuvées, while Brulhié is more dense and structured. L'Heronde is the most polished and complex of the three, with fine, grippy tannins.

Château Thivin

chateau-thivin.com

Château Thivin's roots are deeply embedded in the history of Brouilly and the Côte de Brouilly. There's been a property on this site since the Middle Ages, and the foundations of the château date back to the fourteenth century. What happened next to the château is lost somewhat in the fog of history, although documentation pertaining to the purchase of the property in 1645 by the Marquis of Vichy exists, and the Vichys owned the buildings and the surrounding land right through to the time of the French Revolution. The château passed through several changes of ownership until Zaccharie and Marguerite Geoffray bought it in 1877, and the property is now in the hands of Claude Edouard and Sonja, the sixth generation of the family.

Much has changed since the Geoffrays settled on the slopes of Mount Brouilly. Their landholdings have expanded well beyond the initial couple of hectares that belonged to the property at the time. These days the family farms around 30 hectares of mostly organic vineyards. Of these, 7 hectares are in Brouilly, 3 hectares of Chardonnay are planted on limestone soils in the Beaujolais AOP zone, there are 4 hectares of Beaujolais Villages vineyards, and the rest are in the Côte de Brouilly, on the slopes of the extinct volcano.

Rather unusually, though, not all of the Côte de Brouilly vineyards are planted to Gamay. A small parcel of Chardonnay vines is planted on limestone soils (atypical for the *cru*, which consists mainly of hard blue volcanic rocks) on the eastern fringes of the appellation. And there are a couple of experimental parcels planted with a range of grapes that include Barbera, Nebbiolo, Carménère, Cannaiolo, Mourvèdre and Tempranillo, as well as Syrah, a more typical new introduction. It's early days yet but although Thivin has strong links to the past, its owners are clearly unafraid of experimentation that might ensure a better future for the domaine.

Down in the cellars, alongside the typical array of stainless steel and cement tanks, large wooden vats and smaller barrels (most of which have been used several times – there's very little new oak at the property), there's a line-up of ceramic eggs, which were used for the very first time in 2023. Fine particles of ground rock from the slopes of the Côte de Brouilly were incorporated into the clay used to create the eggs, and the hope of the Geoffrays is that maturation in these vessels will help to enhance the sense of terroir in the wines even further.

Of the 12 cuvées produced by the Geoffrays, the Reverdon, a Brouilly, is the go-to if you're looking for a simple, juicy fruit-driven wine, while the Griottes de Brulhié, a Côte de Brouilly made from grapes on the south-facing slopes of the Mont Brouilly, has more depth and a delightful aromatic profile that blends rose petals with sour cherries and blackberries. The more structured La Chapelle comes from old vines situated in the highest vineyards on the Côte de Brouilly, and this complex wine has a savoury depth and structure somewhat reminiscent of the wines of Côte-Rôtie.

15

BEAUJOLAIS VILLAGES

> **Year in which AOP status was awarded**: 1937
> **Total vineyard area**: 4,090 hectares
> **Number of villages**: 38
> **Notable villages**: Leynes, Blacé, Lantignié, Quincié, Lancié, Le Perréon

There is a deep and widespread misunderstanding of the relationship between the Beaujolais appellation and that of Beaujolais Villages. Many believe that the comparison is analogous in some way to the difference between Bordeaux and Bordeaux Supérieur. In other words, the use of the name 'Beaujolais Villages' implies some kind of supercharged take on the basic Beaujolais appellation. Others draw parallels between the two appellations and the southern Rhône, where wines bearing the Côtes-du-Rhône Villages appellation come from named villages that lie within the broader Côtes-du-Rhône. As ever, though, they like to do things a bit differently in Beaujolais.

The Beaujolais Villages zone is a discrete geographical entity that runs some 40 kilometres from north to south, beginning just north of Leynes and ending at the village of Rivolet, and stretches 15 kilometres from east to west at its widest point. Curled tightly around the western edges of the *crus*, the zone then projects out beneath Brouilly to create a boundary between the *crus* and the *Bas Beaujolais*. The appellation covers 38 named villages and a huge diversity of soil types, and many of the best vineyards in the zone have similar geologies to those found in the *crus*. If you have a taste for the wines based on Fleurie's pink granite sands or the more robust styles generated by the Côte de Brouilly's hard blue diorites you'll find both soils in Lantignié and Vaux-en-Beaujolais. Lovers of Chardonnays grown on Burgundy's limestone soils might want to look towards Charentay or Blacé (the latter has generous deposits of granite and *pierre bleue* too). The soil mapping of the region conducted by Sigales (see p. 20) has given growers in the appellation a much better understanding of their terroir, helping to refine notions of the best sites. Not coincidentally, it may have helped to fuel a growing desire to put their terroir in the spotlight.

And then there are the hills, particularly in the northern sector of the appellation, some of which are so steep that they make the slopes of Chiroubles look positively gentle. (Quincié-en-Beaujolais has over 90 hectares of vineyards with slopes of more than 30 per cent.) The altitude of many vineyards is such that, in a cooler era, growers regularly struggled to ripen their grapes. One suspects that it is largely for this reason that in the past many of the *lieux-dits* of the appellation were never considered to be sufficiently qualitative to merit *cru* status. Nowadays, though, the retention of acidity and the more modest levels of sugar accumulation in the berries are seen as a net benefit to the zone. Those hills not only allow for vineyards to be planted at a variety of altitudes, they also create room for producers to play with differing exposures, bringing opportunities for the creation of complexity and diversity in the wines.

Bush vines in Lantignié

When the varied geology, topography and mesoclimates of the appellation are considered – or, quite possibly, reconsidered – it's little wonder that growers within the zone are keen that the quality of their vineyards be recognized. In the short term this is being achieved by labelling their wines with the name of a specific village – for instance, Beaujolais Leynes or Beaujolais Le Perréon. The danger of this tactic is that most people might assume that these wines are simply AOP Beaujolais, not even giving them the dubious benefit of assuming that they're members of the slightly-better-than-basic-Beaujolais club. Some growers – particularly those in Lantignié and Blacé – are campaigning for their villages to be elevated to *cru* status. Such recognition would not, in and of itself, necessarily bring with it increased financial rewards for the hard work that goes into farming these often tricky terroirs, but at least it would prevent wine lovers from typecasting these potentially complex and refined wines as simple, short-lived quaffers.

Producers

Domaine de Bel Air

dombelair.com

Jean-Marc Lafont grew up in a family of *métayers* very close to where his domaine is now based. Life was tough, he says. The soils were poor and the property's owner didn't give his parents the necessary materials needed to improve the yields, so the family struggled. So much so, in fact, that Lafont's father only smoked on Sunday as he couldn't afford to buy cigarettes the rest of the week. Nevertheless, when Lafont was given the opportunity to take over the *métayage* when his father retired, he jumped at the chance. By then he'd already completed his wine studies, worked for a producer in Brouilly and then returned to his home village to start a *négoce* business. Lafont is clearly talented as both a winemaker and a businessman – within a few years of starting up, he'd bought himself both the magnificent stone house in which he lives and the property his father used to farm. Lafont not only survived the crisis of the early 2000s, his business kept on growing, due at least in part to the amount of work he put into developing export markets for his wines.

These days he sells around 200,000 bottles a year, two-thirds of them overseas. The négociant side of the business has taken a back seat to the wines produced from the domaine's 25 hectares of vineyards in the *villages* zone, Régnié, Fleurie, Moulin-à-Vent and Morgon. He also makes three different Beaujolais Nouveau cuvées, including the dense, potent

Cuvée 100, a Beaujolais Villages Nouveau based on centenarian vines (proof, as if it were required, that not all Nouveau is made in an ephemeral drink-today, gone-tomorrow style).

Lafont likes to vary his winemaking methods according to the style of the wine he's making, with semi-carbonic macerations being used to make wines like his Beaujolais Villages Les Granits Bleues, which has the ripeness, dark fruit and fleshy mid-palate typical of grapes grown on this type of soil. Most of the *crus* are partially de-stemmed, although the proportion varies from one vintage to another, depending on stem ripeness. Lafont says that working like this allows him to perform longer macerations without extracting too much structure or bitterness. This is the technique used to create the focused, fresh Morgon Les Charmes, a wine that balances red berry fruit with liquorice and spice, the latter particularly noticeable on the generous finish. The Moulin-à-Vent Les Burdelines is made in a similar way, although the tight, firm tannins need ageing for a couple of years in bottle in order to loosen up and let the bright raspberry fruit and orange zest shine through. The top cuvées are parcel selections, and these are fully de-stemmed and aged in barrels. Lafont has stepped away from the use of new oak as, he says, he no longer looks for oak character in these wines, preferring to let the fruit express itself more fully. There's a trace of oak spice in the Morgon Grand Charme, but it's subtle and should integrate into the dense, dark-fruited palate over time, as should the generous, velvety tannins.

Frédéric Berne

fredericberne.com

Very occasionally, people become lightning rods for change, the focal point around which shifting attitudes seem to converge. Frédéric Berne, who produces wines in Beaujolais Villages as well as the *crus* of Morgon, Régnié and Chiroubles, appears to be at the confluence of a whole series of trends. Berne, who farms organically, is a founding member of the Vignerons du Vivant, a group of producers who are driving a move towards regenerative viticulture across Beaujolais, as well as being affiliated to the Ceps et Charrues group (see p. 202). He's also a key player in the move towards a reappraisal of the potential for quality in the *villages* zone in general, and in Lantignié in particular.

Berne's family also grew vines, but their business folded in 2002, victims of the collapse in demand for Beaujolais Nouveau and the ensuing economic crisis. Berne says that although he'd learned practical skills from his father, who was also a stonemason, and his grandfather, a smith, he'd always wanted to work in agriculture. He learned his trade as a viticulturist and winemaker by working alongside Robert Perroud (see p. 187) for several years, then decided to go it alone in 2014 and found the vineyards he was looking for on the hillsides above Lantignié.

Lantignié, a village located some 7 kilometres south-west of Villié-Morgon, is at the heart of Berne's beat, although also he makes wines in a number of *crus*. The key to the village's rising fame is its terroir, which is widely recognized as being among some of the most qualitative in the *villages* zone. The soils are composed mainly of the prized pink granites found in some of Beaujolais's most famous *crus*, although some vineyards are planted on the hard blue stones typically found on Morgon's Côte du Py and on the Côte de Brouilly. In the past, the 400-metre altitude of Berne's vineyards might have posed a challenge to anyone seeking to ripen the grapes grown there, but these days the elevation is of considerable benefit when it comes to retaining freshness and aromatic vibrancy in the wines.

Berne is vocal in advocating for *cru* status for his village but, as ever in France, local politics are a challenge. There is little doubt that he will succeed in his aim in the long term. In the interim, he works hard to ensure that his wines merit the status he champions with such great conviction. After he purchased his vineyards, he spent time – lots of time – setting them up to produce reasonable yields while ensuring the health of the vines. This meant, in some instances, grubbing up his old vineyards to replant anew, while in others he adapted the existing structure to allow him to work in a more environmentally friendly fashion. He's widened the inter-row spaces and raised his bush vines off the ground, trellising the canopy along wires. When asked how long it took him to set his vineyard to rights, he replies that he thinks he's just about getting there now. Viticulture is not a short-term project, he says; you need to put in the work in order to reap financial and qualitative benefits in the long term. The proof, he says, lies in the results he saw during the rainy, challenging 2024 vintage. Many producers talked about crop losses of up to 50 per cent on their average yields but Berne says that his yields were close to the norm as his vines were better able to repel the onslaught of fungal spores.

His healthy grapes show evidence of an ability to make some pretty healthy wines. His Beaujolais Lantignié Granit Rose cuvée is crisp, linear and exuberantly fruity, while the Beaujolais Lantignié Pierre Bleue is perhaps more restrained aromatically in its youth, and shows more structured tannins and deeper, darker fruit. The Les Bruyères cuvée comes from a parcel grown on blue stone, too, but the winemaking is different, with a longer maceration on skins and six months of barrel ageing (around 10 per cent of the barrels are new). The oak here gives the wine greater mid-palate breadth, but the finish remains fresh and lively. Harmonie is a selection of the best wines from the pink granite and blue diorite, a reflection of Lantignié's terroir. Matured for a year in barrels, it's a wine that takes its time to get into its stride, but when it does open up it reveals layers of dark cherries, raspberries, rose petals, spice and cocoa nibs, all draped over a framework of gently grippy tannins. New to the range are the bottlings from the *crus*, of which the focused, taut Chiroubles may well be my favourite.

Nicolas Chemarin

Instagram @ptitgrobis

Nicolas Chemarin's winery is situated on the furthest frontier of the Beaujolais Villages zone – travel over the brow of the nearest hills and, depending on your direction of travel, you'll end up in the forests of the Beaujolais Vert or even in the cattle country of the Charolais. Chemarin's vineyards are planted on some of the steepest slopes in Beaujolais at an altitude of more than 500 metres, which helps him retain a good deal of freshness in his wines.

Chemarin started making wine alongside his father in 2005, sharing space in the family winery – if not a common approach to the business of farming and vinification. Chemarin *père* farmed conventionally, seeking to make approachable, fruit-focused wines, often using thermovinification as a technique, along with plenty of cultured yeasts and prophylactic doses of sulphites. Chemarin *fils* prefers an approach that's altogether redder in tooth and claw. His take on farming is about as organic as it gets, while his approach to winemaking is decidedly natural, with temperatures that rarely exceed 25°C, and as little sulphite addition as he feels he can get away with. 'What bothers my father most about my wines,' says Chemarin, 'is the fact that I don't filter them. That and the way that no two bottles ever taste exactly the same, which is what you get when you don't use sulphur. They evolve, they're alive.'

His entry-level wines, a red and a white, are both called P'tit Grobis. La Grobe, Chemarin explains, was the name of the village of Marchampt in the pre-revolutionary era, and the locals were known as

Grobis. Chemarin himself is not the world's tallest man, so as a kid he was known as '*le petit Grobis*', hence the name of his most important cuvées. The white, a Vin de France, has seen some skin contact (half the grapes are fermented with a carbonic maceration), which gives it a deep yellow colour and a little textural grip, while the zippy acidity and bright lemon curd character come from the early-picked grapes. The red, a Beaujolais Villages, is a little stemmy and herbaceous – which is just the way Chemarin wants it – with some nice, crisp raspberry fruit. His Brouilly, which comes from the *lieu-dit* of Saburin, has more depth and structure, but still shows vibrancy and a little edge of greenness and crunch. Le Rocher is a Beaujolais Villages made from old vines growing at altitudes above 600 metres and aged in amphora. There's a distinct volatility here, but there's also plenty of elderberry and peppercorn flavoured fruit on the palate. He also makes a Régnié from the Haut-Ronze parcel, whose clay subsoils lend heft and structure to the mid-palate.

Famille Descombe/Château de Pougelon

descombe.com

The Descombe family have been making wine in Beaujolais for at least five generations, but it wasn't until the early 2020s that François and Marine Descombe, along with Marine's husband, Kevin Jandard, found their dream vineyards and the property that they hope will become their family's home base for the next few generations.

The Château de Pougelon, situated about 6 kilometres due south of Mont Brouilly, is clearly an ambitious project. The property dates back to the latter half of the seventeenth century and was badly in need of restoration when the Descombes took it over. Newly restored, the buildings now house a brand-new winery stocked with all the latest kit – concrete eggs and tapered tanks designed to facilitate the submersion of the whole bunches during fermentation.

There have been investments in the vineyards, too, and the Descombe family's holdings have risen from 12 hectares of Beaujolais Villages to a total of 30 hectares, spread out across not only the *villages* zone, but also the *crus* of Fleurie, Brouilly, Juliénas and Morgon. There's a strong focus on white wines, with 5 hectares of vineyards dedicated to producing a nicely balanced Beaujolais Blanc, and the pretty Miss Gamay rosé packs more punch than most.

The Juliénas Beauvernay, made from grapes grown on steep slopes at high altitude, shows great freshness and minerality, but needs time in bottle to unwind, while the Brouilly Voujon shows the finesse and linearity typical of grapes grown on pink granite – a contrast to the more opulent, approachable Brouilly Reisser, sourced from a plateau with more clay in the soil. The core of Pougelon's production, though, is the Beaujolais Villages Pougelon, based on 80-year-old vines, which gives mid-palate concentration to the bright, red-fruited palate.

It's an impressive line-up of wines from a young team that has only just been given the green light to run a domaine, but the spirit of thoughtful experimentation that has already seen the trio change tack from complete de-stemming to intensive use of whole-bunch fermentations ('We tasted whole-bunch wines of 35 years that stood up so well we completely revised our approach,' says Kevin) seems likely to stand the Château in good stead over the coming years.

Domaine Les Garçons

domainelesgarcons.com

Loïc Crespin's parents, fourth-generation grape growers in Beaujolais, didn't want their son to follow their footsteps into the wine business. They didn't want to see him struggle with the difficult vintages or the financial challenges that they'd had to face themselves. Nevertheless, Crespin was determined to give it a try, although he wanted to find out whether there might be a way of doing things a bit differently. He went to work for a big producer in Châteauneuf-du-Pape, where the sheer scale of production and the unfamiliar way of making wine opened his eyes to a new world of possibilities. If he hadn't met his partner, Savoie-born Fabien Pinguet, however, Crespin's attempts to rethink approaches to making wine might never have taken flight. Pinguet, meanwhile, admits that he'd never really considered wine as a possible career, despite having worked at some of the best restaurants in his native region.

By the time Pinguet had decided to move to Beaujolais, Crespin had already taken over a couple of hectares of Chardonnay vineyards from his parents on a long-term lease, and set to work adapting what had been a conventionally farmed plot to a more nature-friendly system. 'We began to convert it to organic farming,' he says, 'and that dismayed my parents. Then we told them that we planned to push things further and seek biodynamic certification, and that shocked them even more.' Crespin and Pinguet had a long-term game plan, though, and within a short period of time they'd begun selling their grapes to some of the more switched-on, environmentally focused producers in the region.

Then, in 2022, Crespin and Pinguet – who had, by now, taken on a further 0.7 hectares of vineyards in Brouilly and just over 3.5 hectares of Gamay vineyards in the Beaujolais Villages zone – decided to launch their business, the Domaine les Garçons, and make their own wines. Crespin would be the hands-on wine guy, Pinguet (who also helps out in the vineyard and the cellar) would take on responsibility for sales and marketing – a strategy that played to their very different but complementary strengths.

Pinguet had a tough time of it at first. Doors remained resolutely closed to him in Lyon, despite numerous attempts to try and interest restaurants and retailers in their products. Their first piece of luck came when Pinguet found an agent in Paris who opened doors to a number of high-end restaurants for the wines. The next piece of luck came when the English wine writer Jamie Goode tasted one of their wines on a video that went viral on social media. Within a matter of days, the Garçons had found themselves a prestigious US importer.

It's not hard to see why they've scaled such heights. It's clear that their thoughtful approach to grape growing gives them healthy material for Crespin's detailed work in the cellar. The Beaujolais Blanc is made from grapes grown on the kind of stony, limestone-rich soil that helps it retain its lively acidity – an intrinsic characteristic that's well served by Crespin's decision not to put the wine through malolactic conversion. The current vintage combines savoury elements of fennel and celery salt with bright notes of lemon zest and slightly green pineapple; additional complexity is derived from a little reductive smokiness. The Beaujolais Villages has a rounded generosity on the palate, and supple, slightly powdery tannins, as well as noticeably floral aromas. The Brouilly is altogether darker and denser in character, and its peppery spice and sinewy tannins make it reminiscent of an elegant Northern Rhône Syrah. It's a wine that will repay a bit of time in bottle to allow it to unwind and show its full aromatic complexity. Crespin and Pinguet don't plan to expand their vineyard holdings in future, saying that they want to focus on producing the best possible wines from the 7 hectares they currently manage, but they will soon be releasing a cuvée based on a hectare of centenarian vines planted in their *villages* zone vineyard. Only around 4,000 bottles of this wine will be available each year, and the tank sample I tasted suggests that it will share the domaine's hallmark style, which combines bright acidity and polished tannins with precise, elegant fruit.

The Vignerons du Vivant and Ceps et Charrues

vigneronsduvivantenbeaujolais.fr/cepsetcharrues.fr

Although growers in Beaujolais have always supported each other in terms of pooling practical assistance, until fairly recently the exchange of ideas has been relatively rare. Things are changing, though – and pretty rapidly at that. In the same way that some chefs seem to form a nucleus for the training of the next generation – consider the way Hugh Fearnley-Whittingstall, Jamie Oliver and Theo Randall are all alumni of London's River Café, for instance – some wine producers are lightning conductors for those who follow in their foot-steps, both in terms of inspiration and the passing on of technical know-how. Just as Marcel Lapierre influenced a whole cohort of winemakers in the 1980s and 1990s, the talents of today's young producers are fostered by figures like Paul-Henri Thillardon and Julien Sunier.

But the sharing of ideas in Beaujolais is not restricted to work in the *cuvage*. Arguably, the key forums driving the rapid improvement in quality in the region are viticultural. Groups like the Vignerons du Vivant en Beaujolais and Ceps et Charrues are both aimed at improving viticulture in the region. While the former is largely focused on biodiversity and regenerative practices, the latter has a more overt drive towards full organics (although a significant pro-portion of the Vignerons du Vivant group are also working within an organic framework). Many producers belong to both organizations, which not only provide a forum for improving viticultural knowledge, but also end up creat-ing a support network for their members.

The relationships created by these groups ensure that winemakers have ac-cess to the experiences of their peers. Many of them have spoken to me of the reassurance they derive from knowing that they can call up one of their colleagues when they run into a problem, benefiting by finding out how some-one else has solved the issue they're currently trying to address. Members often end up forming informal tasting groups, too, and the constructive criticism of-fered at such times can be critical to the eradication of faults and to continued improvements in the quality of the wines being made in the region.

Eloi Gros

Instagram @eloigros

Eloi Gros grew up in a wine-focused family. His parents were among the pioneers not only of organic viticulture in the region, but also of agroforestry, planting several hundred hedging plants around their vineyards, which lie near the villages of Le Perréon and Blacé, on the southern fringes of Beaujolais's granitic belt. During Eloi's childhood and adolescence his father, who had been a sommelier at some of the most distinguished restaurants in France before he settled down in Beaujolais, opened numerous bottles of well-aged, prestigious wines for his family, but Eloi was unmoved.

He headed up to Reims to train at a business college and it was while he was there that he finally fell in love with wine. Gros credits his growing interest to Fabrice Parisot, the owner of the Caves du Forum, a Reims wine store. Parisot clearly saw the potential in Gros and nurtured his protégé's new-found fascination with a range of eclectic and unusual bottles. Gros, who by this time had decided that he wasn't suited to life in a business suit, returned to Beaujolais fired up with enthusiasm.

Wanting to learn from a team he considered to be among the best in the region, he fired off a letter to Domaine Lapierre in 2019, asking whether they had any need for a cellar hand. He was in luck, and it wasn't long before he found himself at work in the *cuvage*, lending a hand wherever it was needed. One thing led to another, and within a relatively short period of time, Gros found himself employed as the domaine's vineyard manager and cellar master.

After five years spent working full time at Lapierre, Gros decided that it was time to set out by himself. His wanderings through the countryside near his home had led him to the discovery of some promising vineyards, and when he learned that the owners were about to retire, he decided to make his move. He now farms four individual plots, all situated atop steep sites in Vaux and Le Perréon. These vineyards may once have been deemed low in value due to their high altitude, but the fact that the grapes now ripen some two to three weeks after lower-lying vineyards in *crus* like Morgon and Moulin-à-Vent is an asset in an era of climate change.

His first two vineyards, Au Laveur and Sous Montmain, just about scrape in at a solitary hectare's worth of vines. His most recent acquisitions, Champ Bourdon and Chênevert, clock in at 40 and 30 ares respectively. The small scale doesn't bother Gros in the slightest as he intends to lavish detailed and personalized care on his precious vines. Gros's intention to hand cut wooden stakes that will provide support for the foliage of his bush vines and therefore shade for his bunches is going to be a labour of love, not least because he's going to have to cart all the timber he needs up half a kilometre of steep track on foot. He almost fizzes with excitement as he details his plans for the future of these vineyards, which include building a table and bench so that he can sit on his hillside, survey his plants and listen to the choir of birds that nest in the nearby forest.

Back at base – his parents' winery – Gros brings in his freshly harvested grapes (picked early in the morning to ensure they remain fairly cool) and carefully stacks them into a tank before topping them off with a layer of carbon dioxide. If possible, he says, he then does nothing. What he actually means is that his hope is that his grapes will ferment steadily, with a minimal amount of intervention from him. After 10 days to two weeks, he presses the bunches, then allows the fermentation to run to near completion. He racks the juice into barrels while there's still a gram or two of sugar left as he wants to ensure that any headspace fills up with protective gas.

The 2022 vintage – his first – was challenging, and his Sous Montmain is a journeyman's bottling, with a little more volatile acidity than might otherwise be desirable. Gros is clearly a quick study, though, and his 2023s are seamless. Au Laveur, a Beaujolais Villages from Le Perréon, is a lovely, juicy wine with a plush mid-palate, notes of raspberry and pomegranate and a refreshingly bitter twist of orange rind, all held together by fine, fuzzy tannins. Sous Montmain is also a Beaujolais Villages, but from Vaux-en-Beaujolais. It's denser and firmer, with notes of sour cherry and peppery spice, its richness a reflection, perhaps, of the presence of some of the harder diorite soils in the vineyard from which it hails.

Domaine de Gry-Sablon

www.gry-sablon.com

When Dominique Morel took over his family domaine in 1991, it was at the height of the Beaujolais Nouveau boom and it was practically impossible to buy land in the region. So much money was sloshing around in the system, he says, that many wineries in Beaujolais were better equipped than those of their neighbours to the north in Burgundy. At the time, the going price of a hectolitre of wine from one of the *crus* was the equivalent (in francs) of around 500 euros. And then the bottom dropped out of the market (see p. 8 for more about the history of Beaujolais Nouveau and its impact on the region). Now, says Morel, you're lucky if you can get 400 euros for the same amount of wine from the same vineyard – despite nearly 35 years of a rising cost of living.

Morel has seen Beaujolais through its boom years and on into the era when growers struggled to make a living from their vineyards. He believes that many of those who were unwilling to adapt their practices to the demands of the market during the bad times either went bust or slipped quietly into early retirement. Now, says Morel, things are on the up – not only have producers got a better understanding of how to farm their grapes and make good wine, but also the advent of climate change allows for good levels of ripening in a region which once struggled to achieve appropriate levels of maturity in its grapes.

Morel, however, has thrived, an example of a man swimming against the tide. At the start of his career, he and his father shared 6 hectares of vineyards between them, and now he farms 17 hectares, of which six are in the *villages* zone and the remainder distributed across Morgon, Fleurie (he owns 3 hectares in each), Régnié, Moulin-à-Vent, Saint-Amour and Juliénas. His winery is located on a hillside in the village of Emeringes, with panoramic views out over the slopes of four of the *crus* (Fleurie, Morgon, Chénas and Juliénas).

Morel's approach to viticulture and to winemaking is magpie-like – he picks and chooses the elements that seem to him to be best suited to the requirements of the vineyard and the vintage. In 2024, a year in which heavy rainfall throughout the season caused problems for many growers, particularly those working organically (and therefore constrained in terms of the anti-fungal measures they could take), Morel is gratified by the fact that his ability to use fungicides (albeit at low levels) meant that he was able to harvest a normal year's worth of yields. (Many growers were not as lucky, and were forced to triage carefully on already reduced yields.) He's proud of having worked two vintages with Jules Chauvet (see p. 12) and says that he sourced the yeasts with which he inoculates his ferments from Chauvet's *cuvage*, and he prefers to kick his fermentations off at warm temperatures as this allows for both a more efficient process and better extraction of flavours and structure from the skins of his grapes.

The Gry-Sablon wines have a generosity and richness that shows throughout the range. The Beaujolais Villages Emeringes is supple and refreshing, and laden with fruit, while the Morgon from Douby has a meaty, almost bloody note on the palate, which is supported by plush, gently grippy tannins. The Fleurie Vieilles Vignes has slightly darker fruit than many wines from the *cru*, possibly as a result of growing the grapes on the warm, west-facing slope of the Labourons *lieu-dit*, while the St-Amour Les Tines has an almost salty minerality to provide a counterpoint to its red plum and floral notes. The Juliénas La Petite Cabane is the wild card of the pack – almost feral and savage in its savoury intensity, it tastes of sun-warmed stones and herbs, all supported by burly (in the context of Beaujolais) tannins.

Domaine des Jeunes Pousses

www.domainedesjeunespousses.fr

Ever since 2015 Thibault Liger-Belair (see p. 97) has been funding a side project known as the Domaine des Jeunes Pousses (the young shoots). The idea of, as he puts it, 'a nursery for young winemakers', came to him when he was offered the chance to buy 8 hectares of vineyards, only three of which were in Moulin-à-Vent, the *cru* on which he wanted to focus his attentions. He decided that the remaining 5 hectares of vineyards, some in Chénas and some in Emeringes, one of the Beaujolais Villages, should be used to provide a springboard for the career of promising young winemakers.

'I was lucky enough to have been born with the viticultural equivalent of a silver spoon in my mouth,' says Liger-Belair, 'but I see all these young people with a real passion for winemaking coming out of their training knowing all about how to grow grapes and make wine in theory, but without any practical hands-on experience, particularly in terms of the commercial realities of running a domaine.'

Liger-Belair decided to convert his new vineyards to organics, buy a tractor and to find a nearby *cuvage* and house in order to enable a young couple to gain that real-life knowledge without the attendant financial risks. Liger-Belair not only donates tenancy of the estate to the lucky incumbents, he and his partner in the project, Domaine de Belargus's Ivan Massonnat, are also on hand to offer advice and insights, although the final decisions are largely taken by the current crop of Jeunes Pousses. Any profit that they generate over the course of their tenancy, which lasts a maximum of three years, is their own, with the aim of helping them to fund their own domaine, should they choose to do so.

Angela Quibler and Hugo Foizel of Domaine Obora (see p. 82) were the first couple to benefit from Liger-Belair's generosity, and they were succeeded in 2022 by Thaïs Lamy and Juliette Lumeau, who have now moved out of the region to start their own project. The new crop, Olivier Cossec and Naïs Lombard, had recently taken over the domaine at the time of writing (May 2025), so their take on the project has yet to become apparent.

It's worth noting that Liger-Belair and Massonnat have recently taken the decision that, from the 2025 vintage onwards, they will make the final decisions on the vinification of a couple of the property's cuvées. 'We wanted to ensure that customers who are following the project won't feel totally lost, even if the vinification style changes drastically from one generation of Jeunes Pousses to another,' he explains.

Domaine Minhaé

minhae.fr

Lan Bertrand came to France at the age of three, a refugee from the war that was ravaging the former French territory of Indochina. She says that growing up she never really tasted wine as it wasn't part of her culture. It wasn't until she met her husband, who came from the Jura, that she got her first taste of the stuff. Even then, it was hardly a revelatory moment, just a drink to be enjoyed with dinner. Her interest was sparked a few years later, when she and her husband moved to Beaujolais, and Bertrand began working as an accountant for the Vignerons des Pierres Dorées (see p. 228). She began talking to the growers and the cooperative's winemakers and thrilled to the passion these people had for their work. She switched from working with spreadsheets to working as an administrator for the cooperative so that she could spend more time with the *vignerons*, then began studying for a diploma in viticulture and oenology so that she could understand their concerns better. She undertook a *stage* with Philippe Viet (see p. 176) as part of her studies, working for him for the entire year rather than the pre-ordained two months so that she could follow the annual cycle from winter pruning through to harvest and then winemaking. It was while she was working for Viet that she had a moment of life-changing clarity. 'I was in the vineyard in the Haute Ronze [a *lieu-dit* in Régnié], pruning the vines,' she says, 'when I had this absolute magic moment and realized that this was what I wanted to do.'

Bertrand went home and told her husband that she was going to change her career. She started looking for some vineyards to work on, finally finding a hilly 3-hectare parcel in Blacé, so steep that it's unmechanizable. She didn't want to take on the entire parcel, she says, but the owner said that unless she was willing to take the lot on a long-term lease, they were going to be grubbed up. It's her love for these vineyards, she says, that drives her. Bertrand adores working outside, feeling the sun on her face, listening to the birdsong and the buzzing of the bees. She gets a thrill from watching her vines grow, deepening her understanding of their response to the way in which they are managed.

Initially, says Bertrand, she hadn't even thought about making wine, but one of the producers she was trying to interest in buying her grapes came to visit the plot and asked her why on earth she wasn't going to make her own wine from such beautiful grapes. So Bertrand rolled up her sleeves and decided to try her hand at winemaking, with the support and help of friends who let her use some space in their cellar. Since that first vintage in 2022, she's found her own winery, and her vineyard holdings have evolved to include a hectare in Blacé and a smaller parcel of vines in Régnié, both of which are organically certified and in the process of conversion to full biodynamics.

Winemaking, for Bertrand, is mostly about ensuring the high quality of the grapes, right down to hand-plucking undesirable berries from the bunches one by one at harvest time, if she feels it's necessary. She then stacks the bunches in her tanks and leaves them to get on with the fermentation, even if that takes some time. 'In 2024 it took them 10 days to get started,' she laughs, 'but I don't intervene. If I take care of the vines, the grapes will get there in the end.'

Bertrand likes light-bodied wines, and hers rarely clock in at more than around 12% abv. Her Beaujolais cuvée is a little stemmy, but has a nice, crunchy quality to it, and a fresh, vivid finish. The Beaujolais Villages Blacé feels rounder and riper on the palate, with more density of pomegranate and red cherry fruit, and some stony tannins that drag gently on the palate.

Domaine de Mont Joly

jb1129.wixsite.com/website

'Blacé,' says Jean-Baptiste Bachevillier, 'is at the crossroads of the various soil profiles of the Beaujolais region.' As a member of the eighth generation of his family to make wines in Beaujolais, Bachevillier certainly knows what he's talking about when it comes to his local terroir, but his winemaking is inflected by his adventures across a broad swathe of the viticultural world. He's made wine for Yves Cuilleron in the Rhône and Mommessin in Beaujolais (see p. 241), studied at Plumpton College in the UK, spent time working for Australia's Coriole Estate and Robert Oatley before returning to France to work as a brand ambassador for

Boisset and, ultimately, acquiring his own vineyards in Beaujolais. The breadth of Bachevillier's experience is typical of the approach being taken by the new generation of winemakers in Beaujolais, many of whom have sought to broaden their experience beyond the confines of their home region.

Blacé, where Bachevillier's 5 hectares of vineyards are located, does indeed seem to have a representative sprinkling of most of the major soil types found in Beaujolais, from the limestones typical of the southern Beaujolais, to the pink granites and blue stones found in the *crus* (as well as alluvial deposits, clays and marls). Most of Bachevillier's organically farmed vines are planted either on granites in varying degrees of decomposition or on limestones and marls.

Bachevillier's Chardonnays are among the most sophisticated in the region, demonstrating a lightness of touch in the winery and precise balance of fruit and freshness. The unoaked Cerisiers shows a stony minerality that helps balance the ripe peachy flavours, while the oaked Les Blancs has great textural elegance. His flexible approach to winemaking shows in the reds. The joyously fruity Beaujolais Blacé La Pointe is made from grapes grown on gneiss vinified with a semi-carbonic maceration. The Beaujolais Villages Marzy, from grapes grown on a spot at the foot of a hill where alluvial soils are tumbled together with flint and clay, is redolent of bright, crunchy redcurrants, with a counterpoint of liquorice and tea leaves. It's all framed by gently grippy tannins, its balance created by a *millefeuille* vinification that layers whole bunches with de-stemmed fruit. The de-stemmed, oak-aged Beaujolais Blacé 85.45 is an impressively concentrated wine whose firm but fine tannins show evidence of careful extraction during the course of the fermentation.

Bachevillier has big plans for his domaine's future, including the construction of a smart tasting room to show off his wines to day trippers from Lyon as well as visitors from further afield. During the time he spent in the New World he saw what wine tourism can bring to a region, and he's keen to demonstrate the potential benefits it might bring to his small corner of Beaujolais.

Domaine du Penlois/Sébastien Besson

penlois.fr

Sébastien Besson's family moved south from the Mâconnais four generations ago, purchasing their property just outside of the village of Lancié in the 1920s. As with many farms at the time, vineyards were just part of the family's agricultural portfolio, but it became a viticultural domaine under the management of Besson's grandfather. The Bessons were the first to plant Chardonnay in Lancié on Le Chatelard, a limestone outcrop, but the vineyard was uprooted in favour of Gamay, then reconverted to the production of Chardonnay in the 1970s. At around the same time, Besson's father – who was then in charge of the family business – began investing in vineyards in the *crus*. The family now owns 30 hectares, of which five are in Morgon, three each in Juliénas and Chénas and two in Moulin-à-Vent, with the remaining holdings all in the Beaujolais Villages zone of Lancié, of which a shade more than 6 hectares are dedicated to the production of white wines. There's also a small *négoce* side to the business, largely focused on making rosé and white Vins de France.

Besson began working with his father in 2014 and has now taken over the management of the domaine in his own right. Whereas Besson *père* largely focused on selling his wines to small retailers and private clients in the domestic market, Sébastien has long set his sights on a more international arena, and has been busy adapting the domaine's winemaking accordingly. There are now two ranges produced in the Penlois winery, with the wines bottled under Besson's own label, Sébastien Besson, altogether lighter, fresher and more modern in style than the more traditional wines sold as Domaine du Penlois, particularly the reds, many of which I found over-extracted.

I preferred the unoaked version of the Domaine du Penlois's Beaujolais Blanc, the Chardonnay du Chatelard, with its fleshy mid-palate and rich stone fruit character, finding the oaked cuvée, Le Chêne du Chatelard, a little too marked by its time in barrel. Sébastien Besson makes two whites under his own label, of which l'Agrume, a Chardonnay with a little bit of skin contact, which gives it a gentle textural grip, is the more characterful and complex. Besson's Beaujolais Villages red – shortly to become Beaujolais Lancié – is a very pretty, delicate wine with a perfumed floral character and a little stemmy bitterness that provides refreshment on the finish. His Chénas – the first wine he ever made in his own right, back in 2017 – comes from a *cru* he loves and describes as 'overshadowed'. It's a blend from different parcels, as indicated by the use of a white label instead of a black one, which is reserved for parcel selections. It is a nicely balanced wine with a layered palate of mulberries, cranberries and aniseed, brought into focus by a subtle tannic grip. The black label Morgon Douby spends a year in old oak barrels prior to bottling, and shows rich, dark fruit with an undertow of smoke and spice. It's a firmly structured wine, austere in its youth and needing time to open up fully.

Domaine de Romarand

domainederomarand.fr

There's always a feeling of excitement that comes when I visit a property that hasn't really been written up before, and which I've only heard about on the bush telegraph. Leaving the Domaine de Romarand, which is hidden away in the hills behind Quincié, I felt that frisson anew. Anastasia Kritikou is an architect by training, who fell in love with wine and winemaking. With the support of her husband – also an architect – she quit her job and trained in Burgundy and in Beaujolais, where she worked alongside Frédéric Berne (see p. 196) in Lantignié.

She says that it was while working with Berne that she learned the most – and also where she fell in love with the Gamay vines that cling tenaciously to the steep granite slopes. Kritikou says that it's easy to find good vineyards to work with – the challenge is finding a winery in decent working order. She was lucky enough to find a house that not only had a fully equipped cellar, but was also big enough to raise her children and to open a small *chambres d'hôtes* business that helps supplement the family's income.

For the moment she has a little under 3 hectares of vines spread out across the villages of Quincié, Lantignié and in the *cru* of Régnié, and bottled her first wines in the challenging 2021 vintage. Challenging or not, Kritikou has made a success of her wines both in cool, rainy 2021 and in the hot vintage of 2022. Each parcel undergoes separate vinification, and some of these are further split between wines that mature in inert vessels or in oak or her single concrete egg. All the wines have a poise and elegance that usually come with years of experience, but in Kritikou's case it's clear she's a natural.

She makes five cuvées, whose names hint at her Greek origins. The Régnié cuvées (Gamma is the unwooded wine, while Delta is matured in oak) have a signature spiciness, as well as the fine, stony tannins so typical of wines whose origin lie in the granite soils of the *cru*. The richest, densest wine is Epsilon, made from 60-year-old vines grown on the blue stone slopes of Quincié. A quarter of this wine is matured in oak, which helps lend the tannins some real grip and focus. Lantignié is the source of Mu (matured in fibreglass tanks), which layers blueberries and red cherries with notes of peony and tea leaves along a framework of fine, grippy tannins. My favourite, though, is the refined, elegant Alpha, a Lantignié that is matured in the egg. The palate is lush and layered, with great freshness and precision on the finish.

16

BEAUJOLAIS

> **Year in which AOP status was awarded**: 1937
> **Total vineyard area**: 4,090 hectares

When people talk about generic Beaujolais, they usually have in mind the southern part of the region, the area often referred to as the *pierres dorées*, or the *Bas Beaujolais*. It's worth bearing in mind that there are patches of vineyards dotted across the entire length and breadth of Beaujolais that are part of the Beaujolais AOP production zone. In addition, producers can, if they so choose, declassify some of their production into AOP Beaujolais (or, indeed, into Beaujolais Villages if they're in a *cru*). As a result, the vineyard area cited above does not lie exclusively in the south. It is, however, true that most wine labelled as Beaujolais is produced in the *Bas Beaujolais*, an area with a different geology, landscape and culture to that which prevails in the *crus*.

Although granites and diorites start to give way to limestones, schists and clays somewhere around Blacé, it's not until you head south from Villefranche-sur-Saône, the largest town in the region, that you really start to notice the changing landscape. The hills undulate more gently in the south, and the houses are not built of pink granite or blue stone. Instead, blocks of a rich orange-tinged ochre predominate – the *pierres dorées* or golden stones that lend their name to this part of Beaujolais. This, perhaps, creates a mistaken impression about the geology of the area. Although limestone and clay do predominate, there's more geological diversity than the catch-all term for the region suggests. In the west of the region, in particular, you'll find broad swathes of granite, sandstones, gneiss and outcrops of diorite, although the blue stone here often has a greenish tinge. Those gentle rolling hills give way in the west to an altogether wilder countryside, with dense patches of forest and tumbling rivers.

It is somewhat confusing, perhaps, to learn that the producers of this southern zone are currently seeking to create a *Denomination Géographique Complémentaire*, a supplementary geographical designation, that would allow them to add the words '*Pierres Dorées*' to their labels. This new denomination would not be restricted to grapes grown specifically on the golden limestone soils, it would be available to all producers growing grapes in southern Beaujolais. Such labelling might be easily understood by someone born and brought up in France, where the term *pierres dorées* is strongly linked to the wider southern Beaujolais zone. Nevertheless, the use of the designation runs the risk of baffling outsiders, who might not appreciate the cultural nuances and assume a link between terminology and terroir. At the moment the final decision on the matter rests with the INAO.

But let's head back to those golden houses as their presence tells a story not only of the region's geology, but also about its economy. They're often larger in scale than the houses of the north, and many of them seem to be quite grand. Wrought iron gates allow glimpses of substantial mansions hidden behind high walls, and landscaped gardens seem to be

The warm glow cast by Beaujolais's pierres dorées *is clearly visible in the pretty village of Jarnioux, with its golden-hued castle and church*

the norm. Lyon, France's third-largest city, lies less than an hour's drive away. The *pierres dorées* are therefore within easy commuting distance – or at least close enough by for people to have weekend country houses here even if they don't want to commute on a daily basis. There are more big villages than there are in the north (some of them might even be classified as small towns), and, perhaps, a few more restaurants and bars in these villages. The people strolling along the streets don't generally look as if they're dressed for a hard day's labour in the fields.

The south is not all about manicured villages, though. The landscape is rich in fields of wheat, there are meadows where cows graze lazily, and an abundance of woods and orchards, too. The south, far more than the north, is a region in which polyculture is the norm. There are plenty of vineyards, but they don't look like those in the *crus*. They're trellised and planted wide – wide enough to allow for the mechanization of most vineyard tasks. Even harvest is largely mechanized here, which means that semi-carbonic maceration is far from the norm – machine harvesting doesn't allow for whole bunch picking. In addition, come late summer, you'll notice that a significant proportion of these vineyards bear white grapes rather than red. A surprising amount of Chardonnay is grown here – far more than the statistics about the volumes of white wine production in Beaujolais might suggest.

In the aftermath of the Beaujolais Nouveau crash some 20 years ago, most of the growers in southern Beaujolais were casting about desperately for a viable source of income. Gamay, once the cash cow that fed the apparently inexhaustible demand for cheap, fruity red, was no longer required – at least not in anything like the same quantity as before. The solution that offered itself was Crémant de Bourgogne. This traditional method fizz, so beloved of the French market, is currently kept afloat on a sea of Chardonnay grown in the south. Around 60 per cent of the grapes that go into Burgundian bubbly actually come from Beaujolais, although this source is never acknowledged on the label. It's worth noting that Chardonnay may well be better adapted to the generous limestone-rich soils of the south than Gamay, which, given free rein can run wild and over-crop, resulting in the creation of rather thin, weedy wines.

All of this means that the production model in southern Beaujolais differs widely from the one that operates in the *crus* and the Villages. There are very few small-scale (or even mid-sized) wine producers in the *Bas Beaujolais*. Why work your fingers to the bone to farm densely planted vineyards or use your grapes to make artisanal wines when customers aren't prepared to pay big bucks for AOP Beaujolais? It's far more efficient, economically, to farm by machine – often using sprays of all kinds, from herbicides and fungicides to pesticides – and to then hand over responsibility for blending, bottling and marketing the resulting wine to a cooperative or a négociant. It's a pragmatic response to the economic realities and the reason why this particular chapter, despite the sheer scale of the southern region, features a relatively small number of producers.

Producers

Domaine Chasselay/Famille Chasselay

www.domaine-chasselay.com

There are lots of winemakers in Beaujolais who can trace their family's viticultural roots back for several generations. Few, though, have the longevity record of the Chasselays, who have documentary evidence that their family-owned vineyards near the village of Châtillon in 1464. Vineyards were handed down from father to son over the course of centuries. And there's the rub. Claire Chasselay grew up believing that winemaking was a man's job, and that she – like her mother before her – was destined to run the family's *chambres d'hôtes* (bed and breakfast) business and to take care of the domaine's administration. While her brother, Fabien, went off to further his viticultural studies in Australia, Claire stayed at home and dutifully cooked meals for guests, poured wines in the tasting room and manned the family's stand at tastings all around the country.

After eight years of this, though, Claire was bored. What's more, she was tasting wines at the *salons* she was attending that made her appraise the wines being made by her father and brother with a more critical eye. In 2016 she announced that she was leaving the family domaine but Fabien persuaded her to stay and, furthermore, to take on a role alongside him, working in the vineyards and making wines. Claire accepted and, in turn, persuaded Fabien to introduce some lighter, fresher wines to the line-up. Initially sceptical and fearful of losing their traditional clientele, Fabien and Jean-Gilles, their father, agreed to the introduction of one of Claire's wines to the range. Gradually, that one wine was joined by further bottlings, and while the Chasselay family did lose some of their older customers, they gained a far greater number of new ones.

These days Claire and her brother farm 10 hectares of Gamay in Beaujolais, along with a generous couple of hectares of Chardonnay, and a further 4 hectares in Fleurie, Brouilly and the Côte de Brouilly. These vineyards have been farmed organically since 2001 – a bold step to take at the height of the region's Nouveau crisis – but the younger generation has moved things on by adding hedges and other plants in order to encourage greater biodiversity. Winemaking varies from year to year – Claire says that there's no recipe, just an adaptation to the requirements of each vintage, but generally semi-carbonic maceration at cool temperatures of up to 22°C is favoured over de-stemming, and the degree of extraction is restrained.

I love the resulting verve and dash of Beaujolais Is Not Dead, a pretty, precise, easy-drinking cuvée that, served lightly chilled, would be a perfect summer-time wine. The Platière is also a Beaujolais, but a more serious take on the appellation, with rich, ripe cherry fruit enhanced by a dusting of spice, and framed by fine but discreet tannins. The Fleurie cuvée is called III, a reference to the three parcels that are assembled to make it. It's intensely floral on the nose and palate, with juicy blood oranges and delicate, almost lacy tannins that stretch the fruit out onto a hugely lengthy finish. The Brouilly Balloquets is focused and long, while the Côte de Brouilly Chardignon is firmer and denser in style. The Chasselays also make a couple of Beaujolais Blancs, of which the Terroir de Chatillon is the slightly lighter, simpler cuvée, based on a massal selection planted in 2009 and sourced from the 70-year-old vines that go into the rich, rounded Eparcieux Blanc.

Famille Girin

www.famillegirin.fr

As you cross from east to west over the Azergue River, you move from the ochre-coloured limestones that dominate the *Bas Beaujolais* to a landscape of granitic sands reminiscent of the terroir of much of the *crus*. The Girin family domaine is deeply rooted in this alternative geology, and has been since the current generation's great-great-grandfather, Pierre Girin, settled in these hills. A brother and sister team, Audrey and Thibaut have managed the property together since 2020. Thibaut was always destined to become a winemaker, following in his father's footsteps. Along the way he took some time to work for other domaines in Beaujolais as well as in New Zealand, returning home to work with his father and uncle in 2016. Audrey's career path was more meandering, but when Covid struck in 2020, the decision to return home to work alongside her brother became clearer.

Although the family vineyards, which extend out over 36 hectares, are not farmed organically, the use of treatments and sprays is minimal, and herbicides are not used at all. The vines, 95 per cent of which are planted on the granite soils, benefit from altitudes ranging from 250 to 400 metres, which helps ensure good levels of acidity and aromatic development in the grapes. Although a significant proportion of the production is dedicated to the production of musts, which are sold off to make Crémant de Bourgogne, the pair produce an average of around 50,000 bottles of their own wine a year, of which 80 per cent are reds. A quarter of their bottled wine sales are now Beaujolais Nouveau, a figure that has taken the Girins somewhat by surprise, although Audrey notes that these wines are becoming increasingly popular with younger wine drinkers.

Of their white wines, the Séduction de Chardonnay, the simpler, tank-aged wine, is the pick of the crop, with its zesty, attractive, bright-fruited palate. The equivalent bottling in red, the Séduction de Gamay Rouge, is equally appealing, with a brisk, crunchy, slightly stemmy palate. The Côteaux de Razet, an old-vine cuvée, shows some concentration and weight on the mid-palate, with rounded tannins that exert a bit of dusty grip on the finish.

Domaine Célia et David Large

www.davidlarge.fr

Célia and David Large march to the beat of a different drum. This is hardly unusual in Beaujolais, but the Larges don't do things by halves. To begin with, the village in which they're based – Montmelas-Saint-Sorlin – is well off the beaten track, hidden away in wooded hills, right on the border between the Beaujolais Villages and the Beaujolais AOP zones. The location of the vineyards is largely academic, though, as a significant proportion of the wines produced by the Larges is labelled as Vin de France. The decision to do so came about in response to David's experiences of trying to sell wines shortly after he took over the property from his parents in 2010. At the time Beaujolais had fallen from grace, and most people associated the region with cheap industrial plonk. David found himself attending salons with producers from other regions at which he was unable to get people to try his wines once they saw where he was from. Frustrated, he declassified his wines into Vin de France, and found them much easier to sell.

A cement fermentation tank at Domaine Célia et David Large
(photo courtesy of David Large)

Together, the couple farm around 7 hectares of vineyards, mostly in the Beaujolais AOP zone, but with a hectare of vineyards in the *villages*, split more or less equally between white and red, and two tiny parcels of vines on Mont Brouilly. Only 2 hectares of their vineyards are on the flat (and only more or less, at that), the rest are steep – 'As steep as the vineyards in Chiroubles', they explain. The Larges work organically, but find themselves constantly questioning their practices – as well as the conventions dictated by organic certification.

When it comes to white winemaking, the Larges 'keep it classic'. The grapes are pressed and settled before being pumped into tanks to ferment at temperatures of around 15°C (fairly standard for white wines). David would like to age at least some of his whites in barrel, but says he currently doesn't have the space in the winery that would allow him to do so. The Beaujolais Villages Blanc Dos Argenté is, quite simply, one of the most elegant and complex Chardonnays I've tasted in the region.

In terms of reds, there's a spread of vinification styles, ranging from a carbonic maceration with no *remontage* and short macerations of anywhere between four to seven days, to more vigorous semi-carbonic fermentations – some with significant amounts of de-stemmed fruit – lasting up to a couple of weeks, with regular gentle *remontages*. Zombi, bottled in the past as a Beaujolais Nouveau but now as a Vin de France, shows all the signs of being made in the gentlest of manners. It's a lovely light-bodied wine of great freshness and perfume, with little tannin other than a subtle drag on the palate on the length. Gamayhameha is a Beaujolais made from a parcel of vines planted on limestone on the very northernmost edge of the *pierres dorées*. My tasting notes read 'Rose petals!', although there's enough chalky tannin to give this otherwise ethereal wine some substance. Nelson is a Vin de France made from vines planted in the 1970s and named after the Larges' one-eyed cat, who in turn is named in honour of the eighteenth-century British admiral. Nelson – either of them – should be proud of his wine, which is rich and densely fruited, with a complex palate that blends floral notes and tea leaves with plums and salted red liquorice. Les Grands Terriers is a Beaujolais Villages made from 70-year-old Gamay vines grown on south-facing *pierres bleues* and vinified in fibreglass eggs. It's an explosively aromatic wine, rich with dark berry fruit, black pepper, lavender and fennel, all framed by sinewy tannins. The Côte de Brouilly Le Pavé is vinified in the same kinds of vessel as the Grands Terriers, but using whole bunches instead of partial de-stemming. This – and differences in terroir – has resulted in a more linear, structured and less exuberantly fruity wine, but nonetheless a very elegant one.

These wines – along with the names of the cuvées, the poems on the labels and the vibrant, somewhat punkish visual imagery – are all evidence of a truly creative, questioning and restless spirit at Large.

Jean Max

jean-max.org

Maxime Barrot always thought that he'd take over the family domaine in Charnay, but complicated divorces and rifts in relationships meant that he found himself having to reinvent his future. He started off by studying in Beaune, then did a Masters in agronomy, before setting off to do an influential *stage* in Chile. There he found himself working with Roberto Henriquez, a natural winemaker who works with small parcels of very old vines in the country's southern valleys.

Inspired by his experiences, and further work with biodynamic producers back in Beaujolais, most notably the Brets at the Domaine de la Soufrandière (see p. 233), he set up his own *négoce* business in 2018, which allowed him to explore the diversity of terroirs in southern Burgundy. Barrot bought his first parcel of vines in 2020, and now farms just over 4 hectares of vineyards on his own account, having given up his négociant activity in 2024. All his vineyards are worked organically, and he's in the process of conversion to full biodynamics, placing a lot of emphasis on improving the amount of humus in the soil. The ultimate aim, he says, is to create vineyards that are better able to deal with all the challenges the climate is throwing at them, although Barrot warns that it will probably take around a decade to fully achieve his aims.

His Chardonnays are all vinified in barrel, then he ages them in the same vessels to give the wines roundness and complexity. Barrot aims for what he calls a 'proper' carbonic maceration with his reds, saying that it usually takes around 10 days for his grapes – which he chills right down to below 10°C after harvest – to begin to express any juices. In order to extract as little as possible, he does no *remontages* over the course of the two to three weeks of intracellular fermentation, then presses them off to finish the fermentations at a low 20°C to preserve bright fruit characters. Just before the end of the alcoholic fermentation, when there's still a few grams of sugar left, he puts the wines in the vessels in which they will age – enamel-lined concrete tanks, barrels or amphorae. The aim is that the final burst of fermentation will fill the containers with carbon dioxide, allowing the wines to age in a reductive, protective atmosphere.

His L'Exht'hase is a very pale, tangy, unsulphured Gamay cuvée with notes of underripe cherries and hibiscus tea. It would make a wonderfully characterful alternative to a rosé. Dame Jeanne is a darker, riper amphora-aged wine with heady aromas of rose petals. It's a richer wine, with body derived from the shallow clay soils on which the grapes are grown, but it's perhaps a little bit better balanced. Sainte-Paule comes from a parcel of Gamay grown on granite soils. It's a round, fleshy wine with notes of strawberry and smoky tobacco leaves. Le Lievre Blanc is pale gold in colour, the result of a little skin contact early on in the winemaking process and extended ageing in barrel. There's a little textural grip, again from the skin contact, and notes of Golden Delicious apples and stony minerality.

Barrot's labels are striking, featuring drawings of costumed hares, a reference to the *lièvre de course*, the pace-setter in a cycle race or marathon. Barrot draws an analogy between the practice and his own aim, which is to be a pace-setter in terms of drawing attention to the terroirs of Beaujolais's southern hills.

Aurélie et Fabien Romany

aurelie-fabien-romany.web.app

Aurélie and Fabien Romany make their wines in an anonymous modern farm shed that gives no clue to its contents. An uninformed passer-by might well assume that the Romanys, like many of their neighbours, are farming cattle or wheat. Nevertheless, the Romanys are quietly in the process of building a wine business of impressive dimensions. Fabien's parents farmed 11 hectares of vineyards, all of which went to feed the large appetite of the local cooperative, but when the couple took over in 2019, they decided to refocus their efforts on making bottled wines under their own label. They now have some 20 hectares of vineyards, all planted in and around the village of Bully. Around a third of the vineyards are planted to Chardonnay, mostly on soils with generous amounts of clay. There's also a good swathe of granite in the landscape, and even some *pierre bleue*, although Romany says that it's slightly different in both structure and colour from the diorite found in the *crus*, and both are used to grow Gamay. As a pragmatic measure, all but 1 hectare of the Chardonnay is sold off to a négociant who uses the grapes to make crémant, but everything else is vinified on the estate.

All the vineyards are organic. Not, says Romany, because he wants a piece of paper to wave under people's noses but because he truly believes that it produces the best possible raw material for him to work with. The wines are mostly parcel selections, each bunch harvested by hand and then sorted on a vibrating table. Romany is not keen, however, on heating grapes up or chilling them down once they've been loaded into tanks, saying that if you're going to produce organic grapes you should also be paying attention to the carbon footprint involved when vinifying them. The aim is to keep the semi-carbonic fermentations going for around 10 to 14 days, or even up to 18 days in cooler vintages, when you need a bit more time to extract structure.

The couple make a stemmy, crunchy Beaujolais Nouveau, a style they believe is coming back into fashion, albeit with the emphasis firmly on character-driven bottlings rather than the mass-produced examples of yesteryear. There are a couple of Beaujolais Blancs, of which the Palières, vinified and aged in tank, is reminiscent of a blend from the northern Rhône in its rich, rounded fleshiness and the twist of bitterness on the finish. Les Gouttes is the oak-aged wine, although the barrels used are all old, lending the wine a broad mid-palate that gives balance to the bright stone and citrus fruit. Le Moulin, a wine bottled in the spring after harvest, is all rosehips and raspberry on the palate, its exuberance held in check by gently raspy tannins. Aux Ecully comes from a parcel planted on granites. There's considerable tannic grip from a long maceration, but copious fruit provides balance. The year of plantation of their oldest vines, 1918, some of which are Gamay Teinturier, a red-fleshed cousin of the more familiar grape, provides the name for a layered, firmly structured wine. The final cuvée, Into the Wild, is partially de-stemmed to allow for a greater degree of extraction. It's a burly, broad-shouldered wine with plenty of tannin and rich, dark fruit – definitely one for a bit of bottle ageing.

The *nouveau* Beaujolais Nouveau

At the peak of the Beaujolais Nouveau boom in 1988, more than 105 million bottles of the stuff were shipped out of the region and around the world. In 2024, the figure had fallen to 14 million bottles. That's still a lot of wine, but it's also a clear sign that the glory days of Nouveau are well and truly done – isn't it?

Not so fast. There's an argument to be made that Nouveau has made a bit of a comeback in the past few years. Not in terms of volumes produced, but in terms of a growing appreciation for what these *primeur* wines can deliver. The best of the current crop of Nouveaus – not just Beaujolais Nouveau but also Beaujolais Villages Nouveau – are a long way away from the thin, dilute wines that cast such a shadow over the region's reputation. Good examples of the style all have a kind of juicy immediacy to them, but no lack of concentration. All but the poorest examples will not only see you through the dark days of winter, but should also make a bright, characterful alternative to rosé come the next summer. In other words, contrary to widespread opinion, good Nouveau can stay the course for at least a year after bottling.

And although the big guys are still making the bulk of the Nouveaus, the best takes are the *primeurs* made by smaller, more artisanal producers. It's hard to provide a definitive list of the best Nouveaus as not every domaine produces one on a regular basis, but many of the wineries featured elsewhere in this book will make a *primeur* cuvée, at least some of the time. If a producer's approach sounds like your kind of thing, it's worth taking a punt if you stumble across their Nouveau, not least because these wines are often ridiculously cheap.

Around half of all Nouveau is sold in France, but significant quantities are exported. Japan is the key export market for the style. So popular is Beaujolais Nouveau with consumers in Honshu and the other islands that it can be hard for producers of *cru* wines to get a look in on the country's restaurant and retail lists. Other key markets for the wines are big cities in North America, the UK, Scandinavia and Germany.

If you want to track down a bottle, your best place to look is the kind of wine bar, restaurant or retailer that caters to a hip young clientele, suggesting that you don't necessarily need to be old to be wise. The attraction exerted by new Nouveaus might come as a bit of a surprise to those who have spent the past couple of decades pooh-poohing the wines, but there's growing evidence to support the idea that Beaujolais's *primeurs* have turned a reputational corner. Doug Wregg, a director of UK-based wine importer Les Caves de Pyrene, says that he's seen demand for Nouveau growing steadily over the course of the past few years. In the main, he says, the cuvées he imports are being sold to inner-city retailers and restaurants with a strong line in natural wines. As an illustration of the trend, in 2024, Honey Spencer, the author of *Natural Wine, No Drama* and owner of London's fashionable Sune restaurant, commissioned and shipped a barrel of Beaujolais Nouveau from Domaine Obora (see p. 82). The 225-litre *barrique* duly arrived in time for the third Thursday in November, as did around 500 customers, who ate, drank and made merry with huge enthusiasm. By the end of the day, says Spencer, 270 of the 300 bottles of Nouveau had been consumed, and the remainder were all sold on the Friday to diners who hadn't been able to make it to the restaurant the day before. The inspiration behind Spencer's decision to ship Obora's Nouveau came, in turn, from the time she spent working in Copenhagen, where she'd witnessed the huge popularity of the Beaujolais Nouveau parties organized each year by many of the city's wine bars and restaurants. It would appear that, for the most switched-on wine aficionados in both cities, the idea of a race to be the first to pour the Nouveau has largely faded into the background, replaced by the original concept of *primeurs* as a wine to celebrate and enjoy in a spirit of relaxed conviviality.

Domaine Saint-Cyr

www.beaujolais-saintcyr.com

Raphaël Saint-Cyr in all relevant respects looms larger than life, both physically – he's a tall, generously built man – and in terms of his influence on wine production in the southern part of Beaujolais. But although he's best known these days for his organic production and his lightly coloured, fruit-forward wines, his approach to his work has undergone a fairly seismic shift since he first began working on the domaine with his father in 2008.

On returning from a stint working at a large winery in New Zealand where, says Saint-Cyr, he learned how he didn't want to make wine, he converted the family vineyards to organic production. It wasn't that big a step given that his father, although farming conventionally, was a minimalist in terms of his use of sprays compared to many of his neighbours. Winemaking, though, following the pattern set by Saint-Cyr *père*, had a focus on the creation of big, bold wines. Yeasts were cultured and extraction was pushed as far as was feasible, given the grape and the terroirs with which Saint-Cyr was working. His first steps on his own personal road to Damascus came in 2012, when he was invited to participate in the *Biojolaise* tasting (an annual professional wine fair, which later evolved to become part of *Bien Boire en Beaujolais*). Saint-Cyr quickly realized that not only did his wines stand outside the group's norms, but also that he actually preferred the lighter, more delicate cuvées made by his colleagues.

Once back at home, he adapted his style of winemaking, using semi-carbonic macerations and gentler extractions in order to create wines with brighter, fresher palates, but there were still a few steps left on his onwards journey. A few years later and Saint-Cyr was back at the *Biojolaise* event, where an elder statesman of the winemaking community commented while tasting his wines on how he'd rather drink a wine using conventional farming methods but with no use of additives in the winery than a wine made the other way round. Saint-Cyr says that, for him, this was the ultimate revelation. From that stage on he vowed to stop using cultured yeasts or any other winemaking aids. He rarely ever uses sulphites in his wines – not even the minute doses used by most 'natural' producers in the region – saying that there's only one thing that would make him use sulphites, and that's the needs of the wine itself. What he means is that unless he has an active problem with his ferments, he does not believe in adding sulphites to his cuvées, considering that it mutes the vibrant character he now seeks to reveal in his wines.

Of the 18 hectares he now farms – largely biodynamically, albeit without the certification – 5 hectares are in the *crus* of Chénas, Morgon and Moulin-à-Vent. He makes two cuvées in each *cru*, one from younger vines, as denoted by the use of a white label, the other with older vines and a black label. The Moulin-à-Vent Les P'tits Bois, the white label bottling, is pretty and perfumed, with vibrant fruit and gently chalky grip. The La Bruyère is altogether denser, darker and more complex, with an elegant, fresh finish. Chénas Robert is named in memory of a grower who farmed some of the appellation's parcels on behalf of Saint-Cyr, who bought him out on Robert's retirement. Sadly, Robert died within months of selling up, but lives on in a rounded, peppery bottling based, in part, on his vines. Les Journets, from the same *cru*, is made from a parcel of 70-year-old vines, and has dense, compact tannins and a layered, spicy palate.

Saint-Cyr also make a number of white wines. Les Gallong is the entry-level Beaujolais Blanc. Vinified in tank, then aged in a mix of *foudres* and cement tanks for up to 20 months, it's a savoury wine in which salty, stony minerality creates an impression of brightness on the finish. Terroir de Lachassagne is its older brother, made from a parcel grown on a mix of limestone and marl, then aged in large old oak tuns for a couple of years. It's rich and textural, with a piercing acidity Saint-Cyr ascribes to the interaction between long ageing and *Pediococcus*, a strain of lactic acid bacteria. The same acidity is present in Sauvage, a Vin de France made from Sauvignon Blanc. The same long ageing in barrel results in the creation of a sophisticated, textural wine reminiscent of smart white Bordeaux. Most of Saint-Cyr's production is focused on his home terroir of Beaujolais, and the domaine's key cuvée is La Galoche, a rounded, juicy wine whose palate is packed with strawberries and blood oranges, with a bracing twist of smoky tea leaf. The Terroir de Bellevue is the black label Beaujolais, made from a parcel of 70-year-old vines. It's a cuvée that should make you re-evaluate 'basic' Beaujolais, given its layered, dense fruit, its long finish and the supple, chalky grip of its well-integrated tannins.

Séléné/Sylvère Trichard

Sylvère Trichard admits that he was a bit of a firebrand in his youth, full of fierce convictions. These days, he says, he's more interested in asking questions. Trichard's early certainties were constructed slowly, with their foundations built on the time he spent earning his pocket money in his uncles' vineyards. It wasn't until he was 18 that he was allowed to help make wine, and he knew, then and there, that this was what he wanted to do with his life. He went to work for Jean-Claude Lapalu (see p. 186), and refined his calling further. He didn't just want to make wine, he wanted to make natural wine. Somewhere around the time he took over 3 hectares of his family's organic vineyards, he also spent some time working at Domaine Belluard in Savoy, and returned home filled with a passion for biodynamics.

Between his first vintage in 2012 and today, however, he's fallen out of love with at least some of the aspects of biodynamics that would allow him full certification. 'They were sending in assessors who were insisting on the use of silica in my vineyards in hot, dry vintages,' he explains, 'and this ran counter to my *bon sens paysan*.'[6] Trichard's wines are no longer certified, but they are still emphatically biodynamic – so much so that the name of his domaine, Séléné, pays tribute to the Greek goddess of the moon, whose phases influence the timing of his actions in the vineyard and in the *cuvage*. Right now, though, Trichard's current enthusiasm is for agroforestry. He's replanting some of his vineyards and enthuses about how he's surrounding the new plantations with hedges, and interspersing vines with a selection of native and fruit-bearing trees.

Winemaking is fairly minimalist in style, with as little manipulation as Trichard feels he can get away with, although he's prepared to filter or use sulphites if he feels it's necessary. It all comes down to rigorous observation during the course of the process, he says, commenting that it's vital to analyse the ferments all the time, otherwise you're on the fast track to ruining your wine.

His Beaujolais Blanc comes from a parcel of vines planted on lime-stone soils that contain very little clay. The wine doesn't go through malolactic conversion as Trichard wants to preserve acidity. It's a zesty wine with a linear palate and notes of pears and lemons, along with a twist of the savoury celery salt character found so frequently in the whites from the region. The Beaujolais comes from a parcel of vines planted on deep soils that contain clays, limestone and colluvial deposits – 'everything that tumbles down from the hill to come to a rest at

---

6 *Bon sens paysan*, a country man's/peasant's common sense, is a term used frequently by producers, especially in the *Bas Beaujolais*, particularly in the context of a grower digging their heels in and refusing to follow the diktats of bureaucracy.

the bottom,' Trichard explains. It's a rounded, plush wine with fleshy tannins and a ripe cherry cola note tinged with a bit of smoke. The Beaujolais Villages comes from 60-year-old vines planted on granitic soils. A generous third of the wine is aged for a year in a mixture of old barrels and *demi-muids*, creating a deeper, denser wine with layered flavours and a kick of bright acidity that carries the long, potent finish.

Vignerons des Pierres Dorées

www.vignerons-pierres-dorees.fr

Beaujolais used to have a lot of cooperatives, but they've gradually been whittled away and now only nine remain, of which the Vignerons des Pierres Dorées is arguably among the most dynamic. It was born of the fusion of three individual cooperatives, which decided to pool their resources in 2011, and focus on the production of bottled wines rather than bulk sales. (Having said that, only 25–50 per cent of its volume, depending on vintage conditions, is bottled by the cooperative each year. The rest is sold off in bulk, much of it to make Crémant de Bourgogne.)

The Vignerons des Pierres Dorées source their raw material from around 130 individual growers, but of these barely 40 are full-time grape growers. In terms of total vineyard area, the Vignerons are spread out across 400 hectares of vineyards. It sounds like a pretty broad area, but when the cooperative was formed, less than 15 years ago, it bought grapes from over 700 hectares. This vineyard attrition, largely caused by growers retiring without finding anyone to take over their land, is a reflection of broader trends in the region. (Statistics suggest that only around 5 per cent of the children of grape growers across the wider Beaujolais area step into their parents' footsteps to take over the running of their domaines.)

Perhaps confusingly, despite the cooperative's name, which suggests that grapes are sourced from the iron oxide-rich limestone soils that give the *pierres dorées* their ochre colour, its vines are planted on a complex range of geologies that include granites, gneiss, marls and diorite.

Winemaking models are diverse, although fairly unusually, around 80 per cent of the cooperative's grapes are harvested by hand. (Most harvesting in southern Beaujolais is done by machine.) And although a significant proportion of the cooperative's production is exported, sales from their cellar door – a lovely old stone-built négociant's house in one of the (officially) most beautiful villages in France – are also important.

One of the unusual twists to the wines sold by the Vignerons is that the prestige cuvées are aged in bottle for several years prior to release. I'm not sure that this adds much to the sometimes overly rich and rather extractive style of winemaking, preferring instead the lighter, fresher youthful cuvées from the cheaper end of the range. La Rose Blanche is a light, fresh Chardonnay with decent length and some pretty lemon sherbet fruit on the palate, while the Terra Iconia Rouge is a crunchy, refreshing, light-bodied quaffer. Slightly further up the price scale – but not by much – La Rose Pourpre is a bargain of an old-vine cuvée with spicy dark berry fruit, sinewy tannins and a burst of zesty acidity.

17

NÉGOCIANTS

The role of the négociant is fundamental to a French wine region's trading prospects, but what they do – and how they do it – is widely misunderstood. At the most basic level a négociant – a word that can be simply translated as 'trader' – buys product and sells it on. The extent of their impact on the finished product varies widely.

In some instances a négociant in Beaujolais is present throughout the life cycle of a wine, from helping to determine the way in which the vineyard is managed throughout the growing season through to the stage at which wines are sold on to a retailer or a restaurateur. Other négociants have much less involvement with a wine's initial stages of creation, stepping in to buy wine from their suppliers, and assuming responsibility for maturing the wines and the creation of the final blend as well as the sale of the finished product to the end retailer. This is often the case with the largest companies, who typically prefer to distance themselves from the hard labour of wine production. In between the two extremes, you'll also find négociants with varying degrees of involvement in determining the relevant viticultural parameters, but who buy in grapes and then roll up their shirt sleeves to make the wines themselves.

Contrary to popular belief, négociants are not always monolithically large corporate entities. You'll meet all sorts in this chapter, from those who produce and market millions of bottles each year, right down to micro-négociants, whose annual production might only amount to fewer than 100 12-bottle cases. It's worth noting, too, that many self-defined négociants also run their own properties, bottling wines under the names of these domaines rather than under the name of their *négoce* business. Smaller négociants may not run multiple properties, but they may own one or more vineyards themselves, vinifying wines in their own right. In many cases the difference between *négoce* wines – that is, those bought in by the company at some point in their production cycle – and those made from start to finish by the same négociant can be signalled by a difference in the name of the producer used on the label. This can be as subtle as the use of the term 'maison' rather than 'domaine'. Sometimes you don't even get this tiny clue. Conversely, some producers whose main business lies in producing wines made from grapes they have grown themselves may also have a small *négoce* side to their company. Where this is the case, these producers are listed in the relevant *cru* chapter rather than here. Instead, this chapter is dedicated to those producers who are best known as négociants – in the context of wines made in Beaujolais, at least.

Négociants of note

Stéphane Aviron

Stéphane Aviron is obsessed by hygiene, for all the right reasons. A small, wiry man with a ferocious work ethic (my appointment with him was scheduled for 9 a.m. on a Sunday, and by the time I arrived it was clear that he'd already been on site for some time), Aviron grew up in Beaujolais with a father who ran a laboratory that performed analyses for local winemakers. As a result, Aviron was never in any doubt about the need for scrupulous cleanliness in the winery, a need which he believes has become even more important in an age where global warming has raised the pH levels of fermenting musts to a dangerous degree. The lower the levels of acidity in the grapes and the wines they make, he explains, the more susceptible they become to infection by rogue yeasts and other potentially harmful microorganisms, particularly *Acetobacter*. It's all too easy, with very ripe grapes, for levels of phenols (the compounds associated with *Brettanomyces*) and volatile acidity to rise beyond threshold levels, compromising the taste and quality of the wine. And, he warns, once the organisms that cause these problems are present in a winery, they can be very difficult to eliminate.

After graduating from university in Beaune, Aviron spent time working in California – thus becoming a member of the first generation of winemakers in Beaujolais to set out in any numbers to explore the world of wine from a more global perspective. After returning home he spent a few years working for other companies and in the lab with his father. He made the first of his own wines – a Chénas – in 1993.

In 2000, Aviron went into partnership with Nicolas Potel, a class-mate from Beaune and the scion of a famous family of winemakers from the Côte d'Or. Together they built a négociant business that now bottles wines from across the Beaujolais region. This is, in part, testament to foundations built in Aviron's youth – as well as running a technical lab, his father was a broker, an intermediary between growers with grapes to sell and producers or négociants who lacked the required volumes of wine. In addition, the company offers a mobile bottling line service, and 50 per cent of its work is conducted within the Beaujolais region. All of this has allowed Aviron to build relationships with growers that have stood him in good stead in his role as a négociant.

Although Aviron is not responsible for managing the vineyards from which he buys grapes, he keeps a close eye on them throughout the growing season. Grapes are harvested by hand, and where possible this takes place during cooler hours so that the bunches can then be load-ed into the tanks for a prompt start to fermentation. Unlike many of the younger winemakers in the region, Aviron has little truck with notions of minimal intervention in the winery. He adds yeast to the tank as well as sulphites – the aim here, he says, is to get the fermen-tations off to a healthy start and to knock any risk of bad bugs taking hold on the head. He's even ready to acidify whenever he believes it is necessary – an intervention few winemakers are prepared to admit to. Once again this is in the interest of maintaining a healthy pH in the tanks rather than with the organoleptic qualities of the finished wine in mind. Aviron performs a gentle pump-over once a day for the first couple of days, which helps not only to keep the cap moist and start the extraction of tannin and colour, but also introduces some oxygen to the tank, which he believes helps keep the fermentation healthy. The tanks are then left to ferment steadily for another three or four days, at which point Aviron reintroduces more *remontage* during the last couple of days. A week or so into the process the juice is pressed off into ageing vessels – mostly cement tanks, which, as they are porous, allow for sub-tle micro-oxygenation during the maturation period. The end result is a series of cuvées, all labelled as Stéphane Aviron (rather than Potel Aviron, even though that's the name of the parent company), with bright, precise fruit and low levels of fine, supple tannins. My favour-ites are the raspberry-scented Fleurie, the focused and taut Chénas, and the peppery, spicy Moulin-à-Vent, which has a sumptuous, glycerolic richness on the mid-palate.

Bret Brothers

www.bretbrothers.com

The Bret Brothers – Jean-Guillaume and Jean-Philippe – come from a well-established family of winemakers based in Vinzelles, which lies on the Burgundian side of the invisible border with Beaujolais. The wines of Beaujolais were regularly drunk at family gatherings as they grew up, but the thing that really drew them to the region as winemakers was the excitement they felt on drinking bottles made by members of Beaujolais's new generation of producers – people like Paul-Henri Thillardon (see p. 85) and the Dutraives (see p. 111). Instead of investing in their own vineyards in the region – the model on which they base their production at their Burgundian domaine, La Soufrandière – the brothers decided to opt to operate as négociants in the south.

Many négociant purchases are based on personal relationships, but the Brets take it one stage further, and only buy grapes from vineyards owned by their friends. What's at play here isn't just friendship, though, it's also a matter of philosophy. A respectful approach to all matters environmental is intrinsic both to the Bret brothers and their group of friends in Beaujolais, and as a result, all grapes purchased have been farmed organically. The scale of production is, as a result, small – in all, the *négoce* part of their business amounts to, at most, some 12,000 bottles in any one year.

Winemaking is very much in harmony with the organic ethos of the viticulture - the idea is to manipulate the wines as little as possible during the course of a semi-carbonic fermentation. They used to practise a little *remontage*, but have stopped doing so in recent vintages as they've observed that the gentle oxygenation that happens during the process raises the risk of increasing the level of volatility in the wines. The process is one of intense observation, and intervention only when required. If, for instance, they see that fermentation isn't getting off to a healthy start, they'll introduce a *pied de cuve* into the tank.

Their Juliénas comes from a parcel known as La Bottière, and it's surprisingly refined and elegant for a wine from a *cru* usually typified by its density and structure. The Saint-Amour Côte de Besset comes from a north-facing parcel planted on a mix of granite and diorite. It's a fresh, lively wine with very fine tannins and a distinct aniseed note. The Brouilly is rounded, fleshy and generous, with a palate packed full of pretty red fruits and gently chunky tannins. The Fleurie Poncié is sweet and tart, like a raspberry jelly, with a lingering floral aftertaste and surprisingly grippy tannins. Glou des Bret comes from vineyards in the village of Lantignié. Its tannins are fine-grained and well handled, with a gently raspy character, while the fruit character tends towards red plums and spice, with a twist of blood orange. Men in Bret is a Vin de France. It's a blend of all the parcel-based cuvées, but while the parcel wines are derived from liquid drawn off from above the lees, Men in Bret is made from any liquid remaining below. It's a funky, fuzzy, unfiltered wine with a bit more rusticity than the other bottlings, but it's also fun and juicy.

Maison Coquard

www.maison-coquard.com

When Christophe Coquard gave up his job working for a big négociant in 2004 in order to found his own *négoce* company at the height of the economic crisis in Beaujolais, his friends told him he was mad. There were times, he admits, when he wonders whether they were right, saying that his business has never had an easy year. And yet, here he is, more than 20 years later, based at his family home – a magnificent house built of the region's golden stones – with a dynamic and constantly evolving range of wines.

Coquard has always swum against the tide, having left the safety of the *Bas Beaujolais* in his twenties to travel the world and see how wine was made outside his home region. His aim, he says, was to vinify wines on three continents by the time he turned 30, which he achieved by means of *stages* in California, New Zealand and South Africa. But it was the work he'd done in marketing and sales back home in Beaujolais that convinced him that there was room in the market for a modestly sized négociant with the flexibility to explore gaps in the market that the big guys left untapped.

Like many négociants, he buys wine rather than grapes, although he works closely with his growers, who are located across the wider Beaujolais region, to determine both the style and quality of the finished product. Coquard produces a dizzying array of bottlings, each adapted to the demands of a different clientele. Many of these have the punning brand names that are so popular in France and which don't necessarily translate all that well for a foreign audience. Le Coq (a reference to his name, as well as the cockerel that is one of France's national emblems) is one of his entry-level ranges. It includes a vivid rosé whose bright fruit and fresh acidity make it a delightful pool-side summer glugger. Beau(jolais) For You is an equally quaffable red, made for early drinking pleasure. Clochemerle is a French institution, a comedic novel based on life in a small country town in Beaujolais. The book, which was published in the 1930s, inspired a film, a BBC TV series and one of Coquard's most emblematic cuvées, which is made under licence to the author's son (part of his fee is an annual supply of wine). Coquard makes a Beaujolais and a Beaujolais Villages bottling under the name, and the former has more density and weight than many Beaujolais AOP wines. Coquard bottles each of the *crus*, with eye-catching labels that combine a graphic of a house (for Maison Coquard) with a visual representation of each *cru* – for instance, the floral-scented Chiroubles features peonies, while the rich, fleshy Juliénas bears a laurel wreath, a reference to Julius Caesar, who is said to have given his name to the *cru*.

Les Vins Georges Duboeuf

www.duboeuf.com

For many wine lovers around the world, the name Georges Duboeuf is synonymous with Beaujolais. Duboeuf, a canny marketeer, was strongly associated with the Beaujolais Nouveau boom of the late twentieth century (see p. 8). He also created a company that produces around eight million bottles of wine each year, 85 per cent of which come from Beaujolais, with the remainder sourced in the Mâconnais and the wider Burgundian region. Unsurprisingly, given these quantities, Les Vins Georges Duboeuf is one of the biggest négociants – if not the biggest – in the region, and the wines are exported to well over 100 countries worldwide.

Duboeuf was born in Pouilly-Fuissé, on the southern fringes of Burgundy, but as the second son of the family, he was never going to inherit the family vineyards, which were destined for his older brother, Roger. Instead, from a relatively early age, Duboeuf proved himself to be an energetic and compelling salesman, initially selling the family wines and eventually those of Beaujolais to prestigious restaurants in Lyon and the surrounding countryside. The good relationships he enjoyed with some of the men who were fast becoming the celebrity chefs of the post-war period – among them Paul Bocuse and Paul Blanc – stood him in good stead as he built his brand during the 1960s and '70s.

The business model on which the empire was built still operates today. Although the company owns around 60 hectares of vineyards, mainly in Fleurie and Juliénas, most wines are purchased directly from growers shortly after they've finished their fermentations. These wines can be made in a variety of ways, ranging from thermovinification through to semi-carbonic maceration or more extractive practices with full de-stemming. Of the 350 or so vignerons Duboeuf works with, many have been with the company for a long time and know what's expected of them in terms of the way they conduct their work in the vineyard and the standards of vinification. Nevertheless, there's no official checklist of criteria they need to meet as the Duboeuf credo is that the variations in style created by contributing producers serve to add to the complexity and diversity of the company's offering. Duboeuf died in 2020, and after a somewhat rocky period for the company, it is now being steered back into safer commercial territory, although its glory days as a Beaujolais icon appear to be over.

The variety of wines offered by Duboeuf is almost bewildering in its complexity. There's the hallmark 'Flower' range, with about 30 different cuvées. These fruity, approachable wines are the beating heart of the Duboeuf offering – instantly recognizable thanks to the flowers portrayed on the labels and unchallenging in their flavour profiles, these are cuvées designed to please as many people as possible. You'll generally find a more distinctive personality in the 30 or so bottlings in the 'Domaines and Châteaux' range, although you have to look closely at the labels to realize that these are Duboeuf wines. Then there's the 'Signatures', of which there are about six; and the 'Lieux-Dits', whose number and identity changes each year, a bottled reflection of whichever site-specific cuvées the winemaking team feels display exceptional characteristics and great typicity in any particular year. Across the range, the house style is one of fruit-driven wines made to be accessible and easy to drink in their youth.

Jane Eyre

Instagram @janeeyrewines

Australian winemaker Jane Eyre is best known for the elegant, refined Pinots she crafts from grapes grown in Australia and in Burgundy. She says that five years after she began working in France, customers started asking her whether she was going to be making an entry-level wine. Initially she began thinking about adding a Bourgogne Rouge to her range, but the more she thought about it, the more she realized that she wanted to go in a slightly different direction. The decision to make wines in Fleurie came down to two key factors – one was that the cost of grapes that would allow her to make a Bourgogne Rouge was about the same as the price of the equivalent amount of grapes from a *cru* in Beaujolais. The other was that the year in which she decided to make her more affordable cuvée was 2016, and the vintage in Burgundy had been so poor that no grapes were available to her.

Accordingly, she began tasting wines from the different *crus* in Beaujolais, and soon established that the fine-boned elegance of a typical Fleurie held the greatest appeal for her. Initially she'd narrowed her search down to the *lieu-dit* of La Madone, but the young grower from whom she was about to buy her grapes convinced her to take a look at a parcel of centenarian vines in Les Labourons. She immediately fell in love with the vineyard, and the fruit it produced, and although in her first Beaujolais vintage the wine was made up of equal shares of fruit from the two *lieux-dits*, the next year hailstorms meant that Les Labourons became the only option, and she's stuck with this vineyard ever since, producing a wine of great concentration, but also terrific finesse and length. Eyre has flirted with other vineyards in Beaujolais. She produced a Chénas in 2017 as well, and has since added a Juliénas from the Bois de Chat, a vineyard whose blue stone soils gives her a dark, dense, spicy wine with more robust tannins than those found in the more delicate, precise Fleurie.

Once the grapes are picked, she drives them north from Beaujolais to her winery on the outskirts of Beaune, where the grapes destined for her Fleurie and Juliénas cuvées are partially de-stemmed (usually around 40 per cent), then fermented together with whole bunches for around three to four weeks before pressing – a little longer than her Pinots. Decisions about tannin extraction are taken on a tank-by-tank basis, and are largely based on the health of the cap and the homogeneity of the temperature. The wines are then aged in a mix of old barrels, tanks and clayvers (a ceramic ageing vessel).

In response to criticisms that her winemaking style was not sufficiently 'Beaujolais', Eyre also makes a Fleurie by means of a classic semi-carbonic maceration (it's identified on the label as '100% Vendanges Entières'). It's a bright, appealing and eminently drinkable wine, and would be absolutely heavenly on a hot summer's day, especially if lightly chilled.

Le Grappin

www.legrappin.com

Andrew and Emma Nielsen (he's Australian, she's a Brit) set up their négociant business in Burgundy in 2011, buying in grapes from around the region to make their modestly priced, approachable wines. It took them around three years to realize that although they were making Burgundy, what they were actually drinking was Beaujolais because, as Emma says, 'The wines are affordable and delicious'.

The Nielsens started buying grapes from growers in Beaujolais, most of whom work organically, with or without certification. And they're faithful customers, saying that they not only try to buy from the same growers and the same parcels every year, but also try and focus their purchases down to specific rows of vines within each vineyard. Winemaking for grapes from *cru* vineyards takes its cue from the precepts established by Jules Chauvet (see p. 12), and the Nielsens even pay homage to him by detailing the process on the back labels. The Fleurie Poncié is a slightly wild take on the *cru*, redolent with spice and herbs, while the Côte de Brouilly is slightly stemmy, but rounded and generous.

They're a bit more experimental with their Beaujolais Villages Submersion cuvée, which entails separating a parcel of grapes off from the bunches that go into the main tank. This first parcel is pressed and allowed to begin to ferment, and then pumped over the whole bunches in the tank. These bunches then undergo an intracellular fermentation while floating in the fermenting juice, a technique they call a flotation. Finally, the Submersion wine is made from the pressed juice of those whole bunches.

Innovation is not new to the Nielsens. They're probably best known in the UK for their exploration of alternative packaging methods, including 'bagnums', magnum-sized pouches of wine, and kegs, which they supply to restaurants to allow them to serve the Le Grappin wines by the glass or the carafe.

Icy Liu

Instagram @icy_liu_

You don't get much more micro as a négociant than Taipei-born and New York-raised Icy Liu, who currently makes only two barrels of her Beaujolais. Her journey into the world of the négociant was a roundabout one that took in a degree in engineering, with a minor in economics, at Columbia and a fledgling career in finance before some volunteer work at a wine centre in New York put her on the right track. Intensive sommelier training at the Culinary Institute of America was fun, but she knew she didn't want to work in service, so Liu ended up working in sales and distribution. A high achiever from a high-achieving family, she felt the next step was to have something to show for all her hard work, and so she moved to France in order to learn some French and to do a wine MBA. At around the same time she began working in the Beaune offices of Becky Wasserman & Co, the American company famed for its expertise in trading Burgundian wines. Liu felt she was ready to take the next step on her career path, and set her sights on signing up as a student on the Master of Wine programme – and failed the entrance exam. Her ego slightly bruised by the rejection, Liu was casting around for a new challenge, and a fellow MBA student suggested she might like to make some wine with some grapes he had going spare.

Liu's first vintage was 2022, and she was offered space in a friend's winery to make her debut barrels. Liu, who'd always worked as an employee, initially found winemaking on her own to be a strange process. 'It's one thing going to work for someone and being told what to do,' she says, 'so it took me a couple of years to feel comfortable with making consequential decisions by myself. What I learned is that winemaking is about working out what risks you're prepared to take.'

After her first attempt, which focused on grapes from southern Burgundy, Liu decided to broaden her repertoire by making a Beaujolais, and was offered a parcel of grapes from Fleurie. In contrast to Pinot, Liu says that Gamay can be a difficult grape to vinify – it's temperamental and is prone to brett. She manages the challenge by a mixture of hands-on winemaking and close supervision of her ferments. Liu starts by foot treading her bunches to release some juices in order to get fermentation underway, a process she aids with a *pied de cuve*, then tops off the tank with dry ice and carbon dioxide. She'll wait several days before doing both a *pigeage* and a *remontage*, then tastes repeatedly in order to determine the best time to press the juices off. Finally, her wine is aged in old barrels for around nine months. Her Les Fronds is based on a parcel of vines planted on Fleurie's pink granite sands in the 1950s and 1970s. It's a tightly wound wine with a pretty floral character and fine-grained, stony tannins. It shows really well in its youth, although one suspects that more time in bottle would open it up a bit more. It's also testament to Liu's drive to achieve precision. Or, as she puts it, 'When you only make two barrels of each wine, you can't afford to fuck things up.'

Domaines/Maison Jean Loron

www.loron.fr

Domaines Jean Loron has, over the course of its three centuries of existence, cycled its way through a variety of identities. It all began in 1711, when Jean Loron set up shop as a polyculturist in Chénas. The grape-growing side of his business grew, and a century later his descendants decided to start a *négoce* business based in La Chapelle de Guinchay, a village that gave them good access to both the network of canals and, later, the railway. Their success allowed them to invest in viticultural properties, of which the Domaine de Billard in Saint-Amour was the first. For much of the twentieth century, Jean Loron was best known as a négociant, with a range of wines packaged under the Maison Jean Loron umbrella brand. More recently, however, the business has taken a different turn, and the focus is, increasingly, on the wines produced at individual domaines, with only about 30 per cent of the company's production sourced and distributed under the négociant model (a percentage that's due to be scaled back even further in coming years).

Loron now owns eight domaines in Beaujolais, and one in the Mâconnais. There's an additional property – the Domaine de la Vieille Eglise in Juliénas – that's held by a tenant on a long-term lease. The company's total holdings in Beaujolais now amount to 220 hectares of vineyards, spread out across all the *crus*, with the exception of Chiroubles and the Côte de Brouilly. Each of these properties is run on Loron's behalf by a dedicated team which takes on the responsibility for the property's vineyards and the vinification of the wines made from the grapes they grow. They work to an agreed *cahier de charges*, a set of specifications that are fixed in advance, but in general the house style is to de-stem the grapes prior to a Burgundian-style fermentation. Tannin extraction is performed by means of a gentle infusion using a grille, while the maturation of the wines takes place in a wide variety of vessels, ranging from old oak to very contemporary concrete eggs.

Loron's current portfolio includes two properties in Saint-Amour, of which Domaine de la Pirolette makes a generous, rounded La Poulette – a word that can be used either to mean a chicken or as a term of endearment, but which also plays on the wine's *élevage* in concrete eggs. The same domaine's Le Carjot is denser and more structured. The other Saint-Amour property is the Domaine des Billards, Loron's first ever purchase, whose Clos des Billards is richly fruited and generous, with a subtly earthy character. The Château de Fleurie makes a bright-fruited

La Madone, while the Domaine de la Vieille Eglise's Clos des Poulettes, a Juliénas derived from hard diorite soils, is a powerful wine with a smoky dark fruit character and fleshy tannins. It should be noted that all these wines come from a range labelled Héritiers Loron, rather than Domaines Loron.

Mommessin

www.mommessin.com

Mommessin, one of Beaujolais's biggest négociants, is currently owned by Boisset, a Burgundy-based company that also owns properties across France and in California. Mommessin was founded in the Mâconnais in 1865, but like many négociants in southern Burgundy soon got involved in the business of purchasing, bottling and distributing wines from Beaujolais.

Mommessin doesn't buy grapes from its suppliers, only finished wines. It currently has around 25 long-standing partnerships with specific growers and cooperatives, and this – along with supplementary purchases – provides them with wine sourced from around 350 hectares of vineyards spread throughout the region. Wines are also bottled under the label of Pellerin and Maison J Thorin, négociant companies that have been absorbed into the Mommessin fold but which retain their own separate identity (in marketing terms, at least). In addition, Mommessin owns a property in Brouilly, the Château de Pierreux, which tops up the volumes to the tune of around 100 hectares. In total, Mommessin bottles and sells between four and five million bottles of Beaujolais every year.

Some 90 per cent of Mommessin's growers adhere to HVE principles in the vineyards, but winemaking is a diverse process, and each producer is allowed pretty much free rein to make their wines the way they want. Having said that, Mommessin's winemaking team stands ready to provide guidance on request, and will steer winemakers in a suitable direction when appropriate. Most of the tastings are done in producers' cellars in November. The finished wines are shipped to Mommessin's facility in Quincié towards the end of winter for the start of a long, detailed process of blending, which can last right through until July.

As with most big négociants, Mommessin has a number of ranges in its portfolio. The Splendeur Nature is its organic wine, a light, fruity wine with zippy acidity and very little tannin. The J Thorins wines, as exemplified by the Moulin-à-Vent Terres de Silice, offer an easy, approachable take on the sometimes firmly structured *crus*. The domaine-designated wines, bottled under the Pellerin label, are sourced from individual producers. Of these, the Domaine de la Croix Carron, a Saint-Amour, made by means of semi-carbonic maceration with a small portion of thermovinified wine, has supple tannins and rich violet-scented fruit. The Domaine du Vieux Cerisier, in contrast, shows the wild, rather feral nature of Juliénas, albeit with slightly less structure than one might normally expect from this *cru*. The Grandes Mises is Mommessin's prestige range, but to my taste these wines appear to come from the more is more school of winemaking, with too much ripeness (and alcohol), oak and extraction (although some cuvées suffer more from this approach than others).

Christophe Pacalet

christophepacalet.com

If you're going to set yourself up as a wine producer, it probably doesn't hurt to be the nephew of Marcel Lapierre, one of the original Gang of Four (see p. 11). And yet, despite having grown up in the heart of Beaujolais's *crus*, Christophe Pacalet never intended to end up making wine. Instead he studied hospitality, and spent five years working in the Caribbean as a jobbing chef.

Home exerted a pull, however, and he returned and was drawn inexorably towards the world of wine. However, his side of the family had long since sold its vineyards, so Pacalet found himself making wines from bought-in grapes. He quickly discovered that working closely with his growers over the course of the viticultural year resulted in better wines, so he's spent the past twenty or so years building close relationships with growers in vineyards around the region. Pacalet has recently bought his first-ever vineyard, a small parcel in Les Labourons, one of Fleurie's *lieux-dits*. In the past, Les Labourons was not widely considered to be one of the *cru*'s better parcels, but in the face of global warming, the slow-ripening, largely north-west-facing slope looks to be a canny choice.

Pacalet worked closely with his uncle while developing his own business, and unsurprisingly some of Lapierre's approach to both viticulture and vinification has rubbed off onto him. He prefers his growers to work with minimal – if any – chemical treatments, both out of respect for the environment and out of a belief that the resulting wines will benefit from the lack of treatment. For instance, he believes that the use of fertilizers and fungicides makes it more difficult for the indigenous yeasts to ferment efficiently, thereby increasing the risk of the creation of off-aromas.

Pacalet likes to be pretty hands-off in the cellar, too. No yeasts are added, and sulphur is used in judicious measures. The bunches are doused in carbon dioxide and the grapes are then left to ferment for a month or so – quite a long time in the context of fermentation in the region – before being pressed into oak barrels, mostly sourced second-hand from Burgundian growers, to allow the yeasts to finish off the last traces of sugar. The wine is left to mature on the fine lees, a technique Pacalet believes helps the clarification process.

Pacalet's range is small in scale – at least in *négoce* terms – there's a generous, fleshy white, made from Chardonnay grown in the southern part of the region, a Beaujolais Nouveau and a Beaujolais Villages wine, and seven *crus*, one each from Chénas, Chiroubles, Côte de Brouilly, Fleurie, Juliénas, Moulin-à-Vent and Saint-Amour. Of these, the complex Fleurie from Les Labourons and the tightly wound, ageworthy Chénas may well be the pick of the bunch, although the ripe, rounded Saint-Amour is a lot of fun, too. Pacalet is planning on adding a further wine to the range – he's planting Gamay on a parcel of land that lies just outside the Fleurie zone so that he can make an easy-drinking quaffing wine under the more flexible regulations that govern the Vin de France category.

Maison Piron

www.maison-piron.fr

Despite the name, Maison Piron is no longer owned by the Piron family, which now – confusingly, perhaps – owns the Clos du Vieux Bourg in Corcelles, to the east of Morgon. However, there is a historic link as Dominique Piron and the current owner of Maison Piron, Julien Révillon, worked together for a number of years before Piron sold up. Piron was the first *négociant-vinificateur* in Beaujolais, which means that he not only produced wines from grapes grown in his own vineyards but also bought in grapes and wines to bottle under the Maison Piron label. The business model, established in 1971, still holds good, and to-day Maison Piron owns about 25 hectares of vineyards, buys in grapes grown by others from another 25 hectares, and then doubles its annual production by buying in a further 50 hectares-worth of wine made by other producers.

As with a lot of négociants working along these lines, many of the supply contracts are long-standing ones, with both sides understanding their rights and their responsibilities. Ultimately, what counts, Révillon says, is quality – or at least a level of quality appropriate for the required end result, which may be different for grapes or wines destined to become part of an entry-level range than it is for those whose fate is to become part of a premium cuvée. Révillon says his approach is a pragmatic one – 'I don't really care how the wines were made,' he says, 'all I'm interested in is what they taste like.'

When it comes to the wines made from the property's own vineyards, Révillon insists on an initial selection of the bunches in the vineyard, and then a further pass on a vibrating table once the bunches reach the winery. Although he typically looks to retain about 20 per cent whole bunches in his tanks, depending on the cuvée, most grapes are de-stemmed prior to the start of fermentation. Révillon is looking for a bit more extraction than is the norm for many Beaujolais producers, using both *remontage* and *pigeage* as extractive techniques, although he's also started using a Pulsair device, which gently bubbles either carbon dioxide or air through the fermenting must, helping to break up the cap in a delicate fashion.

Of the premium cuvées made at Maison Piron, highlights include the Chiroubles, a pretty, floral wine with elegant, rather stony tannins, and Fructus Agapé (a name that can be translated as 'the unconditional love of fruit'), a Beaujolais Villages from Révillon's home village of Lantignié, which shows pleasingly bright red berry and cherry fruit, and lightly grippy tannins. The Morgon Les Charmes also impresses. Made from fruit grown on a belt of sandstone that runs down the *cru* from north-west to south-east, this shows a little more precision and linearity than many Morgons, along with fine tannins and a burst of vibrant acidity. The Chénas Quartz is another standout bottling – fine-boned and focused, with savoury notes of spice and tobacco leaf, as well as some mid-palate roundness and generosity.

Le Clos des Vignes du Maynes

www.vignes-du-maynes.com

The Clos des Vignes du Mayne has only been owned by Julien Guillot's family since the 1950s, but its history stretches back more than 1,000 years to a site managed by the monks of Cluny. Guillot is best known for the wines he makes in the Mâconnais, but after a year when his production was decimated by devastating hailstorms, he decided to start a small *négoce* business. It wasn't easy, at first, to find growers in Beaujolais, in part because Guillot was only willing to buy organically farmed grapes (his home vineyards are certified biodynamic). He stuck it out, and ended up finding partners to work with in the southern vineyards – not least because he was prepared to share the hard-won expertise he and his father had acquired in the management of organic vineyards in order to help his chosen growers to achieve organic certification.

Winemaking for all Guillot's *négoce* production is a mish-mash of Burgundian and Beaujolais tradition, with a significant percentage being whole bunches – usually around 80 per cent – fermented with de-stemmed berries. These are layered in a *millefeuille* into a large *tronçonnais* oak fermenter, then chilled down to around 12–13°C to ensure that the intracellular fermentation is long and slow, extracting as much bright fruit character as possible before the whole bunches are pressed.

The Ultimatum Climat – a 'simple' AOP Beaujolais bottled with a militant, punkish red label – has had an extended maturation period of five years, but the depth of fruit and fresh acidity ensures an impressive brightness and length. It's not the most elegant wine in the world, but it has great attitude. Although Guillot showed me a Morgon from Les Charmes, the vintage in question – a 2020 – is the last he's going to make. Instead he's decided to focus his attention on Chénas in future. He currently makes two wines in the *cru*. Les Petites Pierres, which is always 100 per cent whole-bunch wine, is a bright, peppery, floral wine whose tannins have a pleasingly fine raspiness to them. The Chénas 2023 was a tank sample, and it's going to be a massive beast of a wine. He's got the balance right, though – a good thing as it's hit an astounding 15.6% abv. Guillot also has a new parcel of Chénas, Les Gondelins, which comes from the *lieu-dit* of Champagne, that he's bringing on-stream in the near future.

18

SLEEP, EAT AND DRINK

Unlike other winemaking regions in France, Beaujolais doesn't get all that many visitors. The hordes of northern Europeans who trek southwards to Provence each summer rarely stop off there, even though it's a natural midway point for many. Instead, Beaujolais is France's equivalent of a flyover state, largely ignored in favour of layovers in Burgundy or an onward push to Lyon. In this instance, the old saw about the wisdom of crowds doesn't hold true, as Beaujolais is the perfect place for a brief (or not-so-brief) wine trip.

Part of the attraction comes from the natural beauty of the region. After the relatively gentle landscape of Burgundy, the slopes of Beaujolais exert a rather more dramatic appeal. There are plenty of hilly tracks for hikers or cyclists to explore, and even those who would rather not exert themselves too strenuously can drink in the landscape from lookout points on Morgon's Côte du Py, Mont Brouilly or beneath the Chapel of the Madonna in Fleurie.

Those whose travel interests turn more towards gastronomy will also find much to celebrate in a region that has recently rediscovered its culinary mojo, and now offers visitors Michelin-starred fare as well as hearty country cooking. And then there are the wineries. Unlike some regions in France, where visits seem to be conducted under sufferance, if at all, many producers in Beaujolais are only too happy to receive visitors, especially those who are genuinely interested in exploring and understanding their wines. As ever, in France, it pays to make an appointment beforehand, rather than just rocking up at a winery and assuming that someone will be able to receive you. It's also considered to be good form to buy at least a bottle or two at the end of a tasting, unless you've paid a fee (even if you really don't like the wines).

It's true that in the past Beaujolais suffered from a lack of good-quality accommodation for holidaymakers. There are gites in the region, but most of them are large, catering to groups celebrating weddings or family reunions, often placing an emphasis on low prices rather than good facilities and modern comforts. Even in some of the region's smaller self-catering venues, standards of accommodation can be pretty basic. But there's a new(ish) generation of small hotels and *chambres d'hôtes* opening up in Beaujolais, and these cater to a more discerning clientele – and to smaller groups.

Working on the assumption that at least some of this book's readers might be interested in visiting Beaujolais, the following pages provide recommendations for some of my favourite places to stay, eat and drink in the region.

PLACES TO STAY

The **Auberge du Paradis** (aubergeduparadis.fr) is a small but sophisticated boutique hotel located in the pretty village of Saint-Amour-Bellevue, and a few minutes' stroll from the vineyards of Saint-Amour. There are a dozen rooms, each spacious and well decorated, and two on-site restaurants. The fine dining venue, Lucienne Fait des Siennes (Lucienne Acts Up, named in honour of the owner's dog), may well take the prize for the world's most oddly named restaurant, while I consider the more informal Joséphine à Table (see below) to be the Platonic ideal of a French country bistro.

The **Auberge de Clochemerle** (www.aubergedeclochemerle.fr) lies on the fringes of the Beaujolais Villages zone, and makes a great base for visiting both the *crus* and the *Bas Beaujolais*. Rooms are comfortable, if fairly standard hotel issue, but the views out over the vineyards are breathtaking. The on-site restaurant (see below) makes it well worth investing in a dinner, bed and breakfast package.

The **Maison de Pagneux** (maisondepagneux.com) can be found on the outskirts of the *pierres dorées* village of Lachassagne. It opened relatively recently, in the post-Covid era, and is part of the new wave of high-end *chambres d'hôtes* in the region. There are three comfortable bedrooms for guests, and the couple who run this B&B are talented cooks, so the *table d'hôtes* option is highly recommended.

Bienvenue en Beaujonomie

Every year, during the third weekend in June, the growers of Beaujolais throw open their doors to members of the public. Around 50 producers, including some of the region's best-known names, hire in chefs and *traiteurs* and treat visitors to relaxed meals, washed down by generous libations of their wines. Tables might be set up in the coolness of the *cuvage* or outdoors, within touching distance of the vineyards. Before you and your fellow guests sit down for lunch or dinner you'll be guided towards a better understanding of the domaine, its history and its winemaking. It's a relaxed and convivial way of learning about the region's wines, and gaining an unusual level of access to the men and women who make them. Find out more – and book your tickets – by visiting bienvenue-en-beaujonomie.fr

Santé! Guests at a Bienvenue en Beaujonomie event enjoy an evening of food, wine and conversation (photo courtesy of Nicolas Dormont/ Beaujolais Wines)

If you're planning a longer stay and would prefer self-catering accommodation, **La Maison du Village** (maisonvillage.fr) is conveniently situated in the heart of Romanèche-Thorins. There are five separate well-appointed apartments for rent, ranging in size from the teeny-tiny (Azurite) to the luxuriously large (Barytine).

While I haven't stayed at any of the following, they come with the wholehearted endorsement of friends and colleagues:

- The **Château des Janroux** (chateaudesjanroux.fr) is a glamorous *chambres d'hôtes* based in a seventeenth-century château in Juliénas.
- The elegant **Hotel Villa Alexandre** (hotelvilla-alexandre.fr) in Régnié-Durette allows for easy access to the *crus* and the *villages*.
- **Les Larmes du Soleil** (leslarmesdusoleil.fr) in Blacé has four separate alluringly decorated self-catering spaces.

PLACES TO DRINK AND EAT

If you just want somewhere with a view where you can enjoy a glass or two of wine, and maybe a simple bite to eat, there are few places that combine panoramas and picnics quite as well as Chiroubles's high-altitude **Maison du Cru** (chiroubles-lecru.com/maison-du-cru-chiroubles).

XVIII sur Vins (Instagram @xviii_sur_vins) is a wine bar and shop in Belleville-en-Beaujolais where you can pick the bottle of your choice from the wide selection of local (and not-so-local) offerings that line the walls. Order from a short menu of simple dishes (charcuterie, salads, cheeses, plat du jour) or not, the choice is yours.

The **Epicerie Saint-Etienne des Oullières** is a small shop on the village's high street that offers groceries, wines made by local producers and a small, ever-changing menu of daily specials at lunchtime during the week as well as at dinner-time on Fridays.

La Mine (la-mine.org) in Romanèche-Thorins is a friendly wine bar that's part owned by winemaker Richard Rottiers (see p. 102). It's only open Thursdays to Saturdays, and there's a regular schedule of events that takes in everything from wine tastings and live music to lectures and Qi Gong.

Joséphine à Table (josephineatable.fr) in Saint-Amour Bellevue is the little French village bistro of my dreams (and, quite possibly, yours). The menu offers hearty portions of classic French country dishes, and the *poulet au vin jaune* (if you want it with morels, you'll have to pay a €10 supplement, but it's worth it) is my regular order. The wine list reads like a who's who of local producers (some of whom may well be there, enjoying a drink at the bar). Always buzzing with energy, it's as popular with locals as it is with travellers, so book early.

Le Port de By (leportdeby.fr) is a neighbourhood restaurant, albeit one that happens to have a splendid view out over the Saône River. Its big floor-to-ceiling windows face west, so book in for dinner just before sunset, and tuck in to simple, well-cooked dishes like a roast leg of lamb or a salad of lentils and cured trout while you watch the sun sink slowly beneath the horizon. (If you've ever hankered to try frogs' legs with lots of garlic and parsley, this might well be the place to do it.)

The **Buffet de la Gare** (lebuffetdelagare-restaurant.com) in Belleville-en-Beaujolais is beloved of locals, especially at lunchtime, when the set meal offers generous portions and amazing value. Evenings are a little more sedate, but only just.

Le Café Terroir Chez Saint-Cyr (www.cafeterroir.fr/cafeterroir-chez-saintcyr) is the *Bas Beaujolais* outpost of a well-known and respected Lyonnais bistro. Housed in a space that was once the site of Domaine Saint-Cyr's (see p. 225) shop, and overlooking the winery's vineyards, this is a great place to stop off for a well-priced *prix fixe* lunch to round off a morning's visits. Alternatively, stop by for a more protracted evening meal on Wednesday through to Saturday.

Les Moblots (Instagram @les_moblots) in Saint-Julien is a noisy, bustling bistro that serves as a canteen for winemakers based nearby. Friendly and informal, with light, modern takes on French classics, the food is prepared with high-quality ingredients from local suppliers. There's also a strong wine list.

Beurre Noisette (beurre-noisette.fr) is housed in one of the cream stone houses so typical of Lucenay (and so unusual in a region where rich ochre is the norm). It offers an equally understated but attractive set menu at lunch and dinner, and dishes change every week according to what's in season at the time. Fairly unusually in a region where meat-eating is the norm, there's always a good vegetarian option on offer. The wine list is interesting and varied.

Ema (emarestaurant.fr) calls itself a *restaurant bistronomique*, but in the eyes of many that term sells the precise, carefully plated food they serve here rather short. The wide-ranging wine list is largely a celebration of all things natural, and – most unusually – sake also features. The view out over the forested hills of the *Beaujolais Vert* only adds to the sheer joyousness of a meal here.

The restaurant at the **Auberge de Clochemerle** (see above) has recently regained its Michelin star, and dinner there is an elegant, refined, if slightly hushed occasion. You can choose to see the menu, or just have the dishes roll over you one by one, like waves crashing on a beach. The basic menu, 'M', appears to suggest that all you'll get is three courses, but it doesn't mention the parade of pre-prandial nibbles or the generous post-dinner procession of petits fours, so count on eating far more than you might otherwise imagine. Inevitably, there's a terrific, rather compendious wine list, too.

The other splurge restaurant in the region is Fleurie's **Auberge du Cep** (aubergeducep.com), which also has received recognition from the Michelin inspectors. In grand French style, the choice consists of a range of set menus of varying proportions and prices, but the lunch menu, served on weekdays, is a bargain by anyone's measure. The wine list features some of the best bottlings from the region, as well as a selection of stellar wines from elsewhere in France.

Finally, I have two shopping recommendations for anyone who enjoys good food. **The Huilerie Beaujolaise** (huilerie-beaujolaise.fr) in Beaujeu, the region's ancient seat of power, offers a world-class line-up of oils and vinegars. You'll find old favourites like a powerful, rich toasted walnut oil or raspberry vinegar, as well as more unusual flavours such as grapeseed oil infused with coffee or the perfumed quince vinegar. I stock up here every time I'm in Beaujolais.

If you enjoy food markets as much as I do, I urge you to visit Chatillon-sur-Chalaronne on a Saturday morning. Located a short drive west from the heart of Beaujolais's wine country, this produce market, voted the third best in France, is held in a fifteenth-century vaulted semi-enclosed structure. You'll find everything from locally produced fruit and vegetables, cheeses, meats and charcuteries to pastries, *pâtes de fruits* and prepared dishes. Admire the cute bunnies and the chickens that strut in the wire cages, but don't think too hard about their inevitable fate.

CONCLUSION: WHERE IS BEAUJOLAIS HEADING?

It's 2045 and in a chic inner-city restaurant somewhere, a smart-looking couple are browsing the wine list. Their attention is focused on the two pages that list some of Beaujolais's best wines, starting with several vintages of *premier cru* bottlings from seven out of the twelve *crus* (Blacé and Lantignié both received the nod from the INAO a decade or so ago), and culminating in a brief selection of more reasonably priced offerings from some of the region's up-and-coming young producers. It seems astonishing to both of them – keen wine aficionados that they are – that Beaujolais was ever considered to be a region fit only for making cheap gluggers for immediate pleasure. Nowadays, the region more than holds its own in the company of appellations once considered to be far more prestigious, and warrants as much space on top restaurant lists and on the shelves of independent merchants as Bordeaux, Piemonte and the northern Rhône. Prices are still relatively affordable for most of the cuvées exported from the region, although bottlings from some of the top producers have hit the kind of heights once reserved for *grand cru* Burgundies and elite-level SuperTuscans.

It's 2045 and the buying director for a major British retail chain is checking the inventory ahead of her next order from Beaujolais. She's already decided against buying any more of the handful of *premier cru* wines produced in the region – they're priced higher than 'regular' wines from the eight *crus* that remain in production, but don't really offer a significant step up in quality. She reflects sadly on the fact that both Chiroubles and Chénas have effectively ceased to exist, producers having largely abandoned the effort to farm their vineyards within the past few years as customers are unwilling to pay enough money for the wines to make it worthwhile for growers to toil up and down the vertiginous hills. Still, she consoles herself with the fact that sales of the new drought-resistant hybrid blends recently permitted in the region under new appellation rules are growing fast, with consumers increasingly interested in wines that are able to tackle the challenges of climate change in an environmentally sustainable way, even though the wines rarely hit qualitative heights. She believes that this is a far better approach for the region to focus on than the push towards Chardonnay that dominated Beaujolais's production a few years ago. The emphasis on white wines proved to be of little interest to her customers, who didn't really see any benefit to buying Beaujolais Blanc given that there was already a glut of more reasonably priced Chardonnay from around the world available to them.

It's 2045 and many of Beaujolais's vineyards have been abandoned. The impact of climate change, coupled with the inability of the region's growers to adapt their practices to the new normal, has meant that the cultivation of Gamay has become largely untenable. The dispensation that producers in the *Bas Beaujolais* received to allow them to irrigate their vines saved their vineyards – and their financial bacon. The *crus* were not so lucky. Held to a higher qualitative standard, the lack of irrigation and the increased incidence of devastating hailstorms made farming these appellations financially unviable. When the average alcohol levels of red wines produced in the region hit 15% abv, the *raison d'être* for Gamay in the minds of most wine lovers – its freshness, perfume and sheer drinkability – was lost. Sales went into a tailspin nearly a decade ago, and have never recovered. Disheartened, many producers simply packed up and left the region, cutting their losses and their ties to Beaujolais. Some have gone on to make a name for themselves in the new vineyards of northern Europe that are attracting so much critical attention. Others have simply retired from the business completely. You can still find the occasional bottle of Beaujolais on supermarket shelves, if you look hard.

When I was invited by my editor to gaze into a crystal ball and speculate, in writing, about Beaujolais's future, a considerable number of potential paths seemed to open up between the present and a time some two decades hence.

Although I very much hope my first, highly optimistic scenario is the most likely – it certainly is a viable outcome of the current trends in both Beaujolais and the fine wine scene around the world – it has to be acknowledged that it is highly contingent on a combination of luck, smart marketing by the region and hard work in both vineyards and cellars to keep quality moving on its current upwards trajectory. It will also require those of us who love wine to shed our preconceptions that Beaujolais is, of necessity, a simple wine for short-term enjoyment and wake up to the sheer joyousness, diversity and complexity of the region's wines.

The middle scenario suggests something that incorporates elements of a flexible approach to wine production in the region in tandem with an inability of Beaujolais and its individual domaines to work towards improving both the quality and image of the wines produced in the region. Favouring short-term gain over long-term strategy was the reason why Beaujolais became tarred with the brush of cheap Nouveau in the late twentieth century, and the region runs a very real risk of repeating the same tactical mistakes in the future. There is also a current move afoot to place more emphasis on the region's Chardonnays. While there are a handful of good wines being made from the grape in the region, I believe that an increased focus on its production would be a strategic error. The world is not short of Chardonnay at all quality levels and price points. I do not believe that Beaujolais has the capacity to make wines from this grape that are stylistically distinctive enough to interest wine buffs at the top end of the market, nor can these wines be produced cheaply enough to make them attractive to a more price-conscious audience. Given this, large volumes of Beaujolais Blanc are unlikely to be competitive in a global marketplace.

The last scenario is, clearly, the doomsday option. At the time of writing (early July 2025) I have just returned from a trip to France during the course of which daytime temperatures rarely dipped below 35°C and often rose above 40°C. Highly unseasonable for June, everyone said, ignoring the fact that this was once the case but that these 'unseasonable' temperatures are increasingly the norm. Most of us acknowledge that climate change will have a major impact on our lives, but we appear to be unable to make the necessary adaptations to curb its effects. Governments and individuals alike will need a drastic change of priorities if Beaujolais and most other viticultural regions are not to become increasingly unviable as a source of high-quality wines. (Of course, all other agricultural activities are equally vulnerable to climate change, so the implications of this development would have profound use of a press. Typically this is more delicate and less tannic than the *jus de presse.*

Lieu-dit (pl. *lieux-dits*) – the literal translation of the term is 'named place', and refers to the designation given to a specific parcel of land within a larger zone, such as a vineyard or appellation. A *lieu-dit* is typically smaller than a *climat.*

Malolactic conversion/fermentation – not a true fermentation (hence the increasing use of the term malolactic conversion rather than fermentation). A process whereby lactic acid bacteria convert sharp malic acid in wines into softer lactic acid. Almost all red wines go through malolactic conversion, but it's widely considered to be optional for most white wines (although it's frequently used when producing Chardonnay).

Métayage – can be roughly translated as 'sharecropping'. A system in which the tenant farms a property and produces the wine in return (usually) for rent-free accommodation and a share of the finished product (the property's owner gets the remainder of the production).

Métayer(s) – tenant(s) in a *métayage.*

Millefeuille – a technique that involves layering whole bunches and destemmed grapes in a fermentation tank.

Natural winemaking – Most 'natural' winemakers aim to farm either organically or biodynamically and then use few or no additives in the winery (the only additives typically permitted in natural winemaking are small doses of sulphites towards the end of maturation/prior to bottling). Natural wines are typically bottled unfined and only lightly filtered, if at all.

Négoce – wine that is traded by a négociant.

Négociant – literally someone who trades in wine. A merchant who buys grapes and vinifies them, or buys made wine to create a larger-volume blend. The resulting wine is then bottled, sold and marketed under the négociant's label.

Phenolic ripeness/ripening – one of the key measures used when deciding when to pick. The term refers to the ripeness/ripening of the tannins contained in the pips, stems and skins of grapes (often used in opposition to sugar ripeness/ripening).

Phytoplasma – a plant pathogen, related to bacteria, that infects cells, particularly the phloem, the tissue that distributes nutrients through the plant.

Demi-muid – a large oak barrel used for maturing wine; these typically contain around 500–650 litres.

Élevage – translated literally, this means the 'raising' of a wine. A term used in France for the period of maturation between the end of fermentation and the final bottling of the wine.

Enrichment – *see* chaptalization.

Enzymatic fermentation – another term for intracellular fermentation.

Flavescence dorée – an incurable phytoplasma disease that, once it has infected a vine, reduces yield and may eventually kill the plant.

Foudre – a large barrel used for maturing wine. These come in a range of sizes.

Foulage – the technique of gently pressing whole bunches in tank to allow juice to be released.

Fût – a wooden barrel in which a wine is aged. A rather vague term not specifically associated with a particular volume.

Grillage – a traditional method used in Beaujolais for gently extracting tannins, in which a grille is inserted in the top of a tank and used to submerge the cap.

HVE – Haute Valeur Environnementale (High Environmental Values) certification covering key areas such as the conservation of biodiversity, water management and the reduction in use of chemical products in the vineyard. Producers who are certified HVE believe that the certificate is proof of their environmental credentials. Producers who work organically largely believe that HVE certification is an instance of greenwashing.

INAO – the Institut National de l'Origine et de la Qualité (the National Institute of Origin and Quality) is a French government agency charged with the oversight and regulation of French agricultural produce, including wine.

Indigenous fermentation – *see* wild fermentation.

Indigenous yeast – *see* wild yeast.

Intracellular fermentation – an anaerobic fermentation conducted by enzymes rather than yeasts inside whole, uncrushed berries; also known as enzymatic fermentation.

Jus de goutte – another term for free-run juice.

Jus de presse – the juice obtained when the whole bunches are pressed at the end of the enzymatic phase of fermentation. Typically this is more robust and structured than the *jus de tire*.

Jus de tire – free-run juice, the juice expressed from berries without the

the berries than would be typical in carbonic or semi-carbonic macerations in addition to a different suite of aromatic characters.

Cahier de charges – a set of agreed-upon specifications, usually relating to viticultural measures or winemaking protocols. Typically used when négociants or cooperatives are buying grapes and/or wines from individual growers.

Cap – in a typical alcoholic fermentation, the cap is the layer of solids composed of skins, pips and other material that floats on top of the fermenting liquid in a tank. In a carbonic or semi-carbonic maceration, the term is typically used for the bunches stacked in the tank, in contrast to any liquid that may have been expressed by crushed grapes at the bottom of the tank.

Carbonic maceration – a winemaking process in which the initial stage of fermentation takes place inside the berry (see intracellular fermentation). The boundary between this and semi-carbonic maceration is vague and ill-defined. (See p. 48 for full details of the process.)

Chaptalization – also known as 'enrichment', the act of adding sugar to grape juice or must before or during fermentation in order to raise alcohol levels or to extend the duration of the fermentation. This technique used to be widely practised in Beaujolais in the past. It still happens, especially in poorer vintages, but producers generally don't like to admit to the practice.

Climat – the designation given to a specific parcel of land within a larger zone, typically an appellation. A *climat* is typically larger than a *lieu-dit*, and may even encompass several *lieux-dits*.

Conventional – a term used in conjunction with farming or winemaking to indicate the use of chemical products or other additives (for instance, herbicides in the vineyard or cultured yeasts in the winery).

Cultured yeast – a proprietary yeast strain, typically used to inoculate a ferment. The advantage of using cultured yeast is that the yeasts tend to ferment efficiently and the end result is predictable (you can even buy yeasts that will give you specific aromatic characteristics). The disadvantage is that wines made using cultured yeasts may lack the complexity found in wines fermented with indigenous yeasts.

Cuvage – the local Beaujolais term for the area in which wine is made, aged and stored. A winery, in other words.

Délestage – a variation on the theme of *remontage*, in which all the juices in the tank are racked off into a separate tank before being pumped back over the solid matter in the first tank.

GLOSSARY

Acetobacter – several genera of bacteria which, individually or as a group, are responsible for wine spoilage, particularly in the presence of oxygen, which allows them to convert alcohol into acetic acid and other undesirable metabolic byproducts.

Bas Beaujolais – the southern bit of the Beaujolais region, also known as the *pierres dorées* region. Source of most of the wines produced as AOP Beaujolais.

Beaujolais Vert – the western part of the Beaujolais region, noted for its forested landscapes and meadows rather than for winegrowing.

Bien Boire en Beaujolais – a two-day tasting event that takes place in April and allows producers to show off their wines to professionals from France and overseas. The producers organize themselves into various groups, including *Beaujol'Art, Beaujol'Wines, Beaujo'Styles, La Biojolaise, La Beaujoloise* and *Biojolab* (what distinguishes one group from another is not always clear).

Bouchon – term used in Lyon for an informal bistro serving local cuisine.

Brett/*Brettanomyces* – a yeast species that can become dominant in an indigenous/wild yeast ferment or infect a barrel. Its presence in a wine results in the production of a range of flavours, variously described as being similar to mouse droppings, sweaty saddles or spice, that are widely considered to be undesirable, especially in Gamay. (A trace of brett in some wines, often richer styles made from other grapes, is considered to be an acceptable complexing agent by some tasters.)

Burgundian winemaking – in Beaujolais the use of the term 'Burgundian winemaking' typically refers to the use of de-stemmed grapes in a ferment, often with the aim of extracting more tannin or colour from